Guide to
CHOOSING A COLLEGE MAJOR

How to Confidently Pick Your Ideal Path

Laurence Shatkin, PhD

jist
Works
America's Career Publisher

PANICKED STUDENT'S GUIDE TO CHOOSING A COLLEGE MAJOR

© 2011 by JIST Publishing
Published by JIST Works, an imprint of JIST Publishing
7321 Shadeland Station, Suite 200
Indianapolis, IN 46256-3923

Phone: 800-648-JIST   Fax: 877-454-7839
E-mail: info@jist.com   Web site: www.jist.com

Some Other Books by Laurence Shatkin, PhD

The Sequel: How to Change Your Career Without Starting Over

Quick Education and Training Options Guide

Quick Green Jobs Guide

Best Jobs for the 21st Century

200 Best Jobs for College Graduates

300 Best Jobs Without a Four-Year Degree

200 Best Jobs Through Apprenticeships

50 Best Jobs for Your Personality

40 Best Fields for Your Career

225 Best Jobs for Baby Boomers

250 Best-Paying Jobs

150 Best Jobs for a Better World

200 Best Jobs for Introverts

Quantity discounts are available for JIST products. Please call 800-648-JIST or visit www.jist.com for a free catalog and more information.

Visit www.jist.com for information on JIST, tables of contents, sample pages, and ordering information on our many products.

Acquisitions Editor: Susan Pines
Development Editor: Stephanie Koutek
Cover Designer: Honeymoon Image & Design, Inc.
Design and Interior Layout: Toi Davis
Proofreaders: Chuck Hutchinson, Jeanne Clark
Indexer: Cheryl Lenser

Printed in the United States of America
16 15 14 13 12 11   9 8 7 6 5 4 3 2 1

Library of Congress Cataloging-in-Publication Data
Shatkin, Laurence.
  Panicked student's guide to choosing a college major : how to confidently pick your ideal path / Laurence Shatkin.
    p. cm.
  Includes index.
  ISBN 978-1-59357-864-0 (alk. paper)
  1. College majors--United States. 2. College student orientation--United States. 3. College students--Vocational guidance--United States. I. Title.
  LB2361.5.S529 2011
  378.2'41--dc22
                              2011007461

We have been careful to provide accurate information throughout this book, but it is possible that errors and omissions have been introduced. Please consider this in making any career plans or other important decisions. Trust your own judgment above all else and in all things.

ISBN 978-1-59357-864-0

Need to declare a major?
Don't panic!

Does the thought of declaring a major make your pulse race? Calm down. This easy-to-follow book breaks a complex decision into manageable parts. It walks you through a series of steps that lead to a thoughtful choice. The book contains several helpful exercises and a wealth of facts about college majors and the careers they lead to. You'll be able to make a decision without breaking a sweat.

Credits and Acknowledgments: While the author created this book, it is based on the work of many others. The occupational information is based on data obtained from the U.S. Department of Labor. This source provides the most authoritative occupational information available.

Contents

Choose Your Major Without Breaking Into a Cold Sweat

Calm down! Take a few deep, slow breaths. Choosing a major doesn't have to be stressful. With the help that this book provides, you can follow a series of steps that will lead you to a rational decision. Instead of biting your fingernails, you will be coolly considering your preferences and needs while calmly surveying the options available to you.

This book's strategy will work no matter why you need to choose a major right now. Maybe your college is telling you that you must declare a major and you haven't yet made up your mind which one to choose. Or maybe you have chosen a major, but it isn't working out and you're thinking about choosing a new one. Perhaps you're not yet in college but you need to choose a major so you can decide on the best college for your education—or whether to go to college at all. Whatever your reason, you are facing a decision that every college student or college-bound student has to make sooner or later.

Perhaps you feel paralyzed because choosing a major seems like such a big decision. But you can do it without hyperventilating if you follow the step-by-step process that this book outlines.

Of course, no one resource can provide all the answers, but this book contains a wealth of facts and, more important, can prompt you to ask the right questions and then help you process the answers you get. And because you will be going about the process in a structured way, you will save precious time that could have been wasted in pursuing unanswerable questions or agonizing over decisions.

Now, slow down your breathing and get started on making a satisfying choice.

The Strategy This Book Uses

Why is it so scary to choose a major? For many people, the problem is that they don't know where to start. They can't figure out which comes first: choosing a college major or choosing a career. The truth is that this is a chicken-and-egg problem that people disagree about.

Some people say that you should first decide what career you want to pursue and then choose a major that helps you prepare for it. They tell you success stories about students who graduated with degrees in accounting, computer science, or some other career-oriented major and got high-paying, fast-track career offers from businesses. (Students tend to prefer this approach.)

Other people take the opposite approach. They say that you should first decide on a major you really love and then choose a career that can take advantage of what you've learned. They tell you horror stories about students who declared a major in a career-oriented field such as engineering or business, only to discover that the coursework was so boring that they dropped out of college or changed majors and delayed graduation by one or more years. (Many academic advisors prefer this approach.)

Both approaches have elements of truth. And *the reason this book is so special* is that it lets you choose a four-year college major and a career *simultaneously,* instead of considering just one or the other. It links 120 majors to 229 careers. It informs you about what the career is like and also about what you would study in the major. It tells you which careers are commonly associated with the major and, in some cases, how graduates may go into careers in unexpected fields. And it can work *for you* because it helps you identify majors and careers that are a good fit with your personal needs and preferences.

So use this strategy and avoid a panic attack. Turn to Chapter 1 and get some background on the parts of the decision. Then, starting with Chapter 2, do some quick exercises to clarify your priorities. You'll be surprised by how quickly you'll start seeing the connections between who you are and where you want to go. Without breaking into a sweat, you'll assemble a Hot List of majors. Then you'll be able to browse descriptions of college majors and related careers so you can make a decision.

How You Can Benefit from This Book

This isn't the only book about careers or college majors, but it is specially designed to knit the two tightly together so that you can decide about both at the same time. You can benefit from using the book in the following ways:

- Do the quick exercises in Chapters 2 through 4 to help you zero in on what is most important to you in a major and a career. Tables and worksheets that accompany the exercises will help you assemble a Hot List in Chapter 5, highlighting the majors and careers that may offer what you want.

- Browse Chapter 6 for quick and effective information. This is easy because the description of each major begins with a brief definition of the major, followed by a table containing the facts about jobs that are related to the major.

- Also in Chapter 6, see specific and up-to-date facts about careers derived from the databases of the U.S. Department of Labor.

- Easily compare majors and careers in Chapter 6 with the consistent naming scheme used for work-related skills and work conditions. These facts are derived from the Department of Labor's O*NET (Occupational Information Network) database.

- Quickly locate more information sources via the Classification of Instructional Programs (CIP) number that appears in the first paragraph of each major in Chapter 6. This number links the college major to the standard coding scheme used for majors. The occupation names listed in the "Related Jobs" section are also standard titles that you can research elsewhere. This book can serve as a jumping-off point for consulting other reference works.

- Use Chapter 7 to make a decision. This chapter helps you pull together what you know about yourself and college majors that look promising.

Sources of the Information in This Book

The information in this book comes from the best and most current sources available.

Department of Labor's O*NET Database

The U.S. Department of Labor (DOL) is the nation's number-one source of information about careers. This book draws on release 15 of the DOL's O*NET database for ratings of occupational features—personality types, skills, and work conditions—that serve as the basis for assigning majors to the tables in Chapters 2 and 3 and for describing the majors in Chapter 6. A crosswalk table from the DOL identifies which careers are associated with each major.

For each feature (personality type, skill, or work condition) of the related occupation, I calculated a score based on the difference between the occupation's O*NET rating on the level of that feature and the average rating for all occupations on the same feature. Then I computed a weighted average of scores. In weighting, one factor I wanted to take into account was the size of the workforce, giving greater weight to occupations with larger workforces. However, I also wanted to diminish the weight of an occupation if graduates from the major are less likely to enter that occupation. Therefore, for each major, I ranked each related occupation by its likelihood as an outcome of the major, based on a general understanding of how people prepare for the occupation, and I divided the workforce size by the square of this ranking. (For example, I divided the workforce of the second-ranked occupation by 4.) I used this weighting, rather than the raw workforce size, in computing the average. Finally, I put all the features in a domain (e.g., all skills) in descending order of their weighted averages, and I selected as many as eight for inclusion in the Chapter 6 description. In the case of personality types, up to three are listed, or fewer if the first- or second-rated personality type has a score much higher than the next-lowest type. With work conditions, it made sense to arrange similar features together (e.g., "more often indoors than outdoors") rather than order them by their scores.

The information regarding average earnings in the careers is from the DOL's Office of Occupational Employment Statistics and applies to May 2009. The information about job growth and openings in a career is based on the most recent data from another office of the DOL, Employment Projections, and it applies to the years from 2008 to 2018. Finally, much of the information about career paths and opportunities is from the DOL's best-selling *Occupational Outlook Handbook*. Taken together, these facts give you a good introduction to the wide range of careers linked to the majors in this book.

College Web Sites

The information for the "Typical Sequence of College Courses" is derived from research in actual college Web sites listing requirements for majors. For each major, I examined and compared several course listings and identified commonly required courses. You may notice some variation in the number of courses listed. Some majors have fairly standard requirements that can be listed in detail; in some cases, a professional association mandates that certain courses be included. For other majors, notably the interdisciplinary subjects, requirements are either so minimal or so varied that it is difficult to list more than a handful of typical courses.

The information in the "Typical Sequence of High School Courses" section is based on a general understanding of which high school courses are considered prerequisites for the college-level courses required by the major. Consider these as suggestions, because often they are helpful for entering the major but are not required.

Final Points

When you read the information in this book about a major or career, keep in mind that the description covers what is *average* or *typical*—but in the real world, plenty of exceptions exist. For example, one college may offer a major with an unusual emphasis not mentioned here. The earnings figures are national averages, so you may find different figures for income where you live. And if you start looking at "help wanted" advertisements, you may learn about jobs that require a somewhat different mix of skills than the ones listed here. Use this book as an introduction to the majors and careers. When you've found some choices that interest you, explore them in greater detail. You may be able to find a way to carve out a niche within a major or career to suit your particular abilities and personality type.

CHAPTER 1

The Parts of a Major Decision

Deciding on a major is a big step, so you may be relieved when I tell you that you're not signing your life away when you decide. Most majors allow some flexibility to tailor your classes to your particular interests. And if the major doesn't work out for you, you can switch majors at a later time. Let's begin the process of decision making by looking at what some of your options are.

What Is a Major?

A *college major* is an organized program of study with some specific requirements that you must complete. Usually the program of study focuses on a subject, and the academic requirements are designed so that you gain some in-depth knowledge of that subject. Typically the subject that is the focus of the major is the same as the department offering the major (e.g., accounting, English, chemistry, or sociology), but many colleges offer interdisciplinary majors, such as American Studies, that bridge several departments. Even majors that are aligned with a specific department have requirements from other departments to help you understand your main focus of interest. For example, to understand physics, you'll need to take courses in the mathematics department. If the goal of the major is to prepare you for a specific career that you can pursue once you have your degree in hand, the major often includes a certain amount of supervised work experience. For example, student teaching is always part of a teacher education program. Majors that are less career-oriented and more academically oriented often include at least one course on research methods.

Some colleges offer a major called "General Studies" or something similar. This kind of major has few specific requirements but also has no connection to any career in particular. This book is based on the assumption that you, like most students, want to find a connection between majors and careers. That's why most of the majors described here have required courses that equip you with knowledge and skills that you'll use on the job.

Four-year colleges typically require you to declare your major by the end of your sophomore year, but you should start thinking about your choice even before you apply to college. You may need to state your intended major when you apply for admission to college. And having some idea of your intended major may also help you decide on a college because many majors are taught considerably better at some colleges than at others. For the particular major you have in mind, one college may have more experienced instructors, more course offerings, better access to instructors, major requirements better suited to careers, better-equipped labs, better library collections, better academic advisors, or better connections with employers.

Another reason to plan your major before you are required to declare it is that some majors are not open to just anyone who expresses interest. They may have specific entry requirements that you need to complete in high school and during your first two years of college, and there may even be competition for entry, meaning that your grades have to be better than simply getting by.

But if you have delayed planning your major or now feel the need to change your plans, don't panic! Brew some herbal tea and keep reading.

What About Concentrations, Minors, and Double Majors?

Majors that are highly career-oriented may give you few opportunities to choose courses that reflect your interests. For example, in some health-care fields the courses you must take are mandated by a professional association or by licensing requirements.

In most majors, however, you can select courses to emphasize an aspect of the subject that interests you—such as ancient history as opposed to modern, nuclear physics as opposed to optics, or international business management as opposed to domestic. Sometimes the department sets the course requirements for the major to reflect two or more possible "concentrations" or "tracks." For each major included in Chapter 6, you can find some of the most popular concentrations listed under the topic Specializations in the Major. Obviously your career goal is an important consideration when you choose a concentration within a major.

Of course, it is possible that you have a special interest that is not well represented by any of the concentrations in the major. For example, if you major in geology, don't expect that the department will offer a concentration in French. In that case, you may consider doing a minor in the second subject or a double major in the two subjects.

Concentrations

A concentration within a major is not simply a matter of which courses you take within the department offering the major. Often a concentration will lead you to take appropriate supporting courses in other departments. For example, an economics major who concentrates in econometrics will probably take additional courses offered by the mathematics and computer science departments, whereas one who concentrates in applied economics will probably take additional business courses.

Students who have a very clear idea of their career goals may create do-it-yourself concentrations by choosing appropriate courses from departments outside their major. For example, a religious studies major who intends to do missionary work in Latin America may take courses in Spanish and Latin American history. A human resources major who intends to do industrial training may take courses in educational psychology.

Minors

If you have a strong interest in some area outside the department of your major, you may be able to minor in that other subject. A *minor* is a set of course requirements that amount to less than a major but that still put you on record as having some depth of knowledge of that field. By combining a major and a minor, you may create a particular niche for yourself in the working world that makes you attractive to employers. For example, with a major in chemistry and a minor in business, you may be a strong candidate for a sales job with a pharmaceuticals company. With a major in computer science and a minor in public relations, you may become the Webmaster at an advertising agency.

Double Majors

In some cases, it may be possible to pursue a double major—that is, to complete the requirements for two majors. This is most feasible when both majors do not load your schedule with large numbers of required courses. If both majors allow for many freely chosen courses (these are called "electives"), you may be able to satisfy the requirements for both.

Some people combine interests by studying one subject in college and a different one in graduate or professional school. For example, most social workers and librarians are expected to enter the workforce with a master's degree, but master's programs in social work do not require you to major in the same subject as an undergraduate, and master's programs in library science actively discourage it. Medical schools require applicants to have completed certain science and math courses as undergraduates, but it is possible to fit these courses into many majors, and a well-rounded academic background may give you an advantage over other med school applicants.

The lesson to take away is that a major does not need to be a straitjacket that confines you to one subject. So if you're nervous about declaring a major partly because you have a variety of interests, try to find creative ways to tailor your major. Look at the college catalog to see what concentrations are available and how much freedom you will have to take electives. Talk to an academic advisor about options for minors, double majors, or graduate study.

Customize Your Major

If you have a special interest, you may even be able to design your own major or minor in consultation with your academic advisor. Will Shortz, now the puzzle editor at the *New York Times,* designed a major in "enigmatology" (the study of puzzles) when he was an undergraduate at Indiana University–Bloomington. Obviously, nobody's going to let you major in "partyology." But if you can devise a program of study that will gain you in-depth knowledge of a particular field that is not covered well by any one department in your college and if you can develop standards for measuring your progress in learning this field, perhaps you and your academic advisor can persuade the appropriate dean to recognize your program of study as a major.

Changing Majors

For one reason or another, you may decide later that you need to change your major. For example, you may earn poor grades in the major because the subject is either harder than you expected or so uninteresting that you aren't really trying to do the work. Or perhaps a course you take in a different field or a new career goal you learn about may capture your interest and lure you away from your original major. Keep in mind that unless the new major has requirements that are very similar to those of your original major, making this change is likely to set back your graduation date by one or more years. The sooner in your college career you decide to make the change, the less ground you'll lose. That's why, when you choose a major, it makes sense to get a realistic idea of what the major is like as soon as possible so you'll know whether it feels right to you. Ask your academic advisor to suggest a course that represents your intended major well and is not watered-down (e.g., Biology with Lab versus Biology for Poets), and take this course sooner rather than later.

The good news is that if you do the exercises in this book honestly and with an open mind, you can focus on the factors that are likely to make you want to stick with your choice of a major.

Factors That Should Be Part of the Decision

The goal of this book is to help you choose a major and a career simultaneously through a process that improves the likelihood that your choice will satisfy you. You'll go through a series of exercises to clarify your **personality type, skills,** and **favorite high school courses.** All of these are important factors in the decision—but before you look at those concerns, here are some other factors you'll probably want to consider.

Time and Expense Required

Some of the majors included in this book take longer than others to bear fruit as a career. People seeking careers in medicine, law, optometry, pharmacy, veterinary medicine, and (often) clergy must complete years of postgraduate study and on-the-job training to earn professional status. These jobs tend to pay well or (especially in the case of clergy) have other outstanding rewards. But before you commit yourself to pursue one of these career goals, you have to be sure you have the determination and ability to go through the long preparatory process. The same is true of careers such as college teaching that require a master's or doctoral degree. You need to be confident that you will enjoy the major itself, not just the rewards at the end of the road, because it will be a long road, and college tuition keeps getting more and more expensive.

Some of the careers listed in this book require more than just a degree. For managerial jobs in particular, college graduates are expected to gain some experience in the workplace, learn the language of the industry, acquire people skills that usually aren't taught in college classrooms, and demonstrate their readiness through some temporary managerial assignments. Don't plan on a managerial career unless you are willing to pay your dues as a management trainee.

In some cases, a career linked to one of these majors may not actually require four years of college. For example, this book includes Agricultural and Food Science Technicians, Chemical Technicians, Dietetic Technicians, and several other technician-level jobs that you can enter with an associate degree. Some other jobs, such as Craft Artists, Dancers, Food Service Managers, Industrial Production Managers, and Lodging Managers, are open to people who have gained work experience in related occupations or who get long-term on-the-job training. For these jobs a college education is not always necessary, but the degree may save you considerable time in getting ahead and may pave the way to further advancement or career shifts not open to those who lack the degree.

The time and expense of getting a college degree can also pay off later in ways that have nothing to do with your career. What you have learned in college may enable you to appreciate a well-designed building, an outstanding movie, or a nature walk better than someone without that background. A vacation in a foreign country, a story on the evening news, or a conversation with a stranger may connect with things you have learned in your major so that the experience is much more meaningful.

Competition

Rewarding careers often attract large numbers of job seekers. The competition can begin in college or, for some careers, even earlier. As part of the decision about a major and a career, you need to get a realistic sense of your chances of entering and succeeding in the job.

This book can help give you an idea of the competition you'll face for jobs because, wherever possible, the descriptions of majors give indications of the job opportunities in the associated careers. In the Career Snapshots, you'll notice statements such as "Competition is expected to be keen" or "Job opportunities are expected to be good." Another clue may be found in the information about how fast an occupation is growing and how many job openings are expected. But keep in mind that these nuggets of information are national averages. At the local level you may find either greater or less competition, so you need to investigate conditions where you plan to seek employment. People who do the hiring or have recently been employed can supply useful insights.

If you are already enrolled in college, you may get some answers from the staff of the career development office or from experienced faculty in the major you are considering. If you are not yet enrolled in college, consider that what recruiters tell you may be slanted as a sales pitch. Confirm what you hear by asking other sources, such as recent graduates, and be sure to ask about the college's recent job-placement track record for your intended major.

Of course, you may face competition long before you hit the job market. Some majors limit the number of people who enroll and admit only high-performing students. If you pursue a graduate or professional degree, expect competition for entry. Professional schools generally create a climate where, once admitted, students work hard but can expect to complete their degree (although often they compete for the best job prospects); many graduate departments, on the other hand, limit the number of students who are allowed to proceed beyond the master's degree into the doctoral program. Graduate students also compete for financial aid, such as fellowships that may pay a stipend.

So, as you make plans, you need to decide whether you have the drive and the ability to withstand the competition that you will face. Talk to people currently in the program and measure your past grades and test scores against their backgrounds. Ask people in the workforce what it takes to succeed. If you expect a small but significant possibility of failure, consider how well you accept risk and construct an alternative plan in case your original goal does not work out. Many people have found success and happiness in their "plan-B" careers.

Key Points: Chapter 1

- A major focuses on a particular subject, but often you can pursue an additional interest through a concentration, a minor, a double major, or graduate study.

- You need to focus on not just the career goal, but also the time and expense that the major will require to reach that goal. Be honest about your commitment to the major.

- Don't forget to consider the amount of competition you will face for entering the major, succeeding in it, and entering the workforce. Everyone needs a dream, but also a realistic plan for reaching it.

CHAPTER 2

What Is Your Personality Type?

Before you can figure out where you're going, it helps to understand who you are. With the help of some quick and easy exercises in this chapter and the two that follow, you'll take a look at yourself and what matters most to you. You'll examine your priorities from several different angles:

- Your personality type

- Your favorite high school courses

- Your skills

Each time you draw conclusions about your priorities, you'll get immediate feedback in terms of **college majors** and **related careers** that you should consider.

Then, in "Your Hot List of College Majors and Careers" in Chapter 5, you'll put together the suggestions from all three factors to create a Hot List of college majors that you should explore in Chapter 6.

Your Personality Type: The Six Holland Types

With dozens of majors to choose from, you probably would appreciate some help with narrowing down your options. That's what this chapter is for. In the following pages you're going to gain some insights into the work-related aspects of your personality and learn which of the college majors and careers in this book best suit your personality. Personality is a good place to start thinking about majors and career because it provides a big-picture view.

The most widely used personality theory about majors and careers was developed by John L. Holland in the early 1950s. The theory rests on the principle that people tend to be happier and more successful in jobs where they feel comfortable with the work tasks and problems, the physical environment, and the kinds of people who are coworkers. Holland identified six personality types that describe basic aspects of work situations. He called them Realistic, Investigative, Artistic, Social, Enterprising, and Conventional. (Some of these labels are difficult to grasp at first glance, but you'll gain a clearer understanding by the time you finish this chapter.) The initials for these personality types spell RIASEC, so that is often used to refer to these types.

To get an understanding of the Holland personality types, read these definitions:

The Holland Types Defined

Personality Type	Definition
Realistic	Realistic occupations frequently involve work activities that include practical, hands-on problems and solutions. They often deal with plants; animals; and real-world materials such as wood, tools, and machinery. Many of the occupations require working outside and do not involve a lot of paperwork or working closely with others.
Investigative	Investigative occupations frequently involve working with ideas and require an extensive amount of thinking. These occupations can involve searching for facts and figuring out problems mentally.
Artistic	Artistic occupations frequently involve working with forms, designs, and patterns. They often require self-expression, and the work can be done without following a clear set of rules.
Social	Social occupations frequently involve working with, communicating with, and teaching people. These occupations often involve helping or providing service to others.
Enterprising	Enterprising occupations frequently involve starting up and carrying out projects. These occupations can involve leading people and making many decisions. They sometimes require risk taking and often deal with business.
Conventional	Conventional occupations frequently involve following set procedures and routines. These occupations can include working with data and details more than with ideas. Usually there is a clear line of authority to follow.

Holland demonstrated the relationships among these personality types by arranging them on a hexagon:

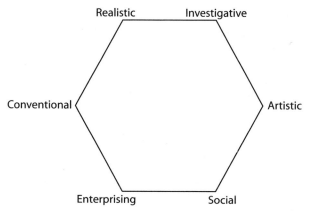

(After Holland, A Theory of Vocational Choice, *1959.)*

Holland used this diagram to explain that people tend to have one dominant personality type but may also identify with one or more other types, and these usually are types that are adjacent to the dominant type on the hexagon. Each personality type tends to have little in common with the types on the opposite side of the hexagon. Therefore, for example, a person might be primarily the Social type, with an additional but smaller identification with the Enterprising type. Such a person's personality would be described by the two-letter code SE and might point this person toward work as a Social Worker (coded SE). This person would probably have little interest in Realistic matters and likely would not be very happy or productive as an Animal Breeder (coded RI).

Perhaps you already know what Holland types describe you best, either based on the earlier definitions or because you have taken an assessment that has had its results reported as Holland types. If so, you can skip the next section and go to "Relating Personality Types to College Majors and Careers" on page 19. But if you are not clear about how to characterize your personality in Holland's terms, try the following exercise.

Personality Types Checklist

The following checklist contains Holland's six work-related personality types and examples of activities for each. Think about which personality type includes one or more activities that have the greatest appeal to you. Keep in mind that these are only *examples,* not an exhaustive list of every activity of that type. You may know you are greatly interested in an activity of this type that is not listed among the examples. (For example, you may be interested in an art form not listed under Artistic.) Similarly, you can choose a personality type as the one that describes you even if you're not interested in *all* the activities listed. Many people have diverse interests; feel free to choose one or two personality types that might be additional ways to describe you.

The psychology of personality is not an exact science, and this quick exercise is not a scientific instrument. Nevertheless, it should give you insights that will help you understand your personality type. Use common sense to combine the results of this exercise with other information you can get about yourself and your academic and work options. Talk to people who know you and are familiar with your school and work experiences.

In the blank spaces to the left, write a "1" to indicate your dominant personality type. You may also write a "2" or "3" to indicate other personality types that feature activities that interest you, but not as much as your principal type.

PERSONALITY TYPES CHECKLIST

___ **Realistic:** Putting out forest fires; laying brick or tile; growing Christmas trees in a nursery; testing the quality of parts before shipment; enforcing fish and game laws; refinishing furniture; applying pesticides and fertilizers to plants.

___ **Investigative:** Making a map of the bottom of an ocean; determining the infection rate of a new disease; investigating crimes; studying the governments of different countries; inventing a replacement for sugar; diagnosing and treating sick animals; studying ways to reduce water pollution.

___ **Artistic:** Playing a musical instrument; creating special effects for movies; writing reviews of books or plays; dancing in a Broadway show; designing artwork for magazines; announcing a radio show; painting sets for plays.

___ **Social:** Teaching children how to read; helping people with family-related problems; organizing activities at a recreational facility; working with juveniles on probation; helping disabled people improve their skills for daily living; helping conduct a group therapy session; teaching children how to play sports.

___ **Enterprising:** Giving a presentation about a product you are selling; managing a department within a large company; marketing a new line of

---

clothing; negotiating business contracts; selling houses; managing the operations of a hotel; buying and selling stocks and bonds.

__ **Conventional:** Organizing and scheduling office meetings; inventorying supplies using a hand-held computer; taking notes during a meeting; developing a spreadsheet using computer software; assisting senior-level accountants in performing bookkeeping tasks; maintaining employee records; using a word processor to edit and format documents.

Relating Personality Types to College Majors and Careers

Now that you have clarified your work-related personality type, it's time to consider majors and careers that go well with this personality type. The following table lists the majors and careers included in this book that are associated with each of the six personality types. Most of the majors have two- or three-letter codes, meaning that they may be able to satisfy one or two secondary personality types as well as a dominant type.

Note that each major is given personality type codes based on the *careers that the major is linked to* and not necessarily on what you focus on while you are studying the major in college. For example, the American Studies major is listed in the Social personality type (with the code SIA) because the major is linked to the job Area, Ethnic, and Cultural Studies Teachers, Postsecondary (also coded SIA). Like most teaching jobs, this one involves a lot of working with and helping people and, therefore, is associated primarily with the Social personality type. While you are pursuing an American Studies major in college, however, you may have limited opportunities to work with and help people. In more career-oriented majors, such as Art (Artistic), Dietetics (Investigative), or Animal Science (Realistic), the activities you engage in as an undergraduate may more often reflect the experience of the job.

Also consider that some people with diverse interests choose majors that are not directly linked to their career goals. For example, a person with an Enterprising personality might major in Russian (classified as Artistic) while intending to pursue a career in international sales; this person could take some business courses in college and learn the rest of the job through on-the-job training. Other people with diverse interests complete a minor related to their secondary personality type. Still others study one thing as an undergraduate and something else in graduate or professional school—or pursue a secondary interest as a hobby at the end of the workday.

With these considerations in mind, browse the following table to find majors and careers associated with your dominant personality type and perhaps with one or more secondary personality types. Write these in the blank spaces in the worksheet that follows the table on page 33, "College Majors and Careers That Relate to My Personality Type."

Personality Types and Related College Majors and Careers

Personality Type: Realistic

Personality Type(s): RIE   **Related Major:** Forestry

Related Careers and Their Personality Types: Conservation Scientists (RIE), Forest and Conservation Technicians (RIE), Forest and Conservation Workers (RCI), Foresters (RIE)

Personality Type(s): RIC   **Related Major:** Civil Engineering

Related Careers and Their Personality Types: Civil Engineers (RIC), Engineering Managers (ERI), Engineering Teachers, Postsecondary (SIR)

Personality Type(s): RIC   **Related Major:** Food Science

Related Careers and Their Personality Types: Agricultural and Food Science Technicians (RIC), Chemical Technicians (IRC), Food Scientists and Technologists (IRC)

Personality Type(s): REC   **Related Major:** Agricultural Business and Economics

Related Careers and Their Personality Types: Farm and Home Management Advisors (SRE), Farm, Ranch, and Other Agricultural Managers (ERC), Farmers and Ranchers (REC), First-Line Supervisors/Managers of Farming, Fishing, and Forestry Workers (ERC), Nonfarm Animal Caretakers (RC), Pest Control Workers (RC), Purchasing Agents and Buyers, Farm Products (ECR)

Personality Type(s): REC   **Related Major:** Agronomy and Crop Science

Related Careers and Their Personality Types: Agricultural and Food Science Technicians (RIC), Agricultural Sciences Teachers, Postsecondary (SIR), Farm, Ranch, and Other Agricultural Managers (ERC), Farmers and Ranchers (REC), First-Line Supervisors/Managers of Farming, Fishing, and Forestry Workers (ERC), Soil and Plant Scientists (IR)

Personality Type(s): REC   **Related Major:** Animal Science

Related Careers and Their Personality Types: Agricultural and Food Science Technicians (RIC), Agricultural Sciences Teachers, Postsecondary (SIR), Animal Scientists (IR), Farm and Home Management Advisors (SRE), Farm, Ranch, and Other Agricultural Managers (ERC), Farmers and Ranchers (REC), First-Line Supervisors/Managers of Farming, Fishing, and Forestry Workers (ERC)

Personality Type: Investigative

Personality Type(s): I   **Related Major:** Astronomy

Related Careers and Their Personality Types: Astronomers (IAR), Atmospheric, Earth, Marine, and Space Sciences Teachers, Postsecondary (SI), Natural Sciences Managers (EI), Physicists (IR)

Personality Type(s): IR   **Related Major:** Chemistry

Related Careers and Their Personality Types: Chemistry Teachers, Postsecondary (SIR), Chemists (IRC), Natural Sciences Managers (EI)

Personality Type(s): IR   **Related Major:** Electrical Engineering

Related Careers and Their Personality Types: Electrical Engineers (IR), Electronics Engineers, Except Computer (IR), Engineering Managers (ERI), Engineering Teachers, Postsecondary (SIR)

Personality Type(s): IR   **Related Major:** Geology

Related Careers and Their Personality Types: Atmospheric, Earth, Marine, and Space Sciences Teachers, Postsecondary (SI), Geoscientists, Except Hydrologists and Geographers (IR), Hydrologists (IR), Natural Sciences Managers (EI)

Personality Type(s): IR   **Related Major:** Geophysics

Related Careers and Their Personality Types: Atmospheric, Earth, Marine, and Space Sciences Teachers, Postsecondary (SI), Geoscientists, Except Hydrologists and Geographers (IR), Natural Sciences Managers (EI)

Personality Type(s): IR   **Related Major:** Microbiology

Related Careers and Their Personality Types: Biological Science Teachers, Postsecondary (SI), Medical Scientists, Except Epidemiologists (IRA), Microbiologists (IR), Natural Sciences Managers (EI)

Personality Type(s): IR   **Related Major:** Oceanography

Related Careers and Their Personality Types: Atmospheric, Earth, Marine, and Space Sciences Teachers, Postsecondary (SI), Biological Science Teachers, Postsecondary (SI), Geoscientists, Except Hydrologists and Geographers (IR), Hydrologists (IR), Natural Sciences Managers (EI)

Personality Type(s): IR   **Related Major:** Soil Science

Related Careers and Their Personality Types: Agricultural Sciences Teachers, Postsecondary (SIR), Biochemists and Biophysicists (IAR), Microbiologists (IR), Soil and Plant Scientists (IR)

Personality Type(s): IRS   **Related Major:** Dentistry

Related Careers and Their Personality Types: Dentists, General (IRS), Health Specialties Teachers, Postsecondary (SI)

(continued)

R=Realistic; I=Investigative; A=Artistic; S=Social; E=Enterprising; C=Conventional

Personality Type: Investigative (continued)

Personality Type(s): IRE   **Related Major:** Aeronautical/Aerospace Engineering
Related Careers and Their Personality Types: Aerospace Engineers (IR), Engineering Managers (ERI), Engineering Teachers, Postsecondary (SIR)

Personality Type(s): IRE   **Related Major:** Chemical Engineering
Related Careers and Their Personality Types: Chemical Engineers (IR), Engineering Managers (ERI), Engineering Teachers, Postsecondary (SIR)

Personality Type(s): IRE   **Related Major:** Wildlife Management
Related Careers and Their Personality Types: Conservation Scientists (RIE), Fish and Game Wardens (RI), Zoologists and Wildlife Biologists (IR)

Personality Type(s): IRE   **Related Major:** Zoology
Related Careers and Their Personality Types: Biological Science Teachers, Postsecondary (SI), Natural Sciences Managers (EI), Zoologists and Wildlife Biologists (IR)

Personality Type(s): IRC   **Related Major:** Computer Engineering
Related Careers and Their Personality Types: Computer Hardware Engineers (IRC), Computer Software Engineers, Applications (IRC), Computer Software Engineers, Systems Software (ICR), Computer Specialists, All Other (CIR), Engineering Managers (ERI), Engineering Teachers, Postsecondary (SIR)

Personality Type(s): IRC   **Related Major:** Environmental Science
Related Careers and Their Personality Types: Environmental Science and Protection Technicians, Including Health (IRC), Environmental Science Teachers, Postsecondary (SIA), Environmental Scientists and Specialists, Including Health (IRC)

Personality Type(s): IRC   **Related Major:** Mechanical Engineering
Related Careers and Their Personality Types: Cost Estimators (CE), Engineering Managers (ERI), Engineering Teachers, Postsecondary (SIR), Mechanical Engineers (IRC)

Personality Type(s): IRC   **Related Major:** Medical Technology
Related Careers and Their Personality Types: Health Specialties Teachers, Postsecondary (SI), Medical and Clinical Laboratory Technologists (IRC)

Personality Type(s): IA   **Related Major:** Anthropology
Related Careers and Their Personality Types: Anthropologists and Archeologists (IA), Anthropology and Archeology Teachers, Postsecondary (SI)

Personality Type(s): IA   **Related Major:** Archeology
Related Careers and Their Personality Types: Anthropologists and Archeologists (IA), Anthropology and Archeology Teachers, Postsecondary (SI)

Personality Type(s): IAR   **Related Major:** Biochemistry
Related Careers and Their Personality Types: Biochemists and Biophysicists (IAR), Biological Science Teachers, Postsecondary (SI), Medical Scientists, Except Epidemiologists (IRA), Natural Sciences Managers (EI)

Personality Type(s): IAS   **Related Major:** Urban Studies
Related Careers and Their Personality Types: Sociologists (IAS)

Personality Type(s): IS   **Related Major:** Biology
Related Careers and Their Personality Types: Biological Science Teachers, Postsecondary (SI), Natural Sciences Managers (EI)

Personality Type(s): IS   **Related Major:** Botany
Related Careers and Their Personality Types: Biological Science Teachers, Postsecondary (SI), Natural Sciences Managers (EI)

Personality Type(s): IS   **Related Major:** Dietetics
Related Careers and Their Personality Types: Dietetic Technicians (SIR), Dietitians and Nutritionists (IS)

Personality Type(s): IS   **Related Major:** History
Related Careers and Their Personality Types: Archivists (CI), Curators (EC), Historians (I), History Teachers, Postsecondary (SIA)

Personality Type(s): ISR   **Related Major:** Medicine
Related Careers and Their Personality Types: Anesthesiologists (ISR), Family and General Practitioners (IS), Internists, General (ISR), Obstetricians and Gynecologists (ISR), Pediatricians, General (IS), Psychiatrists (ISA), Surgeons (IRS)

Personality Type(s): ISR   **Related Major:** Optometry
Related Careers and Their Personality Types: Optometrists (ISR)

Personality Type(s): ISR   **Related Major:** Podiatry
Related Careers and Their Personality Types: Podiatrists (ISR)

Personality Type(s): ISR   **Related Major:** Veterinary Medicine
Related Careers and Their Personality Types: Health Specialties Teachers, Postsecondary (SI), Veterinarians (IR)

Personality Type(s): ISA   **Related Major:** Geography
Related Careers and Their Personality Types: Geographers (IRA), Geography Teachers, Postsecondary (SI)

Personality Type(s): ISA   **Related Major:** Psychology
Related Careers and Their Personality Types: Clinical, Counseling, and School Psychologists (ISA), Industrial-Organizational Psychologists (IES), Psychology Teachers, Postsecondary (SIA)

Personality Type(s): ISA   **Related Major:** Sociology
Related Careers and Their Personality Types: Sociologists (IAS), Sociology Teachers, Postsecondary (SIA)

(continued)

R=Realistic; I=Investigative; A=Artistic; S=Social; E=Enterprising; C=Conventional

Personality Type: Investigative (continued)

Personality Type(s): IE   **Related Major:** Physics

Related Careers and Their Personality Types: Natural Sciences Managers (EI), Physicists (IR), Physics Teachers, Postsecondary (SI)

Personality Type(s): IEC   **Related Major:** Economics

Related Careers and Their Personality Types: Economics Teachers, Postsecondary (SI), Economists (ICE), Market Research Analysts (IEC), Survey Researchers (ICE)

Personality Type(s): IEC   **Related Major:** Industrial Engineering

Related Careers and Their Personality Types: Engineering Managers (ERI), Engineering Teachers, Postsecondary (SIR), Industrial Engineers (ICE), Natural Sciences Managers (EI), Operations Research Analysts (ICE)

Personality Type(s): IC   **Related Major:** Statistics

Related Careers and Their Personality Types: Mathematical Science Teachers, Postsecondary (SIA), Mathematicians (ICA), Natural Sciences Managers (EI), Statisticians (CI)

Personality Type(s): ICR   **Related Major:** Computer Science

Related Careers and Their Personality Types: Computer and Information Scientists, Research (IRC), Computer and Information Systems Managers (ECI), Computer Science Teachers, Postsecondary (SIC), Computer Software Engineers, Applications (IRC), Computer Software Engineers, Systems Software (ICR), Computer Specialists, All Other (CIR), Database Administrators (CI), Network and Computer Systems Administrators (ICR), Network Systems and Data Communications Analysts (IC)

Personality Type(s): ICS   **Related Major:** Mathematics

Related Careers and Their Personality Types: Mathematical Science Teachers, Postsecondary (SIA), Mathematicians (ICA), Natural Sciences Managers (EI), Statisticians (CI)

Personality Type(s): ICS   **Related Major:** Occupational Health and Industrial Hygiene

Related Careers and Their Personality Types: Health Specialties Teachers, Postsecondary (SI), Occupational Health and Safety Specialists (IC), Occupational Health and Safety Technicians (CR)

Personality Type(s): ICS   **Related Major:** Pharmacy

Related Careers and Their Personality Types: Health Specialties Teachers, Postsecondary (SI), Pharmacists (ICS)

Personality Type: Artistic

Personality Type(s): ARE   **Related Major:** Graphic Design, Commercial Art, and Illustration

Related Careers and Their Personality Types: Commercial and Industrial Designers (AER), Computer Programmers (IC), Computer Specialists, All Other (CIR), Graphic Designers (AER), Multi-Media Artists and Animators (AI), Set and Exhibit Designers (AR)

Personality Type(s): AIE   **Related Major:** Architecture

Related Careers and Their Personality Types: Architects, Except Landscape and Naval (AI), Architecture Teachers, Postsecondary (SA), Engineering Managers (ERI)

Personality Type(s): AS   **Related Major:** Chinese

Related Careers and Their Personality Types: Foreign Language and Literature Teachers, Postsecondary (SAI), Interpreters and Translators (AS)

Personality Type(s): AS   **Related Major:** French

Related Careers and Their Personality Types: Foreign Language and Literature Teachers, Postsecondary (SAI), Interpreters and Translators (AS)

Personality Type(s): AS   **Related Major:** German

Related Careers and Their Personality Types: Foreign Language and Literature Teachers, Postsecondary (SAI), Interpreters and Translators (AS)

Personality Type(s): AS   **Related Major:** Japanese

Related Careers and Their Personality Types: Foreign Language and Literature Teachers, Postsecondary (SAI), Interpreters and Translators (AS)

Personality Type(s): AS   **Related Major:** Modern Foreign Language

Related Careers and Their Personality Types: Foreign Language and Literature Teachers, Postsecondary (SAI), Interpreters and Translators (AS)

Personality Type(s): AS   **Related Major:** Russian

Related Careers and Their Personality Types: Foreign Language and Literature Teachers, Postsecondary (SAI), Interpreters and Translators (AS)

Personality Type(s): AS   **Related Major:** Spanish

Related Careers and Their Personality Types: Foreign Language and Literature Teachers, Postsecondary (SAI), Interpreters and Translators (AS)

Personality Type(s): ASR   **Related Major:** Dance

Related Careers and Their Personality Types: Art, Drama, and Music Teachers, Postsecondary (SA), Choreographers (ASE), Dancers (AR)

(continued)

R=Realistic; I=Investigative; A=Artistic; S=Social; E=Enterprising; C=Conventional

Personality Type: Artistic (continued)

Personality Type(s): AE   **Related Major:** Drama/Theater Arts

Related Careers and Their Personality Types: Actors (AE), Art, Drama, and Music Teachers, Postsecondary (SA), Producers and Directors (EAC)

Personality Type(s): AE   **Related Major:** Film/Cinema Studies

Related Careers and Their Personality Types: Art, Drama, and Music Teachers, Postsecondary (SA), Camera Operators, Television, Video, and Motion Picture (RA), Film and Video Editors (AEI), Producers and Directors (EAC)

Personality Type(s): AE   **Related Major:** Music

Related Careers and Their Personality Types: Art, Drama, and Music Teachers, Postsecondary (SA), Music Directors and Composers (AE), Musicians and Singers (AE)

Personality Type(s): AER   **Related Major:** Art

Related Careers and Their Personality Types: Art Directors (AE), Art, Drama, and Music Teachers, Postsecondary (SA), Craft Artists (ARE), Fine Artists, Including Painters, Sculptors, and Illustrators (AR), Multi-Media Artists and Animators (AI)

Personality Type(s): AER   **Related Major:** Industrial Design

Related Careers and Their Personality Types: Commercial and Industrial Designers (AER), Graphic Designers (AER)

Personality Type(s): AEI   **Related Major:** Journalism and Mass Communications

Related Careers and Their Personality Types: Broadcast News Analysts (ASE), Communications Teachers, Postsecondary (SA), Editors (AEC), Reporters and Correspondents (AEI), Writers and Authors (AEI)

Personality Type(s): AES   **Related Major:** Interior Design

Related Careers and Their Personality Types: Art, Drama, and Music Teachers, Postsecondary (SA), Interior Designers (AE)

Personality Type(s): AEC   **Related Major:** English

Related Careers and Their Personality Types: Editors (AEC), English Language and Literature Teachers, Postsecondary (SAI)

Personality Type: Social

Personality Type(s): S   **Related Major:** Industrial/Technology Education

Related Careers and Their Personality Types: Education Teachers, Postsecondary (SAI), Middle School Teachers, Except Special and Vocational Education (SA), Secondary School Teachers, Except Special and Vocational Education (SAE), Vocational Education Teachers, Middle School (SAC), Vocational Education Teachers, Postsecondary (SR), Vocational Education Teachers, Secondary School (S)

Personality Type(s): SI   **Related Major:** Chiropractic
Related Careers and Their Personality Types: Chiropractors (SIR), Health Specialties Teachers, Postsecondary (SI)

Personality Type(s): SI   **Related Major:** Nursing (RN Training)
Related Careers and Their Personality Types: Nursing Instructors and Teachers, Postsecondary (SI), Registered Nurses (SIC)

Personality Type(s): SI   **Related Major:** Occupational Therapy
Related Careers and Their Personality Types: Health Specialties Teachers, Postsecondary (SI), Occupational Therapists (SI)

Personality Type(s): SI   **Related Major:** Orthotics/Prosthetics
Related Careers and Their Personality Types: Health Specialties Teachers, Postsecondary (SI), Medical Appliance Technicians (RIS), Orthotists and Prosthetists (SRI)

Personality Type(s): SI   **Related Major:** Physical Therapy
Related Careers and Their Personality Types: Health Specialties Teachers, Postsecondary (SI), Physical Therapists (SIR)

Personality Type(s): SI   **Related Major:** Physician Assisting
Related Careers and Their Personality Types: Health Specialties Teachers, Postsecondary (SI), Physician Assistants (ISR)

Personality Type(s): SIA   **Related Major:** African-American Studies
Related Careers and Their Personality Types: Area, Ethnic, and Cultural Studies Teachers, Postsecondary (SIA)

Personality Type(s): SIA   **Related Major:** American Studies
Related Careers and Their Personality Types: Area, Ethnic, and Cultural Studies Teachers, Postsecondary (SIA)

Personality Type(s): SIA   **Related Major:** Area Studies
Related Careers and Their Personality Types: Area, Ethnic, and Cultural Studies Teachers, Postsecondary (SIA)

Personality Type(s): SIA   **Related Major:** Political Science
Related Careers and Their Personality Types: Political Science Teachers, Postsecondary (SEA), Political Scientists (IAS)

Personality Type(s): SIA   **Related Major:** Speech-Language Pathology and Audiology
Related Careers and Their Personality Types: Audiologists (IS), Health Specialties Teachers, Postsecondary (SI), Speech-Language Pathologists (SIA)

(continued)

R=Realistic; I=Investigative; A=Artistic; S=Social; E=Enterprising; C=Conventional

Personality Type: Social (continued)

Personality Type(s): SIA   **Related Major:** Women's Studies
Related Careers and Their Personality Types: Area, Ethnic, and Cultural Studies Teachers, Postsecondary (SIA)

Personality Type(s): SA   **Related Major:** Art History
Related Careers and Their Personality Types: Archivists (CI), Art, Drama, and Music Teachers, Postsecondary (SA), Curators (EC), Museum Technicians and Conservators (RA)

Personality Type(s): SA   **Related Major:** Early Childhood Education
Related Careers and Their Personality Types: Kindergarten Teachers, Except Special Education (SA), Preschool Teachers, Except Special Education (SA)

Personality Type(s): SA   **Related Major:** Humanities
Related Careers and Their Personality Types: Anthropology and Archeology Teachers, Postsecondary (SI), Area, Ethnic, and Cultural Studies Teachers, Postsecondary (SIA), Art, Drama, and Music Teachers, Postsecondary (SA), Communications Teachers, Postsecondary (SA), Economics Teachers, Postsecondary (SI), Education Teachers, Postsecondary (SAI), English Language and Literature Teachers, Postsecondary (SAI), Foreign Language and Literature Teachers, Postsecondary (SAI), Geography Teachers, Postsecondary (SI), Graduate Teaching Assistants (SC), History Teachers, Postsecondary (SIA), Library Science Teachers, Postsecondary (SIC), Philosophy and Religion Teachers, Postsecondary (SAI), Political Science Teachers, Postsecondary (SEA), Psychology Teachers, Postsecondary (SIA), Sociology Teachers, Postsecondary (SIA)

Personality Type(s): SA   **Related Major:** Special Education
Related Careers and Their Personality Types: Interpreters and Translators (AS), Special Education Teachers, Middle School (SA), Special Education Teachers, Preschool, Kindergarten, and Elementary School (SA), Special Education Teachers, Secondary School (SI)

Personality Type(s): SAI   **Related Major:** Classics
Related Careers and Their Personality Types: Anthropologists and Archeologists (IA), Foreign Language and Literature Teachers, Postsecondary (SAI), Interpreters and Translators (AS)

Personality Type(s): SAE   **Related Major:** Business Education
Related Careers and Their Personality Types: Business Teachers, Postsecondary (SEI), Education Teachers, Postsecondary (SAI), Secondary School Teachers, Except Special and Vocational Education (SAE), Vocational Education Teachers, Postsecondary (SR)

Personality Type(s): SAE   **Related Major:** Family and Consumer Sciences
Related Careers and Their Personality Types: Editors (AEC), Education Teachers, Postsecondary (SAI), Farm and Home Management Advisors (SRE), First-Line Supervisors/ Managers of Retail Sales Workers (ECS), Home Economics Teachers, Postsecondary (SIA), Marketing Managers (EC), Middle School Teachers, Except Special and Vocational Education (SA), Public Relations Specialists (EAS), Sales Managers (EC), Secondary School Teachers, Except Special and Vocational Education (SAE), Writers and Authors (AEI)

Personality Type(s): SAE   **Related Major:** Religion/Religious Studies
Related Careers and Their Personality Types: Clergy (SEA), Philosophy and Religion Teachers, Postsecondary (SAI)

Personality Type(s): SAE   **Related Major:** Secondary Education
Related Careers and Their Personality Types: Secondary School Teachers, Except Special and Vocational Education (SAE)

Personality Type(s): SAC   **Related Major:** Elementary Education
Related Careers and Their Personality Types: Elementary School Teachers, Except Special Education (SAC)

Personality Type(s): SE   **Related Major:** Physical Education
Related Careers and Their Personality Types: Coaches and Scouts (SRE), Education Teachers, Postsecondary (SAI), Fitness Trainers and Aerobics Instructors (SRE), Middle School Teachers, Except Special and Vocational Education (SA), Secondary School Teachers, Except Special and Vocational Education (SAE)

Personality Type(s): SE   **Related Major:** Social Work
Related Careers and Their Personality Types: Child, Family, and School Social Workers (SE), Marriage and Family Therapists (SAI), Probation Officers and Correctional Treatment Specialists (SEC), Social Work Teachers, Postsecondary (SI)

Personality Type(s): SEA   **Related Major:** Parks and Recreation Management
Related Careers and Their Personality Types: Recreation Workers (SEA)

Personality Type(s): SEA   **Related Major:** Philosophy
Related Careers and Their Personality Types: Clergy (SEA), Directors, Religious Activities and Education (ESC), Philosophy and Religion Teachers, Postsecondary (SAI)

Personality Type: Enterprising

Personality Type(s): ERC   **Related Major:** Criminal Justice/Law Enforcement
Related Careers and Their Personality Types: Bailiffs (RCE), Criminal Justice and Law Enforcement Teachers, Postsecondary (SI), Detectives and Criminal Investigators (ECR), Police and Sheriff's Patrol Officers (ERS), Private Detectives and Investigators (EC)

Personality Type(s): ERC   **Related Major:** Operations Management
Related Careers and Their Personality Types: Business Teachers, Postsecondary (SEI), Computer and Information Systems Managers (ECI), Construction Managers (ERC), First-Line Supervisors/Managers of Mechanics, Installers, and Repairers (ECR), First-Line Supervisors/Managers of Production and Operating Workers (ERC), Industrial Production Managers (EC), Logisticians (EC), Transportation, Storage, and Distribution Managers (EC)

(continued)

R=Realistic; I=Investigative; A=Artistic; S=Social; E=Enterprising; C=Conventional

Personality Type: Enterprising (continued)

Personality Type(s): EI   **Related Major:** Law

Related Careers and Their Personality Types: Administrative Law Judges, Adjudicators, and Hearing Officers (EIS), Arbitrators, Mediators, and Conciliators (SE), Judges, Magistrate Judges, and Magistrates (ES), Law Clerks (CIE), Law Teachers, Postsecondary (SIE), Lawyers (EI)

Personality Type(s): EIR   **Related Major:** Agricultural Engineering

Related Careers and Their Personality Types: Agricultural Engineers (IRE), Engineering Managers (ERI), Engineering Teachers, Postsecondary (SIR)

Personality Type(s): EIR   **Related Major:** Bioengineering

Related Careers and Their Personality Types: Biomedical Engineers (IR), Engineering Managers (ERI), Engineering Teachers, Postsecondary (SIR)

Personality Type(s): EIR   **Related Major:** Landscape Architecture

Related Careers and Their Personality Types: Architecture Teachers, Postsecondary (SA), Engineering Managers (ERI), Landscape Architects (AIR)

Personality Type(s): EIR   **Related Major:** Materials Science

Related Careers and Their Personality Types: Engineering Managers (ERI), Engineering Teachers, Postsecondary (SIR), Materials Scientists (IR)

Personality Type(s): EIR   **Related Major:** Metallurgical Engineering

Related Careers and Their Personality Types: Engineering Managers (ERI), Engineering Teachers, Postsecondary (SIR), Materials Engineers (IRE)

Personality Type(s): EIR   **Related Major:** Petroleum Engineering

Related Careers and Their Personality Types: Engineering Managers (ERI), Engineering Teachers, Postsecondary (SIR), Petroleum Engineers (IRC)

Personality Type(s): EAS   **Related Major:** Communications Studies/Speech

Related Careers and Their Personality Types: Communications Teachers, Postsecondary (SA), Public Address System and Other Announcers (SEA), Public Relations Specialists (EAS), Technical Writers (AIC), Writers and Authors (AEI)

Personality Type(s): EAS   **Related Major:** Public Relations

Related Careers and Their Personality Types: Advertising and Promotions Managers (EAC), Communications Teachers, Postsecondary (SA), Public Relations Managers (EA), Public Relations Specialists (EAS)

Personality Type(s): EAC   **Related Major:** Advertising

Related Careers and Their Personality Types: Advertising and Promotions Managers (EAC), Advertising Sales Agents (ECA), Communications Teachers, Postsecondary (SA)

Personality Type(s): ESC   **Related Major:** Health Information Systems Administration

Related Careers and Their Personality Types: Medical and Health Services Managers (ESC)

Personality Type(s): ESC   **Related Major:** Hospital/Health Facilities Administration

Related Careers and Their Personality Types: Medical and Health Services Managers (ESC)

Personality Type(s): ESC   **Related Major:** Human Resources Management

Related Careers and Their Personality Types: Business Teachers, Postsecondary (SEI), Compensation and Benefits Managers (ECS), Compensation, Benefits, and Job Analysis Specialists (CE), Employment, Recruitment, and Placement Specialists (ESC), Training and Development Managers (ES), Training and Development Specialists (SAC)

Personality Type(s): EC   **Related Major:** Business Management

Related Careers and Their Personality Types: Administrative Services Managers (EC), Business Teachers, Postsecondary (SEI), Chief Executives (EC), Construction Managers (ERC), Cost Estimators (CE), General and Operations Managers (ECS), Industrial Production Managers (EC), Management Analysts (IEC), Sales Managers (EC), Social and Community Service Managers (ES), Transportation, Storage, and Distribution Managers (EC)

Personality Type(s): EC   **Related Major:** Marketing

Related Careers and Their Personality Types: Advertising and Promotions Managers (EAC), Business Teachers, Postsecondary (SEI), Marketing Managers (EC), Sales Managers (EC)

Personality Type(s): EC   **Related Major:** Transportation and Logistics Management

Related Careers and Their Personality Types: Administrative Services Managers (EC), Business Teachers, Postsecondary (SEI), Chief Executives (EC), Logisticians (EC), Transportation, Storage, and Distribution Managers (EC)

Personality Type(s): ECI   **Related Major:** Management Information Systems

Related Careers and Their Personality Types: Computer and Information Systems Managers (ECI), Computer Programmers (IC), Database Administrators (CI)

Personality Type(s): ECS   **Related Major:** Hotel/Motel and Restaurant Management

Related Careers and Their Personality Types: Food Service Managers (ECR), Lodging Managers (ECS)

(continued)

R=Realistic; I=Investigative; A=Artistic; S=Social; E=Enterprising; C=Conventional

Personality Type: Enterprising (continued)

Personality Type(s): ECS   **Related Major:** Industrial and Labor Relations

Related Careers and Their Personality Types: Business Teachers, Postsecondary (SEI), Compensation and Benefits Managers (ECS), Compensation, Benefits, and Job Analysis Specialists (CE), Employment, Recruitment, and Placement Specialists (ESC)

Personality Type(s): ECS   **Related Major:** International Business

Related Careers and Their Personality Types: Business Teachers, Postsecondary (SEI), Chief Executives (EC), General and Operations Managers (ECS)

Personality Type(s): ECS   **Related Major:** International Relations

Related Careers and Their Personality Types: Chief Executives (EC), Political Science Teachers, Postsecondary (SEA), Political Scientists (IAS)

Personality Type(s): ECS   **Related Major:** Public Administration

Related Careers and Their Personality Types: Administrative Services Managers (EC), Chief Executives (EC), Emergency Management Specialists (SE), General and Operations Managers (ECS), Legislators (ES), Postmasters and Mail Superintendents (ECS), Social and Community Service Managers (ES), Transportation, Storage, and Distribution Managers (EC)

Personality Type: Conventional

Personality Type(s): CIS   **Related Major:** Actuarial Science

Related Careers and Their Personality Types: Actuaries (CIE), Business Teachers, Postsecondary (SEI)

Personality Type(s): CSE   **Related Major:** Library Science

Related Careers and Their Personality Types: Librarians (CSE), Library Science Teachers, Postsecondary (SIC)

Personality Type(s): CE   **Related Major:** Insurance

Related Careers and Their Personality Types: Business Teachers, Postsecondary (SEI), Claims Adjusters, Examiners, and Investigators (CE), Insurance Appraisers, Auto Damage (CRE), Insurance Sales Agents (ECS), Insurance Underwriters (CEI), Purchasing Agents, Except Wholesale, Retail, and Farm Products (CE), Sales Representatives, Wholesale and Manufacturing, Except Technical and Scientific Products (CE), Telemarketers (EC), Wholesale and Retail Buyers, Except Farm Products (EC)

Personality Type(s): CEI   **Related Major:** Accounting

Related Careers and Their Personality Types: Accountants and Auditors (CEI), Budget Analysts (CEI), Business Teachers, Postsecondary (SEI), Credit Analysts (CE), Financial Examiners (EC), Tax Examiners, Collectors, and Revenue Agents (CE)

Personality Type(s): CEI   **Related Major:** Finance

Related Careers and Their Personality Types: Budget Analysts (CEI), Business Teachers, Postsecondary (SEI), Credit Analysts (CE), Financial Analysts (CIE), Financial Managers (EC), Loan Officers (CES), Personal Financial Advisors (ECS)

Use the following worksheet to jot down the majors and careers that relate to your main interest or interests.

COLLEGE MAJORS AND CAREERS THAT RELATE TO MY PERSONALITY TYPE

Panicked Student's Guide to Choosing a College Major _____

Key Points: Chapter 2

- People who do work consistent with their personality type tend to be happier and more successful.

- The six Holland types can provide a useful way of organizing work-related personality types into a few large categories. Understanding your Holland type(s) can help you choose a major and a career.

- If you have diverse interests, it is possible to satisfy them by identifying a major that combines them or by rounding out a major with a minor, a graduate program, or an atypical career path.

CHAPTER 3

What Are Your Skills?

Different kinds of work demand different skills, and people vary in what skills they bring to the workplace. Most people want to go into a kind of work where they will be able to handle the skill requirements. Of course, you don't yet *have* all the skills you will need for your career—that's why you are planning to get further education. Nevertheless, based on your experience in school, you probably have a good idea of which skills you learn easily and which come harder. You may also have work experience that indicates some of your skills.

Skills Checklist

The following checklist defines 28 of the skills that the U.S. Department of Labor includes in the O*NET database. For each skill, ask yourself, "What things have I done in which I've used this skill *at a high level* and *enjoyed* using it?" If you can think of several good examples, mark the name of the skill with a plus sign in the blank space at the left; otherwise, move on to another skill.

Some people find it difficult to judge their own skills, so just do your best here. You may ask a friend or relative who knows you well to review your self-ratings.

Skills Checklist

___ **Active Learning:** Understanding the implications of new information for both current and future problem solving and decision making.

___ **Complex Problem Solving:** Identifying complex problems and reviewing related information to develop and evaluate options and implement solutions.

___ **Coordination:** Adjusting actions in relation to others' actions.

(continued)

(continued)

___ **Critical Thinking:** Using logic and reasoning to identify the strengths and weaknesses of alternative solutions, conclusions, or approaches to problems.

___ **Equipment Maintenance:** Performing routine maintenance and determining when and what kind of maintenance is needed.

___ **Equipment Selection:** Determining the kinds of tools and equipment needed to do a job.

___ **Installation:** Installing equipment, machines, wiring, or programs to meet specifications.

___ **Instructing:** Teaching others how to do something.

___ **Judgment and Decision Making:** Considering the relative costs and benefits of potential actions to choose the most appropriate one.

___ **Learning Strategies:** Selecting and using training/instructional methods and procedures appropriate for the situation when learning or teaching new things.

___ **Management of Financial Resources:** Determining how money will be spent to get the work done and accounting for these expenditures.

___ **Management of Material Resources:** Obtaining and seeing to the appropriate use of equipment, facilities, and materials needed to do certain work.

___ **Management of Personnel Resources:** Motivating, developing, and directing people as they work; identifying the best people for the job.

___ **Mathematics:** Using mathematics to solve problems.

___ **Monitoring:** Assessing how well one is doing when learning or doing something.

___ **Negotiation:** Bringing others together and trying to reconcile differences.

___ **Operations Analysis:** Analyzing needs and product requirements to create a design.

___ **Programming:** Writing computer programs for various purposes.

___ **Quality Control Analysis:** Evaluating the quality or performance of products, services, or processes.

___ **Reading Comprehension:** Understanding written sentences and paragraphs in work-related documents.

___ **Repairing:** Repairing machines or systems, using the needed tools.

___ **Science:** Using scientific rules and methods to solve problems.

___ **Service Orientation:** Actively looking for ways to help people.

___ **Social Perceptiveness:** Being aware of others' reactions and understanding why they react as they do.

___ **Speaking:** Talking to others to convey information effectively.

___ **Technology Design:** Generating or adapting equipment and technology to serve user needs.

___ **Time Management:** Managing one's own time and the time of others.

___ **Writing:** Communicating effectively in writing as appropriate for the needs of the audience.

Now that you've looked at all the skills and marked those that you feel most positive about, go back and choose three skills that you would *most* like to use in your career. In the blank spaces to the left, write a "1," "2," and "3" to indicate your top three.

Relating Your Skills to College Majors and Careers

The following table relates these 28 skills to college majors and careers. The majors and careers on the lists are rated high on the skills, but the lists do not always include all the highest-rated majors and careers. For reasons of space, most of the lists show representative examples.

Using the three skills that you marked in the Skills Checklist, find the corresponding college majors and careers and circle the ones that look particularly interesting to you.

Skills and Related College Majors and Careers

Skill: ACTIVE LEARNING

RELATED MAJORS: African-American Studies; American Studies; Astronomy; Biochemistry; Biology; Botany; Dentistry; Geography; International Relations; Mathematics; Medicine; Microbiology; Physics; Podiatry; Political Science; Sociology; Soil Science; Speech-Language Pathology and Audiology; Statistics; Veterinary Medicine

RELATED CAREERS: Area, Ethnic, and Cultural Studies Teachers, Postsecondary; Astronomers; Audiologists; Biochemists and Biophysicists; Biological Science Teachers, Postsecondary; Dentists, General; Family and General Practitioners; Geographers; Mathematical Science Teachers, Postsecondary; Mathematicians; Microbiologists; Natural Sciences Managers; Physicists; Podiatrists; Political Scientists; Sociologists; Soil and Plant Scientists; Speech-Language Pathologists; Statisticians; Veterinarians

Skill: COMPLEX PROBLEM SOLVING

RELATED MAJORS: Aeronautical/Aerospace Engineering; Agricultural Engineering; Architecture; Astronomy; Biochemistry; Bioengineering; Chemical Engineering; Civil Engineering; Dentistry; Environmental Science; Industrial Engineering; International Relations; Landscape Architecture; Materials Science; Mechanical Engineering; Medicine; Microbiology; Petroleum Engineering; Physics; Transportation and Logistics Management

RELATED CAREERS: Aerospace Engineers; Agricultural Engineers; Architects, Except Landscape and Naval; Astronomers; Biochemists and Biophysicists; Biomedical Engineers; Chemical Engineers; Civil Engineers; Dentists, General; Environmental Scientists and Specialists, Including Health; Family and General Practitioners; Industrial Engineers; Landscape Architects; Materials Scientists; Mechanical Engineers; Microbiologists; Petroleum Engineers; Physicists; Political Scientists; Transportation, Storage, and Distribution Managers

Skill: COORDINATION

RELATED MAJORS: Aeronautical/Aerospace Engineering; Agricultural Engineering; Architecture; Astronomy; Bioengineering; Business Management; Chemical Engineering; International Business; International

Relations; Landscape Architecture; Marketing; Materials Science; Metallurgical Engineering; Operations Management; Petroleum Engineering; Philosophy; Physics; Public Administration; Religion/ Religious Studies; Transportation and Logistics Management

RELATED CAREERS: Advertising and Promotions Managers; Aerospace Engineers; Agricultural Engineers; Architects, Except Landscape and Naval; Astronomers; Biomedical Engineers; Chemical Engineers; Chief Executives; Clergy; First-Line Supervisors/Managers of Production and Operating Workers; General and Operations Managers; Landscape Architects; Management Analysts; Marketing Managers; Materials Engineers; Materials Scientists; Petroleum Engineers; Physicists; Political Scientists; Transportation, Storage, and Distribution Managers

Skill: CRITICAL THINKING

RELATED MAJORS: Actuarial Science; African-American Studies; American Studies; Anthropology; Archeology; Area Studies; Biochemistry; Dentistry; International Relations; Law; Medicine; Microbiology; Orthotics/ Prosthetics; Physician Assisting; Physics; Podiatry; Religion/Religious Studies; Soil Science; Urban Studies; Women's Studies

RELATED CAREERS: Actuaries; Anthropologists and Archeologists; Area, Ethnic, and Cultural Studies Teachers, Postsecondary; Biochemists and Biophysicists; Clergy; Dentists, General; Family and General Practitioners; Health Specialties Teachers, Postsecondary; Law Clerks; Lawyers; Medical Appliance Technicians; Microbiologists; Orthotists and Prosthetists; Physician Assistants; Physicists; Podiatrists; Political Scientists; Sociologists; Soil and Plant Scientists; Surgeons

Skill: EQUIPMENT MAINTENANCE

RELATED MAJORS: Agricultural Business and Economics; Agronomy and Crop Science; Animal Science; Chemistry; Computer Engineering; Computer Science; Electrical Engineering; Environmental Science; Food Science; Forestry; Hotel/Motel and Restaurant Management; Management Information Systems; Mechanical Engineering; Medical Technology; Operations Management; Orthotics/Prosthetics; Wildlife Management

RELATED CAREERS: Agricultural and Food Science Technicians; Chemists; Computer and Information Systems Managers; Computer Hardware Engineers; Electrical Engineers; Electronics Engineers, Except Computer;

Skill: EQUIPMENT MAINTENANCE (CONTINUED)

Environmental Science and Protection Technicians, Including Health;
Farm, Ranch, and Other Agricultural Managers; Farmers and Ranchers;
First-Line Supervisors/Managers of Farming, Fishing, and Forestry
Workers; First-Line Supervisors/Managers of Production and Operating
Workers; Fish and Game Wardens; Food Service Managers; Forest and
Conservation Technicians; Forest and Conservation Workers; Lodging
Managers; Mechanical Engineers; Medical and Clinical Laboratory
Technologists; Medical Appliance Technicians

Skill: EQUIPMENT SELECTION

RELATED MAJORS: Agricultural Business and Economics; Agronomy and
Crop Science; Animal Science; Biochemistry; Chemistry; Computer
Engineering; Computer Science; Dentistry; Electrical Engineering;
Environmental Science; Food Science; Forestry; Graphic Design,
Commercial Art, and Illustration; Hotel/Motel and Restaurant
Management; Management Information Systems; Mechanical Engineering;
Medical Technology; Operations Management; Podiatry; Soil Science

RELATED CAREERS: Agricultural and Food Science Technicians; Biochemists
and Biophysicists; Chemists; Commercial and Industrial Designers;
Computer and Information Scientists, Research; Computer and
Information Systems Managers; Computer Hardware Engineers; Computer
Software Engineers, Applications; Computer Software Engineers, Systems
Software; Dentists, General; Electrical Engineers; Environmental Science
and Protection Technicians, Including Health; Farmers and Ranchers;
First-Line Supervisors/Managers of Production and Operating Workers;
Food Service Managers; Foresters; Lodging Managers; Mechanical
Engineers; Medical and Clinical Laboratory Technologists; Multi-Media
Artists and Animators; Podiatrists; Soil and Plant Scientists

Skill: INSTALLATION

RELATED MAJORS: Aeronautical/Aerospace Engineering; Agricultural
Business and Economics; Agronomy and Crop Science; Animal Science;
Art History; Bioengineering; Computer Engineering; Computer Science;
Dentistry; Electrical Engineering; Forestry; Geology; Graphic Design,
Commercial Art, and Illustration; History; Mechanical Engineering;
Operations Management; Soil Science

RELATED CAREERS: Aerospace Engineers; Biomedical Engineers; Commercial and Industrial Designers; Computer Hardware Engineers; Computer Software Engineers, Applications; Computer Software Engineers, Systems Software; Computer Specialists, All Other; Curators; Database Administrators; Dentists, General; Electrical Engineers; Electronics Engineers, Except Computer; Farmers and Ranchers; First-Line Supervisors/Managers of Mechanics, Installers, and Repairers; Forest and Conservation Technicians; Hydrologists; Mechanical Engineers; Museum Technicians and Conservators; Set and Exhibit Designers; Soil and Plant Scientists

Skill: INSTRUCTING

RELATED MAJORS: Art History; Biochemistry; Biology; Botany; Chiropractic; Dance; Dentistry; Geography; Humanities; Microbiology; Orthotics/Prosthetics; Philosophy; Physician Assisting; Podiatry; Political Science; Religion/Religious Studies; Sociology; Speech-Language Pathology and Audiology; Veterinary Medicine

RELATED CAREERS: Art, Drama, and Music Teachers, Postsecondary; Biological Science Teachers, Postsecondary; Chiropractors; Choreographers; Communications Teachers, Postsecondary; Dentists, General; Education Teachers, Postsecondary; English Language and Literature Teachers, Postsecondary; Foreign Language and Literature Teachers, Postsecondary; Geography Teachers, Postsecondary; Health Specialties Teachers, Postsecondary; History Teachers, Postsecondary; Medical Appliance Technicians; Orthotists and Prosthetists; Philosophy and Religion Teachers, Postsecondary; Podiatrists; Political Science Teachers, Postsecondary; Psychology Teachers, Postsecondary; Sociology Teachers, Postsecondary; Veterinarians

Skill: JUDGMENT AND DECISION MAKING

RELATED MAJORS: Actuarial Science; Anthropology; Archeology; Architecture; Astronomy; Biochemistry; Civil Engineering; Dentistry; Environmental Science; International Relations; Law; Marketing; Medicine; Microbiology; Physician Assisting; Physics; Podiatry; Soil Science; Transportation and Logistics Management; Veterinary Medicine

RELATED CAREERS: Actuaries; Anthropologists and Archeologists; Architects, Except Landscape and Naval; Astronomers; Biochemists and Biophysicists; Civil Engineers; Dentists, General; Environmental Scientists and

41

Skill: JUDGMENT AND DECISION MAKING (CONTINUED)

Specialists, Including Health; Family and General Practitioners; Lawyers; Marketing Managers; Microbiologists; Physician Assistants; Physicists; Podiatrists; Political Scientists; Soil and Plant Scientists; Surgeons; Transportation, Storage, and Distribution Managers; Veterinarians

Skill: LEARNING STRATEGIES

RELATED MAJORS: Actuarial Science; Business Education; Chiropractic; Dentistry; Elementary Education; Geography; Industrial/Technology Education; International Relations; Occupational Health and Industrial Hygiene; Orthotics/Prosthetics; Philosophy; Physical Education; Psychology; Religion/Religious Studies; Secondary Education; Sociology; Soil Science; Special Education; Speech-Language Pathology and Audiology; Veterinary Medicine

RELATED CAREERS: Actuaries; Agricultural Sciences Teachers, Postsecondary; Audiologists; Biochemists and Biophysicists; Clinical, Counseling, and School Psychologists; Elementary School Teachers, Except Special Education; Geography Teachers, Postsecondary; Health Specialties Teachers, Postsecondary; Industrial-Organizational Psychologists; Microbiologists; Philosophy and Religion Teachers, Postsecondary; Political Science Teachers, Postsecondary; Psychology Teachers, Postsecondary; Secondary School Teachers, Except Special and Vocational Education; Sociologists; Sociology Teachers, Postsecondary; Soil and Plant Scientists; Special Education Teachers, Secondary School; Speech-Language Pathologists; Vocational Education Teachers, Secondary School

Skill: MANAGEMENT OF FINANCIAL RESOURCES

RELATED MAJORS: Agricultural Engineering; Architecture; Bioengineering; Business Management; Chemical Engineering; Civil Engineering; Dietetics; Hotel/Motel and Restaurant Management; Industrial and Labor Relations; International Business; International Relations; Landscape Architecture; Marketing; Mechanical Engineering; Operations Management; Petroleum Engineering; Philosophy; Podiatry; Public Administration; Transportation and Logistics Management

RELATED CAREERS: Administrative Services Managers; Advertising and Promotions Managers; Chief Executives; Compensation and Benefits Managers; Construction Managers; Cost Estimators; Dietitians and

Nutritionists; Directors, Religious Activities and Education; Emergency Management Specialists; Engineering Managers; Engineering Teachers, Postsecondary; Food Service Managers; General and Operations Managers; Industrial Production Managers; Lodging Managers; Marketing Managers; Podiatrists; Postmasters and Mail Superintendents; Sales Managers; Social and Community Service Managers; Transportation, Storage, and Distribution Managers

Skill: MANAGEMENT OF MATERIAL RESOURCES

RELATED MAJORS: Agricultural Engineering; Architecture; Bioengineering; Business Management; Chemical Engineering; Civil Engineering; Hotel/ Motel and Restaurant Management; International Business; International Relations; Landscape Architecture; Mechanical Engineering; Metallurgical Engineering; Operations Management; Petroleum Engineering; Philosophy; Public Administration; Transportation and Logistics Management

RELATED CAREERS: Administrative Services Managers; Chief Executives; Civil Engineers; Construction Managers; Cost Estimators; Directors, Religious Activities and Education; Emergency Management Specialists; Engineering Managers; First-Line Supervisors/Managers of Mechanics, Installers, and Repairers; First-Line Supervisors/Managers of Production and Operating Workers; Food Service Managers; General and Operations Managers; Lodging Managers; Logisticians; Management Analysts; Materials Engineers; Postmasters and Mail Superintendents; Sales Managers; Social and Community Service Managers; Transportation, Storage, and Distribution Managers

Skill: MANAGEMENT OF PERSONNEL RESOURCES

RELATED MAJORS: Astronomy; Biochemistry; Biology; Botany; Business Management; Civil Engineering; Geology; Geophysics; International Business; International Relations; Landscape Architecture; Marketing; Microbiology; Operations Management; Philosophy; Physics; Public Administration; Transportation and Logistics Management

RELATED CAREERS: Administrative Services Managers; Advertising and Promotions Managers; Business Teachers, Postsecondary; Chief Executives; Construction Managers; Directors, Religious Activities and Education; Emergency Management Specialists; Engineering Managers; First-Line Supervisors/Managers of Mechanics, Installers, and Repairers; First-Line

Skill: MANAGEMENT OF PERSONNEL RESOURCES (CONTINUED)

Supervisors/Managers of Production and Operating Workers; General and Operations Managers; Industrial Production Managers; Logisticians; Management Analysts; Marketing Managers; Natural Sciences Managers; Postmasters and Mail Superintendents; Sales Managers; Social and Community Service Managers; Transportation, Storage, and Distribution Managers

Skill: MATHEMATICS

RELATED MAJORS: Aeronautical/Aerospace Engineering; Agricultural Engineering; Architecture; Astronomy; Bioengineering; Chemical Engineering; Civil Engineering; Electrical Engineering; Geology; Geophysics; Industrial Engineering; Landscape Architecture; Materials Science; Mathematics; Mechanical Engineering; Metallurgical Engineering; Petroleum Engineering; Physics; Soil Science; Statistics

RELATED CAREERS: Aerospace Engineers; Agricultural Engineers; Architects, Except Landscape and Naval; Astronomers; Biomedical Engineers; Chemical Engineers; Civil Engineers; Cost Estimators; Electrical Engineers; Electronics Engineers, Except Computer; Geoscientists, Except Hydrologists and Geographers; Hydrologists; Industrial Engineers; Landscape Architects; Materials Engineers; Materials Scientists; Mathematical Science Teachers, Postsecondary; Mathematicians; Mechanical Engineers; Operations Research Analysts; Petroleum Engineers; Physicists; Soil and Plant Scientists; Statisticians

Skill: MONITORING

RELATED MAJORS: Astronomy; Biochemistry; Business Management; Civil Engineering; Dentistry; Dietetics; International Business; International Relations; Marketing; Microbiology; Nursing (RN Training); Orthotics/Prosthetics; Physics; Sociology; Speech-Language Pathology and Audiology; Transportation and Logistics Management; Veterinary Medicine

RELATED CAREERS: Advertising and Promotions Managers; Astronomers; Audiologists; Biochemists and Biophysicists; Chief Executives; Civil Engineers; Construction Managers; Dentists, General; Dietitians and Nutritionists; General and Operations Managers; Logisticians; Management Analysts; Marketing Managers; Microbiologists; Orthotists and Prosthetists; Physicists; Registered Nurses; Sales Managers; Sociologists; Speech-Language Pathologists; Veterinarians

Skill: NEGOTIATION

RELATED MAJORS: Advertising; Architecture; Business Management; Hospital/Health Facilities Administration; Hotel/Motel and Restaurant Management; Insurance; International Business; International Relations; Law; Marketing; Operations Management; Psychology; Public Administration; Public Relations; Religion/Religious Studies; Social Work; Transportation and Logistics Management

RELATED CAREERS: Administrative Law Judges, Adjudicators, and Hearing Officers; Administrative Services Managers; Advertising Sales Agents; Arbitrators, Mediators, and Conciliators; Architects, Except Landscape and Naval; Chief Executives; Child, Family, and School Social Workers; Claims Adjusters, Examiners, and Investigators; Clergy; Clinical, Counseling, and School Psychologists; Construction Managers; Food Service Managers; General and Operations Managers; Insurance Underwriters; Judges, Magistrate Judges, and Magistrates; Lodging Managers; Logisticians; Marketing Managers; Marriage and Family Therapists; Medical and Health Services Managers; Probation Officers and Correctional Treatment Specialists; Public Relations Managers; Purchasing Agents, Except Wholesale, Retail, and Farm Products; Transportation, Storage, and Distribution Managers

Skill: OPERATIONS ANALYSIS

RELATED MAJORS: Aeronautical/Aerospace Engineering; Agricultural Engineering; Architecture; Astronomy; Bioengineering; Chemical Engineering; Civil Engineering; Computer Engineering; Geophysics; Health Information Systems Administration; Hospital/Health Facilities Administration; Industrial and Labor Relations; International Relations; Landscape Architecture; Materials Science; Mechanical Engineering; Medicine; Metallurgical Engineering; Microbiology; Petroleum Engineering; Physics

RELATED CAREERS: Aerospace Engineers; Agricultural Engineers; Architects, Except Landscape and Naval; Astronomers; Biomedical Engineers; Chemical Engineers; Chief Executives; Civil Engineers; Compensation and Benefits Managers; Computer Hardware Engineers; Computer Software Engineers, Applications; Computer Software Engineers, Systems Software; Cost Estimators; Engineering Managers; Family and General Practitioners; Landscape Architects; Materials Engineers; Materials Scientists; Mechanical Engineers; Medical and Health Services Managers; Microbiologists; Natural Sciences Managers; Physicists; Surgeons

Skill: PROGRAMMING

RELATED MAJORS: Civil Engineering; Computer Engineering; Computer Science; Economics; Electrical Engineering; Environmental Science; Forestry; Geology; Graphic Design, Commercial Art, and Illustration; Industrial Engineering; Management Information Systems; Mathematics; Mechanical Engineering; Physics; Statistics

RELATED CAREERS: Civil Engineers; Computer and Information Scientists, Research; Computer and Information Systems Managers; Computer Hardware Engineers; Computer Programmers; Computer Science Teachers, Postsecondary; Computer Software Engineers, Applications; Computer Software Engineers, Systems Software; Database Administrators; Electrical Engineers; Engineering Teachers, Postsecondary; Environmental Scientists and Specialists, Including Health; Foresters; Geoscientists, Except Hydrologists and Geographers; Industrial Engineers; Market Research Analysts; Mathematicians; Mechanical Engineers; Multi-Media Artists and Animators; Network and Computer Systems Administrators; Network Systems and Data Communications Analysts; Operations Research Analysts; Physicists; Statisticians

Skill: QUALITY CONTROL ANALYSIS

RELATED MAJORS: Aeronautical/Aerospace Engineering; Agronomy and Crop Science; Animal Science; Architecture; Bioengineering; Chemical Engineering; Civil Engineering; Computer Engineering; Computer Science; Dietetics; Electrical Engineering; Environmental Science; Food Science; Landscape Architecture; Management Information Systems; Metallurgical Engineering; Operations Management; Petroleum Engineering; Soil Science

RELATED CAREERS: Aerospace Engineers; Agricultural and Food Science Technicians; Animal Scientists; Architects, Except Landscape and Naval; Biochemists and Biophysicists; Computer and Information Scientists, Research; Computer and Information Systems Managers; Computer Hardware Engineers; Computer Software Engineers, Applications; Computer Software Engineers, Systems Software; Construction Managers; Dietitians and Nutritionists; Engineering Managers; Environmental Science and Protection Technicians, Including Health; Environmental Scientists and Specialists, Including Health; First-Line Supervisors/Managers of Mechanics, Installers, and Repairers; First-Line Supervisors/Managers of Production and Operating Workers; Food Scientists and Technologists;

Industrial Production Managers; Landscape Architects; Logisticians; Materials Engineers; Microbiologists; Soil and Plant Scientists

Skill: READING COMPREHENSION

RELATED MAJORS: Astronomy; Biochemistry; Biology; Botany; Chemistry; Dentistry; English; Geology; Geophysics; Medicine; Microbiology; Oceanography; Orthotics/Prosthetics; Physician Assisting; Physics; Soil Science; Urban Studies; Veterinary Medicine; Zoology

RELATED CAREERS: Agricultural Sciences Teachers, Postsecondary; Astronomers; Biochemists and Biophysicists; Biological Science Teachers, Postsecondary; Chemistry Teachers, Postsecondary; Chemists; Editors; English Language and Literature Teachers, Postsecondary; Family and General Practitioners; Geoscientists, Except Hydrologists and Geographers; Health Specialties Teachers, Postsecondary; Medical Appliance Technicians; Medical Scientists, Except Epidemiologists; Microbiologists; Orthotists and Prosthetists; Physician Assistants; Physicists; Physics Teachers, Postsecondary; Sociologists; Soil and Plant Scientists; Surgeons; Veterinarians; Zoologists and Wildlife Biologists

Skill: REPAIRING

RELATED MAJORS: Agricultural Business and Economics; Agronomy and Crop Science; Animal Science; Chemistry; Computer Engineering; Computer Science; Electrical Engineering; Environmental Science; Food Science; Forestry; Graphic Design, Commercial Art, and Illustration; Hotel/Motel and Restaurant Management; Management Information Systems; Mechanical Engineering; Medical Technology; Operations Management; Orthotics/Prosthetics; Wildlife Management

RELATED CAREERS: Chemical Technicians; Chemists; Computer and Information Systems Managers; Computer Hardware Engineers; Computer Science Teachers, Postsecondary; Electrical Engineers; Electronics Engineers, Except Computer; Environmental Science and Protection Technicians, Including Health; Farm, Ranch, and Other Agricultural Managers; Farmers and Ranchers; First-Line Supervisors/Managers of Farming, Fishing, and Forestry Workers; First-Line Supervisors/Managers of Mechanics, Installers, and Repairers; First-Line Supervisors/Managers of Production and Operating Workers; Fish and Game Wardens; Food Service Managers; Forest and Conservation Technicians; Forest and Conservation Workers; Lodging Managers; Mechanical Engineers; Medical

47

Skill: Repairing (continued)

and Clinical Laboratory Technologists; Medical Appliance Technicians; Network and Computer Systems Administrators; Network Systems and Data Communications Analysts; Set and Exhibit Designers

Skill: Science

Related Majors: African-American Studies; American Studies; Anthropology; Archeology; Area Studies; Astronomy; Biochemistry; Chemistry; Environmental Science; Geography; Geology; Geophysics; Medicine; Microbiology; Optometry; Physics; Sociology; Soil Science; Urban Studies; Women's Studies

Related Careers: Anthropologists and Archeologists; Anthropology and Archeology Teachers, Postsecondary; Area, Ethnic, and Cultural Studies Teachers, Postsecondary; Astronomers; Biochemists and Biophysicists; Biological Science Teachers, Postsecondary; Chemistry Teachers, Postsecondary; Chemists; Environmental Science and Protection Technicians, Including Health; Environmental Science Teachers, Postsecondary; Environmental Scientists and Specialists, Including Health; Family and General Practitioners; Geographers; Geoscientists, Except Hydrologists and Geographers; Hydrologists; Medical Scientists, Except Epidemiologists; Microbiologists; Natural Sciences Managers; Optometrists; Physicists; Physics Teachers, Postsecondary; Sociologists; Soil and Plant Scientists; Surgeons

Skill: Service Orientation

Related Majors: Dietetics; Health Information Systems Administration; Hospital/Health Facilities Administration; Hotel/Motel and Restaurant Management; Law; Library Science; Medicine; Nursing (RN Training); Optometry; Pharmacy; Philosophy; Physician Assisting; Podiatry; Psychology; Religion/Religious Studies; Social Work; Special Education; Speech-Language Pathology and Audiology

Related Careers: Audiologists; Child, Family, and School Social Workers; Clergy; Clinical, Counseling, and School Psychologists; Dietitians and Nutritionists; Directors, Religious Activities and Education; Family and General Practitioners; Food Service Managers; Judges, Magistrate Judges, and Magistrates; Lawyers; Librarians; Lodging Managers; Marriage and Family Therapists; Medical and Health Services Managers; Optometrists; Pharmacists; Physician Assistants; Podiatrists; Probation Officers and

Correctional Treatment Specialists; Registered Nurses; Social Work Teachers, Postsecondary; Special Education Teachers, Secondary School; Speech-Language Pathologists; Surgeons

Skill: SOCIAL PERCEPTIVENESS

RELATED MAJORS: Elementary Education; Hospital/Health Facilities Administration; International Relations; Law; Marketing; Medicine; Nursing (RN Training); Pharmacy; Philosophy; Physician Assisting; Podiatry; Psychology; Public Relations; Religion/Religious Studies; Social Work; Special Education; Speech-Language Pathology and Audiology; Transportation and Logistics Management; Urban Studies

RELATED CAREERS: Advertising and Promotions Managers; Chief Executives; Child, Family, and School Social Workers; Clergy; Clinical, Counseling, and School Psychologists; Elementary School Teachers, Except Special Education; Family and General Practitioners; Industrial-Organizational Psychologists; Judges, Magistrate Judges, and Magistrates; Lawyers; Marriage and Family Therapists; Medical and Health Services Managers; Pharmacists; Physician Assistants; Podiatrists; Political Scientists; Probation Officers and Correctional Treatment Specialists; Psychiatrists; Public Relations Specialists; Registered Nurses; Sales Managers; Sociologists; Special Education Teachers, Secondary School; Speech-Language Pathologists

Skill: SPEAKING

RELATED MAJORS: African-American Studies; American Studies; Anthropology; Archeology; Area Studies; Astronomy; Biology; Botany; Geography; International Relations; Law; Philosophy; Physics; Political Science; Religion/Religious Studies; Sociology; Speech-Language Pathology and Audiology; Urban Studies; Women's Studies; Zoology

RELATED CAREERS: Administrative Law Judges, Adjudicators, and Hearing Officers; Anthropologists and Archeologists; Arbitrators, Mediators, and Conciliators; Area, Ethnic, and Cultural Studies Teachers, Postsecondary; Astronomers; Audiologists; Chief Executives; Clergy; Directors, Religious Activities and Education; Geographers; Geography Teachers, Postsecondary; Judges, Magistrate Judges, and Magistrates; Law Clerks; Lawyers; Natural Sciences Managers; Physicists; Physics Teachers, Postsecondary; Political Science Teachers, Postsecondary; Political Scientists; Sociologists; Speech-Language Pathologists; Zoologists and Wildlife Biologists

49

Skill: TECHNOLOGY DESIGN

RELATED MAJORS: Aeronautical/Aerospace Engineering; Astronomy; Chemical Engineering; Chemistry; Civil Engineering; Computer Engineering; Computer Science; Electrical Engineering; Geology; Geophysics; Graphic Design, Commercial Art, and Illustration; Industrial Design; Industrial Engineering; Management Information Systems; Mathematics; Mechanical Engineering; Physics; Soil Science; Statistics

RELATED CAREERS: Aerospace Engineers; Astronomers; Chemical Engineers; Chemists; Civil Engineers; Commercial and Industrial Designers; Computer and Information Scientists, Research; Computer and Information Systems Managers; Computer Hardware Engineers; Computer Programmers; Computer Software Engineers, Applications; Computer Software Engineers, Systems Software; Database Administrators; Electrical Engineers; Geoscientists, Except Hydrologists and Geographers; Graphic Designers; Industrial Engineers; Mechanical Engineers; Multi-Media Artists and Animators; Network and Computer Systems Administrators; Network Systems and Data Communications Analysts; Physicists; Soil and Plant Scientists; Statisticians

Skill: TIME MANAGEMENT

RELATED MAJORS: Agricultural Engineering; Architecture; Astronomy; Biochemistry; Biology; Botany; Civil Engineering; Geology; Geophysics; International Relations; Landscape Architecture; Marketing; Mathematics; Microbiology; Operations Management; Physics; Statistics; Transportation and Logistics Management; Zoology

RELATED CAREERS: Administrative Services Managers; Agricultural Engineers; Architects, Except Landscape and Naval; Astronomers; Biochemists and Biophysicists; Business Teachers, Postsecondary; Chief Executives; Civil Engineers; Construction Managers; Engineering Managers; Geoscientists, Except Hydrologists and Geographers; Hydrologists; Industrial Production Managers; Landscape Architects; Logisticians; Marketing Managers; Mathematical Science Teachers, Postsecondary; Medical Scientists, Except Epidemiologists; Microbiologists; Natural Sciences Managers; Physicists; Political Scientists; Statisticians; Transportation, Storage, and Distribution Managers

Skill: WRITING

RELATED MAJORS: African-American Studies; American Studies; Anthropology; Archeology; Area Studies; Astronomy; Biochemistry; Biology; Botany; English; Geography; Journalism and Mass Communications; Law; Physics; Political Science; Sociology; Soil Science; Speech-Language Pathology and Audiology; Urban Studies; Women's Studies

RELATED CAREERS: Administrative Law Judges, Adjudicators, and Hearing Officers; Anthropologists and Archeologists; Arbitrators, Mediators, and Conciliators; Area, Ethnic, and Cultural Studies Teachers, Postsecondary; Astronomers; Audiologists; Biochemists and Biophysicists; Broadcast News Analysts; Communications Teachers, Postsecondary; Editors; English Language and Literature Teachers, Postsecondary; Geographers; Judges, Magistrate Judges, and Magistrates; Law Clerks; Lawyers; Microbiologists; Natural Sciences Managers; Physicists; Political Scientists; Reporters and Correspondents; Sociologists; Soil and Plant Scientists; Speech-Language Pathologists; Writers and Authors

Use the following worksheet to write down the most appealing college majors and careers that correspond with the three skills you marked earlier in this chapter.

COLLEGE MAJORS AND CAREERS THAT RELATE TO MY SKILLS

_____

_____

_____

_____

_____

_____

_____

_____

_____

_____

_____

_____

_____

_____

Key Points: Chapter 3

- Part of a good career decision (which will shape your decision about your major) is matching your skills with a career's demands for skills.

- Your past experiences in school and work can help you understand which skills you are good at and enjoy using.

CHAPTER 4

What Were Your Favorite High School Courses?

A good way to predict how well people will like college courses is to ask them how much they liked similar high school courses. In addition, most people earn their highest grades in college courses that are similar to the high school courses in which they did well. Your high school experiences also can help to predict your satisfaction and success in various careers. Therefore, this is a good time for you to give some thought to the high school courses that you liked and in which you earned high grades.

My Favorite High School Courses

In the following worksheet, write down the names of three favorite high school courses.

MY FAVORITE HIGH SCHOOL COURSES
1. _____
2. _____
3. _____

Relating High School Courses to College Majors and Careers

Next, with those courses in mind, look over the information in the following table and circle related college majors and careers.

Tip: Basic high school courses in some subjects, such as math and English, are commonly required for almost every college-bound student. That's why, in the following table, you'll find that these subjects are cross-referenced to higher-level courses, such as pre-calculus and literature, that relate more directly to the requirements of specific majors.

High School Courses and Related College Majors and Careers

High School Course: ALGEBRA, See PRE-CALCULUS OR CALCULUS

High School Course: ART

Related Majors: Advertising; Architecture; Art; Art History; Graphic Design, Commercial Art, and Illustration; Industrial Design; Interior Design; Landscape Architecture

Related Careers: Advertising and Promotions Managers; Architects; Architecture Teachers, Postsecondary; Art Directors; Art, Drama, and Music Teachers, Postsecondary; Commercial and Industrial Designers; Fine Artists, Including Painters, Sculptors, and Illustrators; Graphic Designers; Interior Designers; Landscape Architects; Medical Appliance Technicians; Multi-Media Artists and Animators; Orthotists and Prosthetists

High School Course: BIOLOGY

Related Majors: Agricultural Business and Economics; Agronomy and Crop Science; Animal Science; Biochemistry; Bioengineering; Biology; Botany; Chiropractic; Dentistry; Dietetics; Environmental Science; Food Science; Forestry; Medical Technology; Medicine; Microbiology; Nursing (RN Training); Optometry; Orthotics/Prosthetics; Parks and Recreation Management; Pharmacy; Physician Assisting; Podiatry; Soil Science; Veterinary Medicine; Wildlife Management; Zoology

Related Careers: Agricultural Sciences Teachers, Postsecondary; Agricultural and Food Science Technicians; Anesthesiologists; Biochemists and Biophysicists; Biological Science Teachers, Postsecondary; Chiropractors; Conservation Scientists; Dentists, General; Dietitians and Nutritionists; Environmental Science and Protection Technicians, Including Health; Environmental Science Teachers, Postsecondary; Environmental Scientists and Specialists, Including Health; Family and General Practitioners; Farm, Ranch, and Other Agricultural Managers; First-Line Supervisors/Managers of Farming, Fishing, and Forestry Workers; Food Scientists and Technologists; Foresters; Internists, General; Medical and Clinical Laboratory Technologists; Medical Scientists, Except Epidemiologists; Microbiologists; Obstetricians and Gynecologists; Optometrists; Orthotists and Prosthetists; Pediatricians, General; Pharmacists; Physician Assistants; Podiatrists; Registered Nurses; Soil and

Water Conservationists; Surgeons; Veterinarians; Zoologists and Wildlife Biologists

High School Course: CALCULUS

Related Majors: Actuarial Science; Aeronautical/Aerospace Engineering; Agricultural Engineering; Architecture; Astronomy; Biochemistry; Bioengineering; Chemical Engineering; Chemistry; Civil Engineering; Computer Engineering; Computer Science; Electrical Engineering; Geology; Geophysics; Mathematics; Mechanical Engineering; Metallurgical Engineering; Petroleum Engineering; Pharmacy; Physics; Statistics

Related Careers: Actuaries; Aerospace Engineers; Agricultural Engineers; Architects; Astronomers; Biochemists and Biophysicists; Chemical Engineers; Chemists; Civil Engineers; Computer Hardware Engineers; Computer Software Engineers, Applications; Computer Software Engineers, Systems Software; Economists; Electrical Engineers; Electronics Engineers, Except Computer; Engineering Managers; Engineering Teachers, Postsecondary; Geoscientists, Except Hydrologists and Geographers; Materials Engineers; Mathematical Science Teachers, Postsecondary; Mathematicians; Mechanical Engineers; Petroleum Engineers; Pharmacists; Physicists; Statisticians

High School Course: CHEMISTRY

Related Majors: Agronomy and Crop Science; Animal Science; Biochemistry; Bioengineering; Biology; Botany; Chemical Engineering; Chemistry; Chiropractic; Dentistry; Dietetics; Environmental Science; Food Science; Forestry; Geology; Geophysics; Materials Science; Medical Technology; Medicine; Metallurgical Engineering; Microbiology; Nursing (RN Training); Oceanography; Pharmacy; Soil Science; Wildlife Management; Zoology

Related Careers: Agricultural and Food Science Technicians; Anesthesiologists; Animal Scientists; Atmospheric, Earth, Marine, and Space Sciences Teachers, Postsecondary; Biochemists and Biophysicists; Biological Science Teachers, Postsecondary; Biological Technicians; Chemical Engineers; Chemical Technicians; Chemistry Teachers, Postsecondary; Chemists; Chiropractors; Compliance Officers, Except Agriculture, Construction, Health and Safety, and Transportation; Dentists, General; Dietitians and Nutritionists; Farmers and Ranchers; Forest and Conservation Workers; Food Scientists and Technologists; Foresters; Geoscientists, Except Hydrologists and Geographers; Health

High School Course: CHEMISTRY (CONTINUED)

Specialties Teachers, Postsecondary; Materials Scientists; Medical and Clinical Laboratory Technologists; Medical Scientists, Except Epidemiologists; Natural Sciences Managers; Pharmacists; Registered Nurses; Soil and Plant Scientists; Zoologists and Wildlife Biologists

High School Course: CHINESE, See FOREIGN LANGUAGE

High School Course: COMPUTER SCIENCE

Related Majors: Accounting; Actuarial Science; Aeronautical/Aerospace Engineering; Agricultural Engineering; Architecture; Astronomy; Bioengineering; Chemical Engineering; Civil Engineering; Computer Engineering; Computer Science; Electrical Engineering; Graphic Design, Commercial Art, and Illustration; Health Information Systems Administration; Industrial Design; Industrial Engineering; Library Science; Management Information Systems; Materials Science; Mathematics; Mechanical Engineering; Metallurgical Engineering; Operations Management; Petroleum Engineering; Physics; Statistics; Transportation and Logistics Management

Related Careers: Accountants and Auditors; Actuaries; Aerospace Engineers; Agricultural Engineers; Architects, Except Landscape and Naval; Astronomers; Avionics Technicians; Chemical Engineers; Civil Engineers; Commercial and Industrial Designers; Computer and Information Systems Managers; Computer Hardware Engineers; Computer Operators; Computer Programmers; Computer Science Teachers, Postsecondary; Computer Software Engineers, Applications; Computer Software Engineers, Systems Software; Computer Systems Analysts; Database Administrators; Electrical Engineers; Electronics Engineers, Except Computer; Engineering Managers; Graphic Designers; Industrial Engineers; Librarians; Logisticians; Materials Engineers; Mathematicians; Mechanical Engineers; Medical and Health Services Managers; Network and Computer Systems Administrators; Network Systems and Data Communications Analysts; Petroleum Engineers; Physicists; Statisticians; Transportation, Storage, and Distribution Managers

High School Course: DANCE

Related Majors: Dance

Related Careers: Art, Drama, and Music Teachers, Postsecondary; Choreographers; Dancers; Producers and Directors

High School Course: ENGLISH, See LITERATURE

High School Course: FOREIGN LANGUAGE

Related Majors: African-American Studies; American Studies; Anthropology; Archeology; Area Studies; Chinese; Classics; Communications Studies/Speech; Early Childhood Education; Elementary Education; English; Film/Cinema Studies; French; Geography; German; History; Humanities; International Business; International Relations; Japanese; Journalism and Mass Communications; Library Science; Modern Foreign Language; Music; Philosophy; Public Relations; Religion/Religious Studies; Russian; Secondary Education; Social Work; Spanish; Urban Studies

Related Careers: Anthropologists; Anthropology and Archeology Teachers, Postsecondary; Area, Ethnic, and Cultural Studies Teachers, Postsecondary; Foreign Language and Literature Teachers, Postsecondary; Geographers; History Teachers, Postsecondary; Interpreters and Translators; Philosophy and Religion Teachers, Postsecondary; Political Scientists; Public Relations Managers

High School Course: FRENCH, See FOREIGN LANGUAGE

High School Course: GEOGRAPHY

Related Majors: Environmental Science; Forestry; Geography; International Business; Wildlife Management

Related Careers: Anthropologists; Anthropology and Archeology Teachers, Postsecondary; Atmospheric, Earth, Marine, and Space Sciences Teachers, Postsecondary; Cartographers and Photogrammetrists; Elementary School Teachers, Except Special Education; Environmental Science Teachers, Postsecondary; Environmental Scientists and Specialists, Including Health; Foreign Language and Literature Teachers, Postsecondary; Foresters; Geographers; Geography Teachers, Postsecondary; Geoscientists, Except Hydrologists and Geographers; History Teachers, Postsecondary; Hydrologists; Interpreters and Translators; Surveyors

High School Course: GEOMETRY, See PRE-CALCULUS or CALCULUS

High School Course: GERMAN, See FOREIGN LANGUAGE

High School Course: HISTORY

Related Majors: African-American Studies; American Studies; Anthropology; Archeology; Area Studies; Art History; Chinese; Classics; French; Geography; German; History; Humanities; International Relations; Japanese; Law; Modern Foreign Language; Political Science; Religion/ Religious Studies; Russian; Spanish; Urban Studies; Women's Studies

Related Careers: Administrative Law Judges, Adjudicators, and Hearing Officers; Anthropologists; Anthropology and Archeology Teachers, Postsecondary; Anthropologists and Archeologists; Area, Ethnic, and Cultural Studies Teachers, Postsecondary; Art, Drama, and Music Teachers, Postsecondary; Clergy; Foreign Language and Literature Teachers, Postsecondary; Geographers; Historians; History Teachers, Postsecondary; Interpreters and Translators; Judges, Magistrate Judges, and Magistrates; Lawyers; Museum Technicians and Conservators; Political Science Teachers, Postsecondary; Political Scientists

High School Course: HOME ECONOMICS

Related Majors: Family and Consumer Sciences

Related Careers: Agricultural and Food Science Technicians; Animal Scientists; Dietetic Technicians; Dietitians and Nutritionists; Farm and Home Management Advisors; Food Scientists and Technologists; Food Service Managers; Purchasing Agents and Buyers, Farm Products

High School Course: INDUSTRIAL ARTS

Related Majors: Industrial/Technology Education

Related Careers: Vocational Education Teachers, Middle School; Vocational Education Teachers, Secondary School

High School Course: JAPANESE, See FOREIGN LANGUAGE

High School Course: KEYBOARDING

Related Majors: Business Education; Library Science

Related Careers: Business Teachers, Postsecondary; Education Teachers, Postsecondary; Librarians; Library Science Teachers, Postsecondary; Vocational Education Teachers, Middle School; Vocational Education Teachers, Postsecondary

High School Course: LITERATURE

Related Majors: African-American Studies; American Studies; Area Studies; Art; Art History; Chinese; Classics; Drama/Theater Arts; English; Film/Cinema Studies; French; German; Humanities; Japanese; Journalism and Mass Communications; Russian; Spanish; Women's Studies

Related Careers: Actors; Area, Ethnic, and Cultural Studies Teachers, Postsecondary; Art, Drama, and Music Teachers, Postsecondary; Editors; English Language and Literature Teachers, Postsecondary; Foreign Language and Literature Teachers, Postsecondary; Interpreters and Translators; Producers and Directors; Reporters and Correspondents; Writers and Authors

High School Course: MECHANICAL DRAWING

Related Majors: Graphic Design, Commercial Art, and Illustration; Industrial Design; Industrial/Technology Education

Related Careers: Commercial and Industrial Designers; Graphic Designers; Multi-Media Artists and Animators; Vocational Education Teachers, Middle School; Vocational Education Teachers, Postsecondary; Vocational Education Teachers, Secondary School

High School Course: MUSIC

Related Majors: Dance; Music

Related Careers: Art, Drama, and Music Teachers, Postsecondary; Choreographers; Dancers; Musicians and Singers; Music Directors and Composers; Producers and Directors

High School Course: OFFICE COMPUTER APPLICATIONS

Related Majors: Business Education; Health Information Systems Administration; Hospital/Health Facilities Administration; Library Science

High School Course: OFFICE COMPUTER APPLICATIONS (CONTINUED)

Related Careers: Business Teachers, Postsecondary; Librarians; Library Science Teachers, Postsecondary; Medical and Health Services Managers; Vocational Education Teachers, Middle School; Vocational Education Teachers, Postsecondary; Vocational Education Teachers, Secondary School

High School Course: PHOTOGRAPHY

Related Majors: Film/Cinema Studies; Graphic Design, Commercial Art, and Illustration; Industrial Design

Related Careers: Camera Operators, Television, Video, and Motion Picture; Film and Video Editors; Graphic Designers; Commercial and Industrial Designers; Multi-Media Artists and Animators; Photographers

High School Course: PHYSICS/PRINCIPLES OF TECHNOLOGY

Related Majors: Aeronautical/Aerospace Engineering; Architecture; Astronomy; Bioengineering; Chemical Engineering; Chemistry; Chiropractic; Civil Engineering; Computer Engineering; Computer Science; Dentistry; Electrical Engineering; Geology; Geophysics; Materials Science; Mechanical Engineering; Medicine; Metallurgical Engineering; Oceanography; Optometry; Orthotics/Prosthetics; Petroleum Engineering; Physics; Podiatry; Speech-Language Pathology and Audiology; Veterinary Medicine; Zoology

Related Careers: Aerospace Engineers; Agricultural Engineers; Anesthesiologists; Architects, Except Landscape and Naval; Astronomers; Atmospheric, Earth, Marine, and Space Sciences Teachers, Postsecondary; Audiologists; Chemical Engineers; Chemists; Chiropractors; Civil Engineers; Computer and Information Systems Managers; Computer Hardware Engineers; Computer Science Teachers, Postsecondary; Computer Software Engineers, Applications; Computer Software Engineers, Systems Software; Dentists; Electrical Engineers; Electronics Engineers, Except Computer; Engineering Managers; Engineering Teachers, Postsecondary; Family and General Practitioners; Geoscientists, Except Hydrologists and Geographers; Health Specialties Teachers, Postsecondary; Hydrologists; Internists, General; Materials Engineers; Mechanical Engineers; Natural Sciences Managers; Optometrists; Orthotists and Prosthetists; Petroleum Engineers; Physicists; Physics Teachers, Postsecondary; Podiatrists; Speech-Language Pathologists; Surgeons; Veterinarians

High School Course: PRE-CALCULUS

Related Majors: Actuarial Science; Aeronautical/Aerospace Engineering; Agricultural Engineering; Astronomy; Bioengineering; Chemical Engineering; Chemistry; Civil Engineering; Computer Engineering; Computer Science; Economics; Electrical Engineering; Geology; Geophysics; Industrial Engineering; Materials Science; Mathematics; Mechanical Engineering; Metallurgical Engineering; Oceanography; Operations Management; Optometry; Petroleum Engineering; Physics; Statistics

Related Careers: Actuaries; Aerospace Engineers; Agricultural Engineers; Astronomers; Biomedical Engineers; Chemical Engineers; Chemists; Civil Engineers; Computer Hardware Engineers; Computer Software Engineers, Applications; Computer Software Engineers, Systems Software; Economists; Electrical Engineers; Electronics Engineers, Except Computer; Engineering Managers; Engineering Teachers, Postsecondary; Geoscientists, Except Hydrologists and Geographers; Industrial Engineers; Materials Engineers; Mathematical Science Teachers, Postsecondary; Mathematicians; Mechanical Engineers; Operations Research Analysts; Optometrists; Petroleum Engineers; Physicists; Physics Teachers, Postsecondary; Statisticians

High School Course: PUBLIC SPEAKING

Related Majors: Advertising; African-American Studies; American Studies; Anthropology; Archeology; Business Education; Communications Studies/Speech; Drama/Theater Arts; Early Childhood Education; Elementary Education; Family and Consumer Sciences; French; German; Japanese; Journalism and Mass Communications; Law; Modern Foreign Language; Religion/Religious Studies; Recreation Management; Russian; Secondary Education; Spanish; Special Education; Speech-Language Pathology and Audiology; Women's Studies

Related Careers: Actors; Administrative Law Judges, Adjudicators, and Hearing Officers; Advertising Sales Agents; Anthropologists; Arbitrators, Mediators, and Conciliators; Anthropologists and Archeologists; Area, Ethnic, and Cultural Studies Teachers, Postsecondary; Broadcast News Analysts; Business Teachers, Postsecondary; Clergy; Communications Teachers, Postsecondary; Education Teachers, Postsecondary; Graduate Teaching Assistants; Health Specialties Teachers, Postsecondary; Home Economics Teachers, Postsecondary; Interpreters and Translators; Judges, Magistrate Judges, and Magistrates; Kindergarten Teachers, Except

High School Course: PUBLIC SPEAKING (CONTINUED)

Special Education; Lawyers; Library Science Teachers, Postsecondary; Middle School Teachers, Except Special and Vocational Education; Preschool Teachers, Except Special Education; Public Address System and Other Announcers; Recreation Workers; Reporters and Correspondents; Secondary School Teachers, Except Special and Vocational Education; Special Education Teachers, Middle School; Special Education Teachers, Preschool, Kindergarten, and Elementary School; Special Education Teachers, Secondary School; Speech-Language Pathologists; Telemarketers; Vocational Education Teachers, Middle School; Vocational Education Teachers, Postsecondary; Vocational Education Teachers, Secondary School

High School Course: SOCIAL SCIENCE

Related Majors: Advertising; African-American Studies; American Studies; Anthropology; Archeology; Area Studies; Art History; Communications Studies/Speech; Criminal Justice/Law Enforcement; Dietetics; Economics; Geography; History; Industrial and Labor Relations; International Relations; Law; Parks and Recreation Management; Political Science; Psychology; Religion/Religious Studies; Social Work; Sociology; Spanish; Urban Studies; Women's Studies

Related Careers: Administrative Law Judges, Adjudicators, and Hearing Officers; Advertising Sales Agents; Anthropologists; Anthropology and Archeology Teachers, Postsecondary; Arbitrators, Mediators, and Conciliators; Area, Ethnic, and Cultural Studies Teachers, Postsecondary; Child, Family, and School Social Workers; Clergy; Clinical, Counseling, and School Psychologists; Communications Teachers, Postsecondary; Criminal Justice and Law Enforcement Teachers, Postsecondary; Detectives and Criminal Investigators; Dietitians and Nutritionists; Economists; Employment, Recruitment, and Placement Specialists; Fish and Game Wardens; Geographers; Historians; History Teachers, Postsecondary; Industrial-Organizational Psychologists; Judges, Magistrate Judges, and Magistrates; Law Teachers, Postsecondary; Lawyers; Marriage and Family Therapists; Political Scientists; Probation Officers and Correctional Treatment Specialists; Recreation Workers; Reporters and Correspondents; Social Work Teachers, Postsecondary; Sociologists; Sociology Teachers, Postsecondary

High School Course: SPANISH, See FOREIGN LANGUAGE

High School Course: TRIGONOMETRY, See PRE-CALCULUS or CALCULUS

Find the items in the table that best fit with the three favorite high school courses you listed at the beginning of this chapter. If a lot of majors or careers are listed, try to find some that are linked to more than one of your favorite courses or that otherwise are interesting to you. Then write these college majors and careers in the following worksheet.

COLLEGE MAJORS AND CAREERS THAT RELATE TO MY FAVORITE HIGH SCHOOL COURSES

_____

_____

_____

_____

_____

_____

_____

_____

_____

_____

_____

_____

_____

_____

Key Points: Chapter 4

- Success in a high school course can predict success in a similar college course and therefore in a related college major.

- Your satisfaction with high school courses can also suggest satisfying careers.

CHAPTER 5

Your Hot List of College Majors and Careers

Now that you've done the exercises in the three preceding chapters, it's time for you to assemble a Hot List of College Majors and Careers that deserve your active consideration in Chapter 6.

Compiling Your Hot List

At the end of each of the three exercises in the preceding chapters—concerning personality types, skills, and high school courses—you filled out a worksheet with a list of the college majors and careers that were most strongly suggested by each exercise. Look these over now and decide which of the following statements best characterizes what you see:

- **Certain majors and careers appear in the results from all three exercises.** If this is what you find, congratulations! These majors and careers obviously correspond well to your preferences, and you should write them in your Hot List on page 67.

- **Certain majors and careers appear in your results from two of the exercises, but none appears in three.** This is still a meaningful finding; these majors and careers probably belong on your Hot List. If many majors and careers fit this description, you might ask yourself whether you feel more confident about one kind of exercise than another. For example, do you feel you have a clearer notion of your personality type and favorite high school courses than of your skills? In that case, you might want to give greater weight to the majors and careers that are shared by the results of the exercises relating to your personality and favorite high school courses.

- **There's no pattern at all—no majors or careers appear in the results from more than one of the exercises.** In this case, you need to decide which exercise you trust the most. Different people have different styles of thinking about themselves; for example, some have a much keener awareness of their personality type than their skills. Or perhaps the terms used in one exercise seem easier to understand than the terms in the others. Go with the results of the exercise that you feel most confident about. Write those majors and careers in your Hot List.

- **One of the preceding three statements applies to you, but you have a *very* large number of majors on your Hot List.** Here's where the careers can help you—they can help you narrow down the majors you're considering. Find the career that appears most often in your results. (If no career appears more than once, pick one that seems especially interesting to you.) Then go back to the personality exercise in Chapter 2 and find that career in the table. Make a note of its one-, two-, or three-letter personality code and find majors that have this same personality type code or a code similar to it. These majors are strong candidates for your Hot List.

After you have filled in your Hot List and have started investigating the listed majors in Chapter 6, you can also use the Hot List as an informal way of recording your impressions:

- If a major appeals to you when you read about it, put a few stars next to the name on the Hot List. The stars can serve to remind you which majors are the hottest of the hot!

- One of the important facts you'll read about the major is what careers it is linked to. When you see a career that looks interesting to you, write its name next to the name of the major on the Hot List (if it's not there already). Later you can use other resources to investigate these jobs in greater detail.

MY HOT LIST OF COLLEGE MAJORS AND CAREERS

_____

_____

_____

_____

_____

_____

_____

_____

_____

_____

_____

_____

_____

Key Points: Chapter 5

- If a major or career appeals to you for multiple reasons (for example, because of both your personality and your skills), it deserves further exploration and consideration.

- If the exercises in the preceding chapters did not produce consistently "hot" majors or careers, focus on the results of the one or two exercises that you felt most confident doing.

CHAPTER 6

Review College Majors and Related Careers

In this chapter, you can get the facts about 120 college majors and the 229 careers related to them. You may learn new things about majors that you thought you knew all about. You may also encounter majors that you never heard of before or that you don't know well.

The Hot List you created in Chapter 5 can help you choose majors to explore here. It may also suggest careers that you can look up in the index to identify related majors in this chapter. But even if you just browse this chapter at random, the facts are organized in a way that makes it easy for you to get an understanding of the major and related careers.

Here's what you'll find for each major:

- **Title, Definition, and CIP Code:** The title is a name that is frequently used for the major, although some majors may also be known under other names. The brief definition is derived from the Classification of Instructional Programs (CIP), a system developed by the U.S. Department of Education to catalog every major. The code number(s) of the related CIP program(s) completes this section.

- **Specializations in the Major:** Most majors allow students to select a "concentration," a "track," or some other way of specializing in one aspect of the field. This list identifies some but may not be exhaustive. The specialization you choose may turn into your future career path.

- **Typical Sequence of College Courses:** This section shows a list of courses often required for this major, ordered in a way they might logically be taken. Of course, colleges vary on what specific courses they require, what courses they offer, and what sequences they allow. Also, students usually have some freedom to tailor the course content and sequence to their interests and needs. In some cases, a course listed here may span more than one semester.

- **Typical Sequence of High School Courses:** These are high school courses that are considered good preparation for the major. High schools vary on their requirements and offerings, and colleges vary on what courses they prefer as prerequisites. Many of the courses here are subjects you'll need to study for more than one year.

- **Career Snapshot:** This briefly describes what careers are related to the major. Outlook information that appears here is based on the Department of Labor's *Occupational Outlook Handbook*.

- **Related Job(s):** Here you can see specific facts about the jobs related to the major. The facts are derived from the U.S. Department of Labor and reflect the national average for all workers in the occupation. To help you make sense of the figures, you should know that the average income for all the occupations in this book is about $65,000 and the average rate of growth is 11.8%. (Compare that to the averages of $33,190 income and 10.1% growth for all wage-earning occupations in the economy, and you can see that a college education is a good investment!) Job-growth projections are through 2018. Job openings are average annual figures.

- **Characteristics of the Related Jobs:** This section shows the personality type(s) and the most significant skills and work conditions for the related jobs.

Accounting

Prepares individuals to practice the profession of accounting and to perform related business functions. **Related CIP Program:** 52.0301 Accounting.

Specializations in the Major: Cost accounting, auditing, accounting computer systems, taxation, forensic accounting, financial reporting.

Typical Sequence of College Courses: English composition, business writing, introduction to psychology, principles of microeconomics, principles of macroeconomics, calculus for business and social sciences, statistics for business and social sciences, introduction to management information systems, introduction to accounting, legal environment of business, principles of management and organization, operations management, strategic management, business finance, introduction to marketing, cost accounting, auditing, taxation of individuals, taxation of corporations, partnerships and estates. **Typical Sequence of High School Courses:** English, algebra, geometry, trigonometry, science, foreign language, computer science.

Career Snapshot: Accountants maintain the financial records of an organization and supervise the recording of transactions. They provide information about the fiscal condition and trends of the organization, as well as figures for tax forms and financial reports. They advise management and therefore need good communication skills. A bachelor's degree is sufficient preparation for many entry-level jobs, but some employers prefer a master's degree. Accountants with diverse skills may advance to management after a few years. The job outlook is generally good.

Related Jobs

Job Title	Average Earnings	Job Growth	Job Openings
1. Accountants and Auditors	$60,340	21.6%	50,000
2. Budget Analysts	$66,660	15.1%	2,000
3. Business Teachers, Postsecondary	$73,320	15.1%	ROUGHLY 2,000
4. Credit Analysts	$57,470	15.0%	2,000
5. Financial Examiners	$71,750	41.2%	2,000
6. Tax Examiners, Collectors, and Revenue Agents	$48,550	13.0%	4,000

Characteristics of the Related Jobs: Personality Type—Conventional, Enterprising, Investigative. **Skills**—Mathematics, management of financial resources, operations analysis, critical thinking, writing, active learning, speaking, judgment and decision making. **Work Conditions**—Indoors; sitting.

Actuarial Science

Focuses on the mathematical and statistical analysis of risk and their applications to insurance and other business management problems. **Related CIP Program:** 52.1304 Actuarial Science.

Specializations in the Major: Insurance, investment.

Typical Sequence of College Courses: Calculus, linear algebra, advanced calculus, introduction to computer science, introduction to probability, introduction to actuarial mathematics, mathematical statistics, applied regression, actuarial models, introduction to accounting, principles of microeconomics, principles of macroeconomics, financial management, programming in C++, investment analysis, price theory, income and employment theory. **Typical Sequence of High School Courses:** English, algebra, geometry, trigonometry, science, pre-calculus, calculus, computer science.

Career Snapshot: Actuarial science is the analysis of mathematical data to predict the likelihood of certain events, such as death, accident, or disability. Insurance companies are the main employers of actuaries; actuaries determine how much the insurers charge for policies. The usual entry route is a bachelor's degree, but actuaries continue to study and sit for exams to upgrade their professional standing over the course of 5 to 10 years. The occupation is expected to grow at a good pace, and there will probably be many openings for those who are able to pass the series of exams.

Related Jobs

Job Title	Average Earnings	Job Growth	Job Openings
1. Actuaries	$87,210	21.4%	1,000
2. Business Teachers, Postsecondary	$73,320	15.1%	Roughly 2,000

Characteristics of the Related Jobs: Personality Type—Conventional, Investigative, Social. **Skills**—Mathematics, judgment and decision making, operations analysis, learning strategies, reading comprehension, writing, active learning, critical thinking. **Work Conditions**—Indoors; sitting.

Advertising

Focuses on the creation, execution, transmission, and evaluation of commercial messages in various media intended to promote and sell products, services, and brands and prepares individuals to function as advertising assistants, technicians, and managers. **Related CIP Program:** 09.0903 Advertising.

Specializations in the Major: Management, creative process.

Typical Sequence of College Courses: English composition, oral communication, statistics for business and social sciences, introduction to marketing, introduction to advertising, communications theory, advertising message strategy, communication ethics, advertising media, advertising copy and layout, advertising account planning and research, advertising campaign management, mass communication law, introduction to communication research. **Typical Sequence of High School Courses:** English, algebra, foreign language, art, literature, public speaking, social science.

Career Snapshot: Advertising is a combination of writing, art, and business. Graduates with a bachelor's degree in advertising often go on to jobs in advertising agencies, mostly in large cities. They may start as copywriters and advance to management. Competition can be keen because the industry is considered glamorous. A knowledge of how to advertise on the Internet can be an advantage.

Related Jobs

Job Title	Average Earnings	Job Growth	Job Openings
1. Advertising and Promotions Managers	$82,370	–1.7%	1,000
2. Advertising Sales Agents	$43,360	7.2%	5,000
3. Communications Teachers, Postsecondary	$58,890	15.1%	Roughly 800

Characteristics of the Related Jobs: Personality Type—Enterprising, Artistic, Conventional. **Skills**—Management of financial resources, negotiation, speaking, operations analysis, service orientation, coordination, active learning, management of material resources. **Work Conditions**—More often indoors than outdoors; in a vehicle; sitting.

Aeronautical/Aerospace Engineering

Prepares individuals to apply mathematical and scientific principles to the design, development, and operational evaluation of aircraft, missiles, space vehicles, and their systems; applied research on flight and orbital characteristics; and the development of systems and procedures for the launching, guidance, and control of air and space vehicles. **Related CIP Program:** 14.0201 Aerospace, Aeronautical and Astronautical/Space Engineering.

Specializations in the Major: Propulsion, airframes and aerodynamics, testing, spacecraft.

Typical Sequence of College Courses: English composition, technical writing, calculus, differential equations, introduction to computer science, general chemistry, general physics, thermodynamics, introduction to electric circuits, introduction to aerospace engineering, statics, dynamics, materials engineering, fluid mechanics, aircraft systems and propulsion, flight control systems, aerodynamics, aircraft structural design, aircraft stability and control, experimental aerodynamics, senior design project. **Typical Sequence of High School Courses:** English, algebra, geometry, trigonometry, pre-calculus, calculus, chemistry, physics, computer science.

Career Snapshot: Engineers apply scientific principles to real-world problems, finding the optimal solution that balances elegant technology with realistic cost. Aeronautical/aerospace engineers need to learn the specific principles of air flow and resistance and the workings of various kinds of propulsion systems. Most enter the job market with a bachelor's degree. Some later move into managerial positions. New technologies and new designs for commercial and military aircraft and spacecraft should spur demand for aerospace engineers. Job outlook is good because new grads are needed to replace aerospace engineers who are retiring or leaving the occupation for other reasons.

Related Jobs

Job Title	Average Earnings	Job Growth	Job Openings
1. Aerospace Engineers	$94,780	10.4%	2,000
2. Engineering Managers	$117,000	6.2%	5,000
3. Engineering Teachers, Postsecondary	$85,830	15.1%	ROUGHLY 1,000

Characteristics of the Related Jobs: Personality Type—Investigative, Realistic, Enterprising. **Skills**—Operations analysis, science, mathematics, technology design, quality control analysis, reading comprehension, writing, complex problem solving. **Work Conditions**—Indoors; sitting; common protective or safety equipment.

African-American Studies

Focuses on the history, sociology, politics, culture, and economics of the North American peoples descended from the African diaspora, focusing on the United States, Canada, and the Caribbean but also including reference to Latin American elements of the diaspora. **Related CIP Program:** 05.0201 African-American/Black Studies.

Specializations in the Major: History and culture; behavioral and social inquiry; literature, language, and the arts.

Typical Sequence of College Courses: English composition, foreign language, American history, introduction to African-American studies, African-American literature, African-American history, African Diaspora studies, research methods in African-American studies, seminar (reporting on research). **Typical Sequence of High School Courses:** English, algebra, foreign language, history, literature, public speaking, social science.

Career Snapshot: African-American studies draws on a number of disciplines, including history, sociology, literature, linguistics, and political science. Usually you can shape the program to emphasize whichever appeals most to you. Graduates frequently pursue higher degrees as a means of establishing a career in a field such as college teaching or the law.

Related Jobs

Job Title	Average Earnings	Job Growth	Job Openings
1. Area, Ethnic, and Cultural Studies Teachers, Postsecondary	$65,030	15.1%	Roughly 200

Characteristics of the Related Jobs: Personality Type—Social, Investigative, Artistic. **Skills**—Science, writing, operations analysis, learning strategies, speaking, reading comprehension, active learning, instructing. **Work Conditions**—Indoors; sitting; exposed to disease or infections.

Agricultural Business and Economics

Focuses on modern business and economic principles involved in the organization, operation, and management of agricultural enterprises. **Related CIP Programs:** 01.0101 Agricultural Business and Management, General; 01.0105 Agricultural/Farm Supplies Retailing and Wholesaling; 01.0104 Farm/Farm and Ranch Management.

Specializations in the Major: Farm business management, ranch business management, agricultural marketing and sales, agricultural finance, agricultural economics, natural resources management, computer applications and data management, public policy.

Typical Sequence of College Courses: English composition, oral communication, business math, general biology, introduction to economics, introduction to accounting, introduction to agricultural economics and business, farm/ranch management, computer applications in agriculture,

75

legal and social environment of agriculture, statistics for business and social sciences, microeconomic theory, macroeconomic theory, natural resource economics, agribusiness financial management, introduction to marketing, marketing and pricing agricultural products, technical writing, agricultural policy, quantitative methods in agricultural business. **Typical Sequence of High School Courses:** English, algebra, geometry, trigonometry, biology, chemistry, computer science.

Career Snapshot: Agriculture is a major business in the United States, and graduates of agricultural business and economics programs often work far away from a farm or ranch. They may be employed by a bank that lends to farmers; by a food company that purchases large amounts of agricultural products; by a government agency that sets agricultural policies; or by a manufacturer that sells agricultural equipment, chemicals, or seed. They need to know how agricultural products are produced and how the markets for these products (increasingly global) behave. A bachelor's degree is a common entry route, although a graduate degree is useful for teaching or research positions.

Related Jobs

Job Title	Average Earnings	Job Growth	Job Openings
1. Farm and Home Management Advisors	$44,180	1.1%	FEWER THAN 500
2. Farm, Ranch, and Other Agricultural Managers	$59,450	5.9%	6,000
3. Farmers and Ranchers	$32,350	–8.0%	6,000
4. First-Line Supervisors/Managers of Farming, Fishing, and Forestry Workers	$40,500	7.8%	2,000
5. Nonfarm Animal Caretakers	$19,550	20.7%	7,000
6. Pest Control Workers	$30,410	15.3%	3,000
7. Purchasing Agents and Buyers, Farm Products	$53,150	–1.1%	FEWER THAN 500

Characteristics of the Related Jobs: Personality Type—Realistic, Enterprising, Conventional. **Skills**—Management of financial resources, management of material resources, equipment maintenance, repairing, equipment selection, science, installation, operations analysis. **Work Conditions**—More often outdoors than indoors; in a vehicle; very hot or cold; minor burns, cuts, bites, or stings; hazardous equipment; extremely bright or inadequate lighting.

Agricultural Engineering

Prepares individuals to apply mathematical and scientific principles to the design, development, and operational evaluation of systems, equipment, and facilities for production, processing, storage, handling, distribution, and use of food, feed, and fiber. **Related CIP Program:** 14.0301 Agricultural Engineering.

Specializations in the Major: Agricultural machinery, agricultural structures, irrigation, environmental engineering, food and fiber processing.

Typical Sequence of College Courses: English composition, technical writing, calculus, differential equations, general biology, introduction to computer science, general chemistry, general physics, statics, dynamics, introduction to electric circuits, thermodynamics, numerical analysis, introduction to agricultural engineering, engineering properties of biological materials, fluid mechanics, microcomputer applications, materials engineering, soil and water engineering, agricultural power and machines, biological materials processing, senior design project. **Typical Sequence of High School Courses:** English, algebra, geometry, trigonometry, pre-calculus, biology, calculus, chemistry, computer science.

Career Snapshot: Agricultural engineers use scientific knowledge to solve problems of growing food and fiber crops, building and maintaining agricultural equipment and structures, and processing agricultural products. A bachelor's degree is usually sufficient preparation to enter this field. Often an engineering job can be a springboard for a managerial position. Employment growth should result from the need to increase crop yields to feed an expanding population and to produce crops used as renewable energy sources. Moreover, engineers will be needed to develop more efficient agricultural production and to conserve resources. In addition, engineers will be needed to meet the increasing demand for biosensors, used to determine the optimal treatment of crops.

Related Jobs

Job Title	Average Earnings	Job Growth	Job Openings
1. Agricultural Engineers	$69,560	12.1%	FEWER THAN 500
2. Engineering Managers	$117,000	6.2%	5,000
3. Engineering Teachers, Postsecondary	$85,830	15.1%	ROUGHLY 1,000

Characteristics of the Related Jobs: Personality Type—Enterprising, Investigative, Realistic. **Skills**—Operations analysis, management of financial resources, science, mathematics, management of material resources, management of personnel resources, complex problem solving, coordination. **Work Conditions**—Indoors; sitting; noisy; exposed to radiation; hazardous equipment.

Agronomy and Crop Science

Focuses on the chemical, physical, and biological relationships of crops and the soils nurturing them. **Related CIP Program:** 01.1102 Agronomy and Crop Science.

Specializations in the Major: Agro-industry, soil and crop management, turfgrass management.

Typical Sequence of College Courses: English composition, college algebra, general biology, general chemistry, organic chemistry, genetics, introduction to agricultural economics and business, introduction to soil science, botany, computer applications in agriculture, plant pathology, seed production, crop production, soil fertility, plant nutrition and fertilizers, plant breeding, general entomology, weed control. **Typical Sequence of High School Courses:** Biology, chemistry, algebra, geometry, trigonometry, computer science, English, public speaking.

Career Snapshot: Agronomists and crop scientists look for ways to improve the production and quality of food, feed, and fiber crops. They need to understand the chemical requirements of soils and growing plants and the genetic basis of plant development—especially now that genetic engineering is growing in importance. Those with a bachelor's degree may work in applied research, as managers in businesses that market to farmers and ranchers, or as agricultural products inspectors. A graduate degree is useful to do basic research and necessary for college teaching. Because agriculture is a vital U.S. industry supported by agricultural extension pro-grams, a large number of agronomists and crop scientists, many of them with bachelor's degrees, work for federal, state, and local governments.

Related Jobs

Job Title	Average Earnings	Job Growth	Job Openings
1. Agricultural and Food Science Technicians	$34,410	8.8%	1,000
2. Agricultural Sciences Teachers, Postsecondary	$77,210	15.1%	Roughly 300
3. Farm, Ranch, and Other Agricultural Managers	$59,450	5.9%	6,000
4. Farmers and Ranchers	$32,350	−8.0%	6,000
5. First-Line Supervisors/Managers of Farming, Fishing, and Forestry Workers	$40,500	7.8%	2,000
6. Soil and Plant Scientists	$59,180	15.5%	500

Characteristics of the Related Jobs: Personality Type—Realistic, Enterprising, Conventional. **Skills**—Science, management of financial resources, equipment maintenance, management of material resources, repairing, equipment selection, installation, quality control analysis. **Work Conditions**—More often outdoors than indoors; in a vehicle; very hot or cold; hazardous equipment; minor burns, cuts, bites, or stings; contaminants.

American Studies

Focuses on the history, society, politics, culture, and economics of the United States and its Pre-Columbian and colonial predecessors, includ-ing the flow of immigrants from other societies. **Related CIP Program:** 05.0102 American/United States Studies/Civilization.

Specializations in the Major: History and political science; literature, language, and the arts; popular culture.

Typical Sequence of College Courses: English composition, American history, American government, American literature, American popular cul-ture, seminar (reporting on research). **Typical Sequence of High School**

Courses: English, algebra, foreign language, history, literature, public speaking, social science.

Career Snapshot: American studies is an interdisciplinary major that allows you to concentrate on the aspect of American culture that is of greatest interest to you—for example, history, the arts, or social and ethnic groups. Many, perhaps most, graduates use this major as a springboard to postgraduate or professional training that prepares for a career in college teaching, business, law, the arts, politics, or some other field.

Related Jobs

Job Title	Average Earnings	Job Growth	Job Openings
1. Area, Ethnic, and Cultural Studies Teachers, Postsecondary	$65,030	15.1%	ROUGHLY 200

Characteristics of the Related Jobs: Personality Type—Social, Investigative, Artistic. **Skills**—Science, writing, operations analysis, learning strategies, speaking, reading comprehension, active learning, instructing. **Work Conditions**—Indoors; sitting; exposed to disease or infections.

Animal Science

Focuses on the scientific principles that underlie the breeding and management of agricultural animals and the production, processing, and distribution of agricultural animal products. **Related CIP Programs:** 01.0902 Agricultural Animal Breeding; 01.0903 Animal Health; 01.0904 Animal Nutrition; 01.0901 Animal Sciences, General; 01.0905 Dairy Science; 01.0906 Livestock Management; 01.0907 Poultry Science.

Specializations in the Major: Production, veterinary research.

Typical Sequence of College Courses: English composition, college algebra, statistics, general biology, general chemistry, organic chemistry, genetics, introduction to agricultural economics and business, introduction to animal science, meats and other animal products, plant physiology, anatomy and physiology of farm animals, animal nutrition and nutritional diseases, feeds and feeding, reproduction of farm animals, animal breeding, marking and grading of livestock and meats. **Typical Sequence of High School Courses:** Biology, chemistry, algebra, geometry, trigonometry, computer science, English, public speaking.

Career Snapshot: Animal science graduates may work directly for farms and ranches that raise animals, or they may work in research, marketing, or sales for pharmaceutical or feed companies that supply farmers, ranchers, and veterinarians. About one-third go on to veterinary school, medical school, or another postgraduate scientific field.

Related Jobs

Job Title	Average Earnings	Job Growth	Job Openings
1. Agricultural and Food Science Technicians	$34,410	8.8%	1,000
2. Agricultural Sciences Teachers, Postsecondary	$77,210	15.1%	ROUGHLY 300
3. Animal Scientists	$56,960	13.1%	FEWER THAN 500
4. Farm and Home Management Advisors	$44,180	1.1%	FEWER THAN 500
5. Farm, Ranch, and Other Agricultural Managers	$59,450	5.9%	6,000
6. Farmers and Ranchers	$32,350	–8.0%	6,000
7. First-Line Supervisors/Managers of Farming, Fishing, and Forestry Workers	$40,500	7.8%	2,000

Characteristics of the Related Jobs: Personality Type—Realistic, Enterprising, Conventional. **Skills**—Equipment maintenance, management of financial resources, repairing, management of material resources, science, equipment selection, installation, quality control analysis. **Work Conditions**—In a vehicle; more often outdoors than indoors; very hot or cold; hazardous equipment; contaminants; minor burns, cuts, bites, or stings.

Anthropology

Focuses on the systematic study of human beings, their antecedents and related primates, and their cultural behavior and institutions, in comparative perspective. **Related CIP Program:** 45.0201 Anthropology.

Specializations in the Major: Cultural, biological/forensic, archaeology.

Typical Sequence of College Courses: English composition, general biology, statistics for business and social sciences, human growth and development, introduction to sociology, foreign language, cultural anthropology, physical anthropology, introduction to archeology, language and culture, history of anthropological theory, research methods in anthropology, current issues in anthropology. **Typical Sequence of High School Courses:** Algebra, English, foreign language, social science, history, biology, public speaking, chemistry.

Career Snapshot: Some anthropologists study the social and cultural behavior of people. They investigate communities throughout the world, focusing on their arts, religions, and economic and social institutions. A graduate degree is usually needed to do research or college teaching in this field, but some graduates with bachelor's degrees find their skills useful in business, such as in marketing research. Other anthropologists specialize in human physical characteristics and may study human remains to understand history or evolution or to provide evidence in criminal investigations. A graduate degree is usually required for this specialization.

Related Jobs

Job Title	Average Earnings	Job Growth	Job Openings
1. Anthropologists and Archeologists	$53,460	28.1%	Fewer than 500
2. Anthropology and Archeology Teachers, Postsecondary	$69,520	15.1%	Roughly 200

Characteristics of the Related Jobs: Personality Type—Investigative, Artistic. **Skills**—Science, writing, reading comprehension, operations analysis, speaking, active learning, critical thinking, learning strategies. **Work Conditions**—More often indoors than outdoors; sitting; in a vehicle; very hot or cold.

Archeology

Focuses on the systematic study of extinct societies and the past of living societies via the excavation, analysis, and interpretation of their artifactual, human, and associated remains. **Related CIP Program:** 45.0301 Archeology.

Specializations in the Major: Field work, preservation, ancient civilizations, prehistoric archeology.

Typical Sequence of College Courses: English composition, statistics for business and social sciences, foreign language, introduction to archeology, world prehistory, ancient literate civilizations, field methods in archeology, new world archeology, seminar (reporting on research). **Typical Sequence of High School Courses:** Algebra, English, foreign language, social science, history, biology, public speaking.

Career Snapshot: Archeology (also spelled archaeology) is the study of prehistoric and historic cultures through the discovery, preservation, and interpretation of their material remains. As a major, it is sometimes offered as a specialization within anthropology or classics. Students work with languages as well as physical objects, so they develop a number of skills that are appreciated in the business world. They may also get higher degrees in archeology in order to do museum work, field work, or college teaching.

Related Jobs

Job Title	Average Earnings	Job Growth	Job Openings
1. Anthropologists and Archeologists	$53,460	28.1%	FEWER THAN 500
2. Anthropology and Archeology Teachers, Postsecondary	$69,520	15.1%	ROUGHLY 200

Characteristics of the Related Jobs: Personality Type—Investigative, Artistic. **Skills**—Science, writing, reading comprehension, operations analysis, speaking, active learning, critical thinking, learning strategies. **Work Conditions**—More often indoors than outdoors; sitting; in a vehicle; very hot or cold.

Architecture

Prepares individuals for the independent professional practice of architecture and for conducting research in various aspects of the field. **Related CIP Program:** 04.0201 Architecture (BArch, BA/BS, MArch, MA/MS, PhD).

Specializations in the Major: Design, history, theory and criticism, urban studies, architectural engineering.

Typical Sequence of College Courses: English composition, basic drawing, art history: Renaissance to modern, calculus, introduction to computer science, general physics, history of architecture, structures, building science,

83

visual analysis of architecture, architectural graphics, architectural design, architectural computer graphics, site analysis, introduction to urban planning. **Typical Sequence of High School Courses:** English, algebra, geometry, trigonometry, pre-calculus, calculus, physics, computer science, art.

Career Snapshot: Architects design buildings and the spaces between them. They must have a combination of artistic, technical, and business skills. In order to be licensed, they must obtain a professional degree in architecture (sometimes a five-year bachelor's degree, sometimes a master's degree after a bachelor's in another field); work as an intern, typically for three years; and pass a licensing exam. About one-third are self-employed, and most architectural firms are quite small. Computer skills can be a big advantage for new graduates. Best internship opportunities will be for those who have interned while still in school. Demand for architectural services depends on the amount of building construction and therefore varies with economic ups and downs and by geographic region. Job competition is expected to be keen.

Related Jobs

Job Title	Average Earnings	Job Growth	Job Openings
1. Architects, Except Landscape and Naval	$72,700	16.2%	5,000
2. Architecture Teachers, Postsecondary	$73,550	15.1%	Roughly 200
3. Engineering Managers	$117,000	6.2%	5,000

Characteristics of the Related Jobs: Personality Type—Artistic, Investigative, Enterprising. **Skills**—Operations analysis, management of financial resources, management of material resources, mathematics, science, judgment and decision making, complex problem solving, negotiation. **Work Conditions**—More often indoors than outdoors; in a vehicle; sitting; high places; climbing ladders, scaffolds, or poles.

Area Studies

Focuses on the history, society, politics, culture, and economics of one or more of the peoples within a geographic region and the subcultures within modern and historical countries and societies. **Related CIP Programs:** 05.0103 Asian Studies/Civilization; 05.0122 Regional Studies (U.S.,

Canadian, Foreign); 05.0101 African Studies; 05.0102 American/United States Studies/Civilization; 05.0115 Canadian Studies; 05.0105 Russian, Central European, East European and Eurasian Studies; 05.0104 East Asian Studies; 05.0106 European Studies/Civilization; 05.0107 Latin American Studies; 05.0109 Pacific Area/Pacific Rim Studies; 05.0110 Russian Studies; 05.0112 South Asian Studies; 05.0113 Southeast Asian Studies; 05.0114 Western European Studies; 05.0108 Near and Middle Eastern Studies; others.

Specializations in the Major: History and culture, economics and trade, political science, language and literature.

Typical Sequence of College Courses: English composition, foreign language, foreign literature and culture, comparative governments, introduction to economics, international economics, seminar (reporting on research). **Typical Sequence of High School Courses:** English, foreign language, history, literature, social science, algebra.

Career Snapshot: Certain very popular area studies—African-American studies, American studies, and women's studies—are described elsewhere in this book. But many colleges offer other area studies majors, usually defined in terms of a region of the world: East Asian studies, European studies, Latin American studies, and so on. These are interdisciplinary majors that may involve some combination of linguistics, literature, history, sociology, political science, economic development, or other disciplines. Usually you can emphasize whichever aspects interest you most. Graduates of area studies may go into a business or government career where knowledge of a foreign culture is an advantage. Many get higher degrees to prepare for a career in law or college teaching.

Related Jobs

Job Title	Average Earnings	Job Growth	Job Openings
1. Area, Ethnic, and Cultural Studies Teachers, Postsecondary	$65,030	15.1%	Roughly 200

Characteristics of the Related Jobs: Personality Type—Social, Investigative, Artistic. **Skills**—Science, writing, operations analysis, learning strategies, speaking, reading comprehension, active learning, instructing. **Work Conditions**—Indoors; sitting; exposed to disease or infections.

Art

Focuses on the study and appreciation of the visual arts and prepares individuals to function as creative artists in the visual and plastic media. **Related CIP Programs:** 50.0712 Fiber, Textile, and Weaving Arts; 50.0711 Ceramic Arts and Ceramics; 50.0713 Metal and Jewelry Arts; 50.0708 Painting; 50.0710 Printmaking; 50.0709 Sculpture; 50.0701 Art/Art Studies, General; 50.0702 Fine/Studio Arts, General; 50.0705 Drawing; 50.0706 Intermedia/Multimedia.

Specializations in the Major: Studio art, art education, painting, sculpture, screenprinting, ceramics.

Typical Sequence of College Courses: English composition, foreign language, art and culture, basic drawing, color and design, two-dimensional design, three-dimensional design, art history: prehistoric to Renaissance, art history: Renaissance to modern, figure drawing, a medium (e.g., painting, sculpture, ceramics), art practicum. **Typical Sequence of High School Courses:** English, foreign language, literature, history, art.

Career Snapshot: Only a few highly talented and motivated artists are able to support themselves by producing and selling their artwork. But many other graduates of art programs find work in education—as private instructors, school teachers, and university instructors of art and art history. College teaching requires a master's degree. Some graduates apply their artistic skills to crafts or to commercial applications such as illustration or cartooning.

Related Jobs

Job Title	Average Earnings	Job Growth	Job Openings
1. Art Directors	$78,580	11.7%	3,000
2. Art, Drama, and Music Teachers, Postsecondary	$60,400	15.1%	Roughly 2,500
3. Craft Artists	$28,960	7.2%	Fewer than 500
4. Fine Artists, Including Painters, Sculptors, and Illustrators	$44,160	9.0%	500
5. Multi-Media Artists and Animators	$58,250	14.1%	3,000

Characteristics of the Related Jobs: Personality Type—Artistic, Enterprising, Realistic. **Skills**—Management of financial resources, operations analysis, management of material resources, technology design, active learning, learning strategies, speaking, critical thinking. **Work Conditions**—Indoors; sitting; using hands; making repetitive motions.

Art History

Focuses on the study of the historical development of art as social and intellectual phenomenon, the analysis of works of art, and art conservation. **Related CIP Program:** 50.0703 Art History, Criticism, and Conservation.

Specializations in the Major: Criticism, a historical period, a particular artistic medium, a region of the world.

Typical Sequence of College Courses: English composition, foreign language, art and culture, studio art, world history to the early modern era, world history in the modern era, art history: prehistoric to Renaissance, art history: Renaissance to modern, non-Western art, critical study of visual art. **Typical Sequence of High School Courses:** English, art, foreign language, history, literature, social science.

Career Snapshot: Art has been important to humans since people painted on cave walls, and art history majors learn how art forms, techniques, and traditions have developed since then within their historical and cultural contexts. Study abroad is often part of the curriculum. Graduates of art history programs with a bachelor's degree may work for museums, auction houses, or publishers. With additional education or training, they may work as college teachers or restorers.

Related Jobs

Job Title	Average Earnings	Job Growth	Job Openings
1. Archivists	$46,470	6.5%	Fewer than 500
2. Art, Drama, and Music Teachers, Postsecondary	$60,400	15.1%	Roughly 2,500
3. Curators	$47,930	23.0%	500
4. Museum Technicians and Conservators	$37,120	25.5%	500

Characteristics of the Related Jobs: Personality Type—Social, Artistic. **Skills**—Instructing, learning strategies, speaking, writing, reading comprehension, monitoring, management of material resources, active learning. **Work Conditions**—Indoors; sitting; close to coworkers.

Astronomy

Focuses on the planetary, galactic, and stellar phenomena occurring in outer space. **Related CIP Programs:** 40.0203 Planetary Astronomy and Science; 40.0201 Astronomy; 40.0202 Astrophysics.

Specializations in the Major: Astrophysics, cosmology.

Typical Sequence of College Courses: English composition, introduction to computer science, calculus, differential equations, general chemistry, general physics, mechanics, electricity and magnetism, thermal physics, introduction to astrophysics, astrophysical processes, quantum and atomic physics, observational astronomy. **Typical Sequence of High School Courses:** English, algebra, geometry, trigonometry, chemistry, physics, precalculus, computer science, calculus.

Career Snapshot: Almost every year, astronomers make important discoveries that challenge existing theories about the planets, stars, and galaxies and the forces that formed them. Astronomers typically spend only a small fraction of their time actually observing and much more time analyzing data and comparing it to theoretical models. Many are college faculty members with teaching responsibilities. A PhD is the usual requirement for astronomers, and most new PhDs find a postdoctoral research appointment helpful for future employment. The occupation has only a small workforce, and some graduates of astronomy programs apply their skills to more earthbound pursuits, such as research and development in private industry.

Related Jobs

Job Title	Average Earnings	Job Growth	Job Openings
1. Astronomers	$104,720	16.0%	FEWER THAN 500
2. Atmospheric, Earth, Marine, and Space Sciences Teachers, Postsecondary	$78,660	15.1%	ROUGHLY 300
3. Natural Sciences Managers	$114,560	15.4%	2,000
4. Physicists	$106,390	15.9%	500

Characteristics of the Related Jobs: Personality Type—Investigative. **Skills**—Science, mathematics, operations analysis, reading comprehension, active learning, writing, technology design, learning strategies. **Work Conditions**—Indoors; sitting.

Biochemistry

Focuses on the scientific study of the chemistry of living systems, their fundamental chemical substances and reactions, and their chemical pathways and information transfer systems, with particular reference to carbohydrates, proteins, lipids, and nucleic acids. **Related CIP Program:** 26.0202 Biochemistry.

Specializations in the Major: Research, forensic chemistry, pharmacological chemistry, recombinant DNA.

Typical Sequence of College Courses: English composition, calculus, introduction to computer science, general chemistry, general biology, organic chemistry, general physics, analytical chemistry, general microbiology, introduction to biochemistry, cell biology, molecular biology, physical chemistry, genetics. **Typical Sequence of High School Courses:** English, algebra, trigonometry, biology, geometry, chemistry, physics, computer science, pre-calculus, calculus.

Career Snapshot: Biochemistry studies the fundamental chemical processes that support life. The recent growth of the pharmaceutical industry and of genetic engineering technology has fueled the demand for biochemistry majors, especially at the graduate level, but there will be a lot of competition for independent research positions that are supported by grants—as are many university jobs. Better opportunities are expected for those with bachelor's degrees who seek work in nonresearch jobs such as sales, marketing, and clinical laboratory testing.

Related Jobs

Job Title	Average Earnings	Job Growth	Job Openings
1. Biochemists and Biophysicists	$82,390	37.4%	2,000
2. Biological Science Teachers, Postsecondary	$73,980	15.1%	Roughly 1,700
3. Medical Scientists, Except Epidemiologists	$74,590	40.3%	7,000
4. Natural Sciences Managers	$114,560	15.4%	2,000

Characteristics of the Related Jobs: Personality Type—Investigative, Artistic, Realistic. **Skills**—Science, reading comprehension, active learning, writing, learning strategies, operations analysis, mathematics, instructing. **Work Conditions**—Indoors; sitting; exposed to disease or infections; hazardous conditions; common protective or safety equipment; wear specialized protective or safety equipment; exposed to radiation.

Bioengineering

Prepares individuals to apply mathematical and scientific principles to the design, development, and operational evaluation of biomedical and health systems and products such as integrated biomedical systems, instrumentation, medical information systems, artificial organs and prostheses, and health management and care delivery systems. **Related CIP Program:** 14.0501 Bioengineering and Biomedical Engineering.

Specializations in the Major: Biomedical engineering, molecular bioengineering, computational bioengineering, engineered biomaterials, medical imaging, biomechanics, prosthetics and artificial organs, controlled drug delivery.

Typical Sequence of College Courses: English composition, technical writing, calculus, differential equations, general chemistry, introduction to computer science, general physics, introduction to electric circuits, general biology, mechanics, introduction to bioengineering, bioinstrumentation, biomaterials, biomechanics, business information processing. **Typical Sequence of High School Courses:** English, algebra, geometry, trigonometry, pre-calculus, calculus, chemistry, biology, physics, computer science.

Career Snapshot: Bioengineering uses engineering principles of analysis and design to solve problems in medicine and biology. It finds ways to improve health care, agriculture, and industrial processes. Graduates with a bachelor's may work in industry, but increasing competition is making an advanced degree more important, and it is needed to prepare for a career in research or college teaching. Some graduates go on to medical school. This is one of the fastest-moving fields in engineering, so people in this field need to learn continuously to keep up with new technologies.

Related Jobs

Job Title	Average Earnings	Job Growth	Job Openings
1. Biomedical Engineers	$78,860	72.0%	1,000
2. Engineering Managers	$117,000	6.2%	5,000
3. Engineering Teachers, Postsecondary	$85,830	15.1%	Roughly 1,000

Characteristics of the Related Jobs: Personality Type—Enterprising, Investigative, Realistic. **Skills**—Operations analysis, science, mathematics, management of financial resources, management of material resources, technology design, reading comprehension, complex problem solving. **Work Conditions**—Indoors; sitting; exposed to radiation; hazardous conditions.

Biology

Focuses on the scientific study of plants, animals, microbial organisms, and habitats and ecosystem relations of living things. **Related CIP Program:** 26.0101 Biology/Biological Sciences, General.

Specializations in the Major: Botany, zoology, biochemistry, genetics, cell biology, microbiology, ecology.

Typical Sequence of College Courses: English composition, calculus, introduction to computer science, general chemistry, statistics, general biology, organic chemistry, genetics, general physics, cell biology, introduction to biochemistry, general microbiology, ecology, organisms and populations, animal anatomy and physiology, plant anatomy. **Typical Sequence of High School Courses:** Algebra, English, biology, geometry, trigonometry, chemistry, physics, pre-calculus, computer science, calculus.

Career Snapshot: Although it is often possible to study a specialization—such as botany, zoology, or biochemistry—many colleges offer a major in the general field of biology. With a bachelor's degree in biology, one may work as a technician or entry-level researcher in a medical, pharmaceutical, or governmental regulatory setting or as a sales representative in a technical field such as pharmaceuticals. Such job opportunities are expected to be good. Teaching biology in high school or middle school almost always requires additional coursework (perhaps a master's) in teaching theory and methods, plus supervised classroom experience. A large number of biology majors go on to pursue graduate or professional degrees and thus prepare for careers as researchers, college teachers, physicians, dentists, and veterinarians.

Related Jobs

Job Title	Average Earnings	Job Growth	Job Openings
1. Biological Science Teachers, Postsecondary	$73,980	15.1%	Roughly 1,700
2. Natural Sciences Managers	$114,560	15.4%	2,000

Characteristics of the Related Jobs: Personality Type—Investigative, Social. **Skills**—Science, instructing, reading comprehension, writing, speaking, learning strategies, operations analysis, active learning. **Work Conditions**—Indoors; sitting; hazardous conditions; exposed to disease or infections.

Botany

Focuses on the scientific study of plants, related microbial organisms, and plant habitats and ecosystem relations. **Related CIP Program:** 26.0301 Botany/Plant Biology.

Specializations in the Major: Forestry, plant genetics, phytopathology (plant disease).

Typical Sequence of College Courses: English composition, calculus, introduction to computer science, general chemistry, statistics, general biology, organic chemistry, genetics, general physics, cell biology, introduction to biochemistry, general microbiology, taxonomy of flowering plants, ecology, plant anatomy, plant physiology. **Typical Sequence of High School Courses:** English, algebra, biology, geometry, trigonometry, chemistry, physics, pre-calculus, computer science, calculus.

Career Snapshot: Botany is the science of plants. Since all of our food resources and the very air we breathe ultimately depend on the growth of plants, botany is a vital field of knowledge. A bachelor's degree in this field prepares you for some nonresearch jobs in industry, agriculture, forestry, and environmental protection. Best opportunities are in agricultural research, where a graduate degree is expected.

Related Jobs

Job Title	Average Earnings	Job Growth	Job Openings
1. Biological Science Teachers, Postsecondary	$73,980	15.1%	ROUGHLY 1,700
2. Natural Sciences Managers	$114,560	15.4%	2,000

Characteristics of the Related Jobs: Personality Type—Investigative, Social. **Skills**—Science, instructing, reading comprehension, writing, speaking, learning strategies, operations analysis, active learning. **Work Conditions**—Indoors; sitting; hazardous conditions; exposed to disease or infections.

Business Education

Prepares individuals to teach vocational business programs at various educational levels. **Related CIP Program:** 13.1303 Business Teacher Education.

Specializations in the Major: Distributive education, office skills.

Typical Sequence of College Courses: Introduction to psychology, English composition, oral communication, history and philosophy of education, human growth and development, introduction to accounting, legal environment of business, introduction to business management, business math, business information processing, keyboarding, statistics, business reports and communication, introduction to marketing, methods of teaching business subjects, student teaching. **Typical Sequence of High School Courses:** English, algebra, geometry, trigonometry, science, foreign language, industrial arts, keyboarding, office computer applications, public speaking.

Career Snapshot: Business educators teach secondary school students skills and knowledge they will need to succeed in the business world. Therefore, they must know about one or more specific business fields—such as bookkeeping, retailing, or office computer applications—as well as about techniques for teaching and for managing the classroom. A bachelor's degree is often an entry route to the first teaching job, but job security and pay raises often require a master's degree.

Related Jobs

Job Title	Average Earnings	Job Growth	Job Openings
1. Business Teachers, Postsecondary	$73,320	15.1%	ROUGHLY 2,000
2. Education Teachers, Postsecondary	$58,300	15.1%	ROUGHLY 1,800
3. Secondary School Teachers, Except Special and Vocational Education	$52,200	8.9%	41,000
4. Vocational Education Teachers, Postsecondary	$47,950	15.1%	ROUGHLY 4,000

Characteristics of the Related Jobs: Personality Type—Social, Artistic, Enterprising. **Skills**—Learning strategies, instructing, social perceptiveness, writing, service orientation, speaking, judgment and decision making, monitoring. **Work Conditions**—Indoors; standing; exposed to disease or infections; close to coworkers.

Business Management

Prepares individuals to plan, organize, direct, and control the functions and processes of a firm or organization. **Related CIP Program:** 52.0201 Business Administration and Management, General.

Specializations in the Major: Marketing, management, operations, international business.

Typical Sequence of College Courses: English composition, business writing, introduction to psychology, principles of microeconomics, principles of macroeconomics, calculus for business and social sciences, statistics for business and social sciences, introduction to management information systems, introduction to accounting, legal environment of business, principles of management and organization, operations management, strategic management, business finance, introduction to marketing, organizational behavior, human resource management, international management, organizational theory. **Typical Sequence of High School Courses:**

English, algebra, geometry, trigonometry, science, foreign language, computer science, public speaking.

Career Snapshot: Students of business management learn about the principles of economics, the legal and social environment in which business operates, and quantitative methods for measuring and projecting business activity. Graduates may enter the business world directly or pursue a master's degree. Some get a bachelor's degree in a nonbusiness field and enter a master's of business administration program after getting some entry-level work experience.

Related Jobs

Job Title	Average Earnings	Job Growth	Job Openings
1. Administrative Services Managers	$75,520	12.5%	9,000
2. Business Teachers, Postsecondary	$73,320	15.1%	ROUGHLY 2,000
3. Chief Executives	$160,720	–1.4%	11,000
4. Construction Managers	$82,330	17.2%	14,000
5. Cost Estimators	$57,300	25.3%	10,000
6. General and Operations Managers	$92,650	–0.1%	50,000
7. Industrial Production Managers	$85,080	–7.6%	5,000
8. Management Analysts	$75,250	23.9%	31,000
9. Sales Managers	$96,790	14.9%	13,000
10. Social and Community Service Managers	$56,600	13.8%	5,000
11. Transportation, Storage, and Distribution Managers	$79,490	–5.3%	3,000

Characteristics of the Related Jobs: Personality Type—Enterprising, Conventional. **Skills**—Management of financial resources, management of material resources, operations analysis, management of personnel resources, negotiation, judgment and decision making, coordination, monitoring. **Work Conditions**—Indoors; sitting; in a vehicle.

Chemical Engineering

Prepares individuals to apply mathematical and scientific principles to the design, development, and operational evaluation of systems employing chemical processes, such as chemical reactors, kinetic systems,

95

electrochemical systems, energy conservation processes, heat and mass transfer systems, and separation processes, and the applied analysis of chemical problems such as corrosion, particle abrasion, energy loss, pollution, and fluid mechanics. **Related CIP Program:** 14.0701 Chemical Engineering.

Specializations in the Major: Bioengineering, pharmaceuticals, nuclear engineering, quality control.

Typical Sequence of College Courses: English composition, technical writing, calculus, differential equations, general chemistry, general physics, introduction to computer science, introduction to electric circuits, organic chemistry, introduction to chemical engineering, thermodynamics, numerical analysis, materials engineering, chemical engineering thermodynamics, kinetics and reactor design, mass transfer operations, plant design, process dynamics and controls, process design and optimization, senior design project. **Typical Sequence of High School Courses:** English, algebra, geometry, trigonometry, pre-calculus, calculus, chemistry, physics, computer science.

Career Snapshot: Chemical engineers apply principles of chemistry to solve engineering problems, such as how to prepare large batches of chemical compounds economically and with uniform consistency and quality. A bachelor's degree is the usual entry route for this field. Among manufacturing industries, best opportunities are expected in pharmaceuticals, but most job growth is expected in research and development. Engineers often move on to managerial jobs.

Related Jobs

Job Title	Average Earnings	Job Growth	Job Openings
1. Chemical Engineers	$88,280	−2.0%	1,000
2. Engineering Managers	$117,000	6.2%	5,000
3. Engineering Teachers, Postsecondary	$85,830	15.1%	Roughly 1,000

Characteristics of the Related Jobs: Personality Type—Investigative, Realistic, Enterprising. **Skills**—Operations analysis, science, management of financial resources, mathematics, management of material resources, technology design, quality control analysis, complex problem solving.

Work Conditions—More often indoors than outdoors; sitting; common protective or safety equipment; hazardous conditions; wear specialized protective or safety equipment; high places.

Chemistry

Focuses on the scientific study of the composition and behavior of matter, including its micro- and macro-structure, the processes of chemical change, and the theoretical description and laboratory simulation of these phenomena. **Related CIP Program:** 40.0501 Chemistry, General.

Specializations in the Major: Research, quality control, geological/ocean chemistry, forensic chemistry.

Typical Sequence of College Courses: English composition, calculus, introduction to computer science, general chemistry, molecular structure and bonding, organic chemistry, qualitative analysis, quantitative analysis, general physics, statistics, physical chemistry, inorganic chemistry, undergraduate research project. **Typical Sequence of High School Courses:** English, algebra, geometry, trigonometry, pre-calculus, calculus, chemistry, physics, computer science.

Career Snapshot: Everything around us and within us is composed of chemicals, and chemists search for and put to use new knowledge about the nature and properties of matter. Chemists develop new fibers, paints, pharmaceuticals, solvents, fuels, and countless other materials that are used in industry and the home. A bachelor's degree is usually required for entry to this field, but a PhD is often needed for research or college teaching. Best job opportunities and the greatest security are expected in companies that manufacture pharmaceuticals or do chemical testing. Companies that provide chemicals for industrial purposes are more sensitive to economic ups and downs. Some bachelor's-degree holders find work in sales, marketing, or middle management in companies that value knowledge of chemistry.

Related Jobs

Job Title	Average Earnings	Job Growth	Job Openings
1. Chemistry Teachers, Postsecondary	$68,760	15.1%	Roughly 600
2. Chemists	$68,220	2.5%	3,000
3. Natural Sciences Managers	$114,560	15.4%	2,000

Characteristics of the Related Jobs: Personality Type—Investigative, Realistic. **Skills**—Science, operations analysis, mathematics, reading comprehension, writing, repairing, equipment maintenance, complex problem solving. **Work Conditions**—Indoors; sitting; common protective or safety equipment; hazardous conditions; contaminants; wear specialized protective or safety equipment; hazardous equipment.

Chinese

Focuses on the Chinese language and its associated dialects and literature. **Related CIP Program:** 16.0301 Chinese Language and Literature.

Specializations in the Major: Literature, translation, history and culture, language education.

Typical Sequence of College Courses: Chinese language, conversation, composition, linguistics, Chinese literature, East Asian literature, East Asian studies, grammar, phonetics. **Typical Sequence of High School Courses:** English, public speaking, foreign language, history, literature, social science.

Career Snapshot: Because Chinese is spoken by more people than any other language and China now has the world's second-biggest economy, there is a growing need for Americans with knowledge of the Chinese language and culture. A bachelor's degree in Chinese, perhaps with additional education in business or law, may lead to an Asia-centered career in business or government. A graduate degree is good preparation for translation or college teaching.

Related Jobs

Job Title	Average Earnings	Job Growth	Job Openings
1. Foreign Language and Literature Teachers, Postsecondary	$56,740	15.1%	ROUGHLY 900
2. Interpreters and Translators	$40,860	22.2%	2,000

Characteristics of the Related Jobs: Personality Type—Artistic, Social. **Skills**—Writing, reading comprehension, speaking, social perceptiveness, learning strategies, service orientation, active learning, monitoring. **Work Conditions**—Indoors; sitting; close to coworkers; exposed to disease or infections; exposed to radiation; making repetitive motions.

Chiropractic

Prepares individuals for the independent professional practice of chiropractic, a health-care and healing system based on the application of non-
invasive treatments and spinal adjustments to alleviate health problems
caused by vertebral misalignments affecting bodily function as derived
from the philosophy of Daniel Palmer. **Related CIP Program:** 51.0101
Chiropractic (DC).

Specializations in the Major: Sports medicine, orthopedics, diagnostic
imaging.

Typical Sequence of College Courses: English composition, introduction to psychology, college algebra, calculus, introduction to sociology,
oral communication, general chemistry, general biology, introduction to
computer science, organic chemistry, human anatomy and physiology, general microbiology, genetics, introduction to biochemistry, veterinary gross
anatomy, spinal anatomy, histology, biomechanics, physical diagnosis,
neuroanatomy, neurophysiology, radiographic anatomy, emergency care,
nutrition, neuromusculoskeletal diagnosis and treatment, chiropractic
manipulative therapeutics, pathology, public health, patient examination and evaluation, pharmacology, minor surgery, clinical experience in
obstetrics/gynecology, clinical experience in pediatrics, clinical experience
in geriatrics, mental health, ethics in health care, professional practice management. **Typical Sequence of High School Courses:** English, algebra,
geometry, trigonometry, biology, computer science, public speaking, chemistry, foreign language, physics, pre-calculus.

Career Snapshot: Chiropractors are health practitioners who specialize
in health problems associated with the muscular, nervous, and skeletal
systems, especially the spine. They learn a variety of specialized diagnostic
and treatment techniques but also tend to emphasize the patient's overall
health and wellness, recommending changes in diet and lifestyle that can
help the body's own healing powers. The educational program includes not
only theory and laboratory work, but also a lot of supervised clinical work
with patients. With the aging of the population and increased acceptance
of chiropractic medicine, job opportunities for graduates are expected to be
good, especially for those who enter a multidisciplined practice.

Related Jobs

Job Title	Average Earnings	Job Growth	Job Openings
1. Chiropractors	$67,650	19.5%	2,000
2. Health Specialties Teachers, Postsecondary	$84,840	15.1%	Roughly 4,000

Characteristics of the Related Jobs: Personality Type—Social, Investigative. **Skills**—Science, writing, reading comprehension, instructing, learning strategies, active learning, speaking, operations analysis. **Work Conditions**—Indoors; exposed to disease or infections; exposed to radiation; close to coworkers; standing; bending or twisting the body.

Civil Engineering

Prepares individuals to apply mathematical and scientific principles to the design, development, and operational evaluation of structural, load-bearing, material moving, transportation, water resource, and material control systems and environmental safety measures. **Related CIP Program:** 14.0801 Civil Engineering, General.

Specializations in the Major: Transportation engineering, geotechnical engineering, environmental engineering, water resources, structural engineering.

Typical Sequence of College Courses: English composition, technical writing, calculus, differential equations, general chemistry, introduction to computer science, general physics, introduction to electric circuits, engineering graphics, statics, dynamics, materials engineering, introduction to civil engineering, numerical analysis, fluid mechanics, engineering surveying and measurement, environmental engineering and design, soil mechanics, engineering economics, analysis of structures, highway and transportation engineering, reinforced concrete design, steel design, water resources and hydraulic engineering, senior design project. **Typical Sequence of High School Courses:** English, algebra, geometry, trigonometry, precalculus, calculus, chemistry, physics, computer science.

Career Snapshot: Civil engineers design and supervise construction of roads, buildings, bridges, dams, airports, water-supply systems, and many other projects that affect the quality of our environment. They apply principles of physics and other sciences to devise engineering solutions that are technically effective as well as being economically and environmentally sound. A bachelor's degree is the usual way to enter the field. Engineering is also a good way to prepare for a later position in management. Employment opportunities tend to rise and fall with the economy.

Related Jobs

Job Title	Average Earnings	Job Growth	Job Openings
1. Civil Engineers	$76,590	24.3%	11,000
2. Engineering Managers	$117,000	6.2%	5,000
3. Engineering Teachers, Postsecondary	$85,830	15.1%	ROUGHLY 1,000

Characteristics of the Related Jobs: Personality Type—Realistic, Investigative, Conventional. **Skills**—Operations analysis, mathematics, science, management of financial resources, management of material resources, quality control analysis, programming, reading comprehension. **Work Conditions**—More often indoors than outdoors; in a vehicle; sitting; high places; wear specialized protective or safety equipment; climbing ladders, scaffolds, or poles.

Classics

Focuses on the literary culture of the ancient Graeco-Roman world, as well as the Greek and Latin languages and literatures and their development prior to the fall of the Roman Empire. **Related CIP Programs:** 16.1203 Latin Language and Literature; 16.1202 Ancient/Classical Greek Language and Literature; 16.1200 Classics and Classical Languages, Literatures, and Linguistics, General.

Specializations in the Major: Classical literature/mythology, classical civilization, classical linguistics, Greek, Latin, archeology.

Typical Sequence of College Courses: Latin, Greek, grammar, linguistics, literature of the Roman Empire, literature in ancient Greek, history of the ancient world. **Typical Sequence of High School Courses:** English, public speaking, foreign language, history, literature, social science.

Career Snapshot: The classical languages—Latin and Greek—may be dead, but students who study them often end up in very lively careers. The mental discipline and critical-thinking skills learned in the classics can be first-rate preparation for law school and medical school, and business recruiters report that classics graduates have an exceptional breadth of view. The demand for Latin teachers in secondary schools is strong. A classics major is also a good first step to graduate training in archeology, history, or theology.

Related Jobs

Job Title	Average Earnings	Job Growth	Job Openings
1. Anthropologists and Archeologists	$53,460	28.1%	FEWER THAN 500
2. Foreign Language and Literature Teachers, Postsecondary	$56,740	15.1%	ROUGHLY 900
3. Interpreters and Translators	$40,860	22.2%	2,000

Characteristics of the Related Jobs: Personality Type—Social, Artistic, Investigative. **Skills**—Writing, reading comprehension, learning strategies, speaking, instructing, active learning, monitoring, operations analysis. **Work Conditions**—Indoors; sitting; close to coworkers; exposed to disease or infections.

Communications Studies/Speech

Focuses on the scientific, humanistic, and critical study of human communication in a variety of formats, media, and contexts. **Related CIP Program:** 09.0101 Speech Communication and Rhetoric.

Specializations in the Major: Speech/rhetoric, business communications.

Typical Sequence of College Courses: Public speaking, introduction to psychology, English composition, communications theory, introduction to mass communication, argumentation and critical thinking, interpersonal communication, rhetorical tradition and techniques. **Typical Sequence of High School Courses:** English, public speaking, foreign language, applied communications, social science.

Career Snapshot: This major is sometimes offered in the same department as mass communications or theater, but it is not designed to teach a technical skill such as television production or acting. Instead, it teaches how effective communication depends on a combination of verbal and nonverbal elements. Students work in various media and learn how to strike a balance between covering the subject matter, appealing to the listener

102

or reader, and projecting the intended image of the speaker or writer. Graduates of communication and speech programs may go on to careers in sales, public relations, law, or teaching.

Related Jobs

Job Title	Average Earnings	Job Growth	Job Openings
1. Communications Teachers, Postsecondary	$58,890	15.1%	Roughly 800
2. Public Address System and Other Announcers	$27,210	8.2%	Fewer than 500
3. Public Relations Specialists	$51,960	24.0%	13,000
4. Technical Writers	$62,730	18.2%	2,000
5. Writers and Authors	$53,900	14.8%	5,000

Characteristics of the Related Jobs: Personality Type—Enterprising, Artistic, Social. **Skills**—Operations analysis, writing, social perceptiveness, negotiation, speaking, time management, service orientation, judgment and decision making. **Work Conditions**—Indoors; sitting; in a vehicle.

Computer Engineering

Prepares individuals to apply mathematical and scientific principles to the design, development, and operational evaluation of computer hardware and software systems and related equipment and facilities and the analysis of specific problems of computer applications to various tasks. **Related CIP Programs:** 14.0901 Computer Engineering, General; 14.0902 Computer Hardware Engineering; 14.0903 Computer Software Engineering.

Specializations in the Major: Software/systems design, hardware design, systems analysis.

Typical Sequence of College Courses: English composition, technical writing, calculus, differential equations, general chemistry, introduction to computer science, general physics, introduction to engineering, introduction to electric circuits, engineering circuit analysis, numerical analysis, electrical networks, electronics, computer architecture, algorithms and data structures, digital system design, software engineering, operating systems, microcomputer systems, senior design project. **Typical Sequence of High School Courses:** English, algebra, geometry, trigonometry, pre-calculus, calculus, chemistry, physics, computer science.

103

Career Snapshot: Computer engineers use their knowledge of scientific principles to design computers, networks of computers, and systems (such as telecommunications or GPS) that include computers. They need to understand both hardware and software, and they may build prototypes of new systems. The usual entry route is via a bachelor's degree. Opportunities for employment are good despite foreign competition, especially in nonmanufacturing jobs related to systems design. Some engineers go into management, and the computer industry provides many opportunities for creative and motivated engineers to become entrepreneurs.

Related Jobs

Job Title	Average Earnings	Job Growth	Job Openings
1. Computer Hardware Engineers	$98,820	3.8%	2,000
2. Computer Software Engineers, Applications	$87,480	34.0%	22,000
3. Computer Software Engineers, Systems Software	$93,470	30.4%	15,000
4. Computer Specialists, All Other	$77,010	13.1%	7,000
5. Engineering Managers	$117,000	6.2%	5,000
6. Engineering Teachers, Postsecondary	$85,830	15.1%	Roughly 1,000

Characteristics of the Related Jobs: Personality Type—Investigative, Realistic, Conventional. **Skills**—Programming, technology design, operations analysis, science, quality control analysis, mathematics, installation, complex problem solving. **Work Conditions**—Indoors; sitting.

Computer Science

Focuses on computers, computing problems and solutions, and the design of computer systems and user interfaces from a scientific perspective. **Related CIP Programs:** 11.0701 Computer Science; 11.0802 Data Modeling/Warehousing and Database Administration; 11.1003 Computer and Information Systems Security/Information Assurance; 11.1001 Network and System Administration/Administrator.

Specializations in the Major: Business programming, scientific programming, database programming, systems programming, programming for the Internet, security and disaster recovery.

Typical Sequence of College Courses: English composition, calculus, introduction to economics, statistics for business and social sciences, introduction to computer science, programming in a language (e.g., C, Pascal, COBOL), algorithms and data structures, software engineering, operating systems, database systems, theory of computer languages, computer architecture, artificial intelligence. **Typical Sequence of High School Courses:** English, algebra, geometry, trigonometry, pre-calculus, calculus, chemistry, physics, computer science.

Career Snapshot: Computer science teaches you not only specific languages, but the principles by which languages are created, the structures used to store data, and the logical structures by which programs solve problems. Job outlook is best for roles that are not easily outsourced to overseas workers, such as systems administration and information security.

Related Jobs

Job Title	Average Earnings	Job Growth	Job Openings
1. Computer and Information Scientists, Research	$101,570	24.2%	1,000
2. Computer and Information Systems Managers	$113,720	16.9%	10,000
3. Computer Science Teachers, Postsecondary	$68,580	15.1%	Roughly 1,000
4. Computer Software Engineers, Applications	$87,480	34.0%	22,000
5. Computer Software Engineers, Systems Software	$93,470	30.4%	15,000
6. Computer Specialists, All Other	$77,010	13.1%	7,000
7. Database Administrators	$71,550	20.3%	4,000
8. Network and Computer Systems Administrators	$67,710	23.2%	14,000
9. Network Systems and Data Communications Analysts	$73,250	53.4%	21,000

Characteristics of the Related Jobs: Personality Type—Investigative, Conventional, Realistic. **Skills**—Programming, technology design, operations analysis, management of financial resources, equipment selection, management of material resources, mathematics, active learning. **Work Conditions**—Indoors; sitting.

Criminal Justice/Law Enforcement

Prepares individuals to perform the duties of police and public security officers, including patrol and investigative activities, traffic control, crowd control and public relations, witness interviewing, evidence collection and management, basic crime prevention methods, weapon and equipment operation and maintenance, report preparation, and other routine law enforcement responsibilities. **Related CIP Program:** 43.0107 Criminal Justice/Police Science.

Specializations in the Major: Police work, business security, police administration, homeland security.

Typical Sequence of College Courses: Technical writing, introduction to criminal justice, introduction to psychology, American government, criminal law, criminal investigation, introduction to sociology, police organization and administration, criminal procedures, police-community relations, ethics, diversity and conflict, seminar (reporting on research). **Typical Sequence of High School Courses:** Algebra, English, foreign language, social science, history, public speaking, computer science.

Career Snapshot: We live in a society that is governed by laws at the municipal, state, and federal levels. These laws are enforced by people who understand the laws themselves; the workings of the agencies that are empowered to enforce them; and the techniques for detecting violation of the laws, arresting violators, and processing them through the court system. Public concern about crime has created many job opportunities in this field, especially at the local level. Graduates of this program need to enter a police academy to complete training as police officers.

Related Jobs

Job Title	Average Earnings	Job Growth	Job Openings
1. Bailiffs	$37,950	8.4%	500
2. Criminal Justice and Law Enforcement Teachers, Postsecondary	$57,500	15.1%	Roughly 400
3. Detectives and Criminal Investigators	$62,110	16.6%	4,000
4. Police and Sheriff's Patrol Officers	$53,210	8.7%	23,000
5. Private Detectives and Investigators	$42,110	22.0%	2,000

Characteristics of the Related Jobs: Personality Type—Enterprising, Realistic, Conventional. **Skills**—Negotiation, social perceptiveness, service orientation, critical thinking, speaking, reading comprehension, coordination, complex problem solving. **Work Conditions**—Outdoors; in a vehicle; exposed to disease or infections; very hot or cold; hazardous equipment; extremely bright or inadequate lighting; wear specialized protective or safety equipment; outdoors; cramped work space, awkward positions.

Dance

Prepares individuals to express ideas, feelings, and/or inner visions through the performance of one or more of the dance disciplines and focuses on the study and analysis of dance as a cultural phenomenon. **Related CIP Program:** 50.0301 Dance, General.

Specializations in the Major: Ballet, ballroom dance, composite dance, modern dance, dance education, folk dance.

Typical Sequence of College Courses: Introduction to music, anatomy and kinesiology for dance, history of dance, dance improvisation, methods of teaching dance, dance composition, dance notation, dance technique (e.g., ballet, tap, modern). **Typical Sequence of High School Courses:** Biology, foreign language, dance, music.

Career Snapshot: Dance is one of the most basic arts of all because the medium is the dancer's own body. This means that dance is also a physical discipline as demanding as any sport. Most dancers start training at a very early age and often must give up performing as their bodies age. However, many find continuing satisfaction and employment in dance instruction and choreography. This is a very competitive field, and only the most talented find regular employment as dancers or choreographers. Job opportunities are better for dance teachers.

Related Jobs

Job Title	Average Earnings	Job Growth	Job Openings
1. Art, Drama, and Music Teachers, Postsecondary	$60,400	15.1%	Roughly 2,500
2. Choreographers	$37,860	5.3%	1,000
3. Dancers	No data available	6.8%	500

Characteristics of the Related Jobs: Personality Type—Artistic, Social, Realistic. **Skills**—Instructing, learning strategies, coordination, speaking, monitoring, social perceptiveness, active learning, management of personnel resources. **Work Conditions**—Indoors; keeping or regaining balance; kneeling, crouching, stooping, or crawling; close to coworkers; making repetitive motions; walking and running; bending or twisting the body; standing; extremely bright or inadequate lighting.

Dentistry

Prepares individuals for the independent professional practice of dentistry/ dental medicine, encompassing the evaluation, diagnosis, prevention, and treatment of diseases, disorders, and conditions of the oral cavity, maxillofacial area, and adjacent structures and their impact on the human body and health. **Related CIP Program:** 51.0401 Dentistry (DDS, DMD).

Specializations in the Major: Oral and maxillofacial surgery, periodontics, endodontics, orthodontics, public health dentistry, oral pathology.

Typical Sequence of College Courses: English composition, introduction to psychology, college algebra, introduction to business management, introduction to sociology, oral communication, general chemistry, general biology, organic chemistry, nutrition, introduction to accounting, introduction to biochemistry, dental morphology and function, occlusion, dental materials, ethics in health care, head and neck anatomy, oral radiology, assessment and treatment planning, dental anesthesia, pharmacology, prosthodontics (fixed/removable, partial/complete), community dentistry programs, endodontics, oral pathology, pediatric dentistry, dental emergency diagnosis and treatment, chronic orofacial pain, oral implantology, professional practice management, clinical experience in dentistry. **Typical Sequence of High School Courses:** English, algebra, geometry, trigonometry, biology, computer science, public speaking, chemistry, foreign language, physics, pre-calculus.

Career Snapshot: Dentists generally get at least eight years of education beyond high school. Those who want to teach or do research usually must get additional education. Besides academic ability, students of dentistry need good eye-hand coordination and communication skills. Although it seems unlikely that a vaccine against decay germs will be developed anytime soon, tooth sealants and fluoridation have reduced the incidence of tooth decay among young people, which means that dentistry's emphasis has shifted to prevention and maintenance. Note that as long as you take the courses that dentistry schools require for admissions, you have quite a lot of choice about your undergraduate major.

Related Jobs

Job Title	Average Earnings	Job Growth	Job Openings
1. Dentists, All Other Specialists	$153,290	27.1%	290
2. Dentists, General	$142,090	15.3%	5,000
3. Health Specialties Teachers, Postsecondary	$84,840	15.1%	ROUGHLY 4,000
4. Oral and Maxillofacial Surgeons	$166,400+	28.1%	290
5. Orthodontists	$166,400+	28.1%	360
6. Prosthodontists	$111,110	27.7%	30

Characteristics of the Related Jobs: Personality Type—Investigative, Realistic, Social. **Skills**—Science, management of financial resources, active learning, reading comprehension, management of material resources, judgment and decision making, instructing, complex problem solving. **Work Conditions**—Indoors; sitting; exposed to disease or infections; common protective or safety equipment; exposed to radiation; close to coworkers; using hands; bending or twisting the body; making repetitive motions; cramped work space, awkward positions.

Dietetics

Prepares individuals to apply the principles of dietetics and the biomedical and nutrition sciences to design and manage effective nutrition programs in clinical and other settings. **Related CIP Programs:** 51.3101 Dietetics/Dietitian (RD); 51.3102 Clinical Nutrition/Nutritionist.

Specializations in the Major: Food service management, clinical dietetics, research dietetics, community dietetics, dietetics education.

Typical Sequence of College Courses: English composition, college algebra, general biology, general chemistry, organic chemistry, oral communication, statistics, introduction to computer science, microbiology, introduction to economics, introduction to business management, introduction to biochemistry, introduction to food science and technology, human anatomy, human physiology, nutrition through life, food service operational management, diet therapy, menu management, community nutrition. **Typical Sequence of High School Courses:** English, algebra, social science, biology, trigonometry, chemistry, physics, geometry.

Career Snapshot: Dietitians plan food and nutrition programs and supervise the preparation and serving of food. They are concerned with creating diets that are healthful, appetizing, and within budget. They need to know about human nutritional needs in sickness and health, cultural preferences for foods, the nutritional properties of various foods and how they are affected by preparation techniques, and the business or health-care environment in which food is prepared and served. A bachelor's degree is good preparation for entering this field; for research, teaching, advanced management, or public health, a graduate degree is helpful or required. Job opportunities are expected to be good, especially for those who have specialized in nutritional needs of elderly people or people with kidney or diabetes problems. Specialized training, an advanced degree, or certifications beyond the particular state's minimum requirement will improve your job opportunities.

Related Jobs

Job Title	Average Earnings	Job Growth	Job Openings
1. Dietetic Technicians	$26,990	13.9%	1,000
2. Dietitians and Nutritionists	$52,150	9.2%	3,000

Characteristics of the Related Jobs: Personality Type—Investigative, Social. **Skills**—Management of financial resources, science, management of material resources, operations analysis, social perceptiveness, learning strategies, quality control analysis, writing. **Work Conditions**—Indoors; sitting; exposed to disease or infections; close to coworkers.

Drama/Theater Arts

Focuses on the study of dramatic works and their performance. **Related CIP Program:** 50.0501 Drama and Dramatics/Theatre Arts, General.

Specializations in the Major: Acting, directing, design and technology.

Typical Sequence of College Courses: English composition, foreign language, history of theater, acting technique, dramatic literature, performance techniques, theater technology (e.g., set/costume/lighting), theater practicum. **Typical Sequence of High School Courses:** English, foreign language, literature, public speaking.

Career Snapshot: Drama is one of the most ancient art forms and continues to entertain audiences today. As in all performing arts, there are better opportunities for teachers than for performers. Teaching at the postsecondary level usually requires a master's degree. The technical aspects of theater—set design, lighting, costume design, and makeup—also offer jobs for nonperformers. The academic program includes many opportunities to learn through student performances.

Related Jobs

Job Title	Average Earnings	Job Growth	Job Openings
1. Actors	No data available	12.8%	2,000
2. Art, Drama, and Music Teachers, Postsecondary	$60,400	15.1%	Roughly 2,500
3. Producers and Directors	$66,720	9.8%	4,000

Characteristics of the Related Jobs: Personality Type—Artistic, Enterprising. **Skills**—Reading comprehension, social perceptiveness, writing, speaking, coordination, monitoring, management of personnel resources, time management. **Work Conditions**—Indoors; close to coworkers; extremely bright or inadequate lighting; climbing ladders, scaffolds, or poles.

Early Childhood Education

Prepares individuals to teach students ranging in age from infancy through eight years (grade three), depending on the school system or state regulations. **Related CIP Programs:** 13.1210 Early Childhood Education and Teaching; 13.1209 Kindergarten/Preschool Education and Teaching.

Specializations in the Major: Reading readiness, music education, art education, bilingual education.

Typical Sequence of College Courses: Introduction to psychology, English composition, oral communication, history and philosophy of education, human growth and development, teaching methods, educational alternatives for exceptional students, educational psychology, reading assessment and teaching, mathematics education, art education, music education, physical education, health education, science education, children's literature, student teaching. **Typical Sequence of High School Courses:**

English, algebra, geometry, trigonometry, science, foreign language, public speaking.

Career Snapshot: Because very young children do not think exactly the same way as we do, an important part of an early childhood education major is learning effective educational techniques for this age group. As in any other teaching major, a bachelor's degree is the minimum requirement for employment, and a master's degree is often needed for job security and a pay raise. Although enrollments of very young students are expected to decline for some time, jobs will open to replace teachers who are retiring. Best opportunities are expected in high-growth regions of the country and in inner-city and rural schools.

Related Jobs

Job Title	Average Earnings	Job Growth	Job Openings
1. Kindergarten Teachers, Except Special Education	$47,830	15.0%	6,000
2. Preschool Teachers, Except Special Education	$24,540	19.0%	18,000

Characteristics of the Related Jobs: Personality Type—Social, Artistic. **Skills**—Learning strategies, social perceptiveness, negotiation, service orientation, monitoring, coordination, management of personnel resources, active learning. **Work Conditions**—Outdoors; standing; close to coworkers; exposed to disease or infections; kneeling, crouching, stooping, or crawling.

Economics

Focuses on the systematic study of the production, conservation, and allocation of resources in conditions of scarcity, together with the organizational frameworks related to these processes. **Related CIP Program:** 45.0601 Economics, General.

Specializations in the Major: Economic theory, applied economics, econometrics.

Typical Sequence of College Courses: English composition, introduction to psychology, introduction to sociology, American government, foreign language, statistics, calculus, introduction to economics, statistics for business and social sciences, introduction to computer science, microeconomic theory, macroeconomic theory, mathematical methods in economics, econometrics. **Typical Sequence of High School Courses:** Algebra, English, foreign language, social science, trigonometry, pre-calculus.

Career Snapshot: Economics is most basically the study of human needs and how they are satisfied. Therefore, it looks at how goods and services are produced, distributed, and consumed; how markets for these goods and services are created and behave; and how the actions of individuals, businesses, and governments affect these markets. Graduates of economics programs may work for business, government, or universities. With teacher training, some may find jobs in secondary schools, where economics is becoming a popular course. The best job opportunities should be in the private sector for those with graduate degrees.

Related Jobs

Job Title	Average Earnings	Job Growth	Job Openings
1. Economics Teachers, Postsecondary	$81,170	15.1%	ROUGHLY 400
2. Economists	$86,930	5.8%	500
3. Market Research Analysts	$61,580	28.1%	14,000
4. Survey Researchers	$35,380	30.4%	1,000

Characteristics of the Related Jobs: Personality Type—Investigative, Enterprising, Conventional. **Skills**—Programming, operations analysis, mathematics, reading comprehension, writing, science, judgment and decision making, management of financial resources. **Work Conditions**—Indoors; sitting.

Electrical Engineering

Prepares individuals to apply mathematical and scientific principles to the design, development, and operational evaluation of electrical, electronic, and related communications systems and their components, including electrical power generation systems, and the analysis of problems such as superconductor, wave propagation, energy storage and retrieval, and reception and amplification. **Related CIP Program:** 14.1001 Electrical and Electronics Engineering.

Specializations in the Major: Communications, computers, power generation/transmission, broadcasting, aerospace applications, controls.

Typical Sequence of College Courses: English composition, technical writing, calculus, differential equations, introduction to computer science, general chemistry, general physics, introduction to engineering, introduction to electric circuits, engineering circuit analysis, signals and systems, semiconductor devices, digital systems, logic design, electromagnetic fields, communication systems, control systems, senior design project. **Typical Sequence of High School Courses:** English, algebra, geometry, trigonometry, pre-calculus, calculus, chemistry, physics, computer science.

Career Snapshot: Electrical engineers apply principles of physics, chemistry, and materials science to the generation, transmission, and use of electric power. They may develop huge dynamos or tiny chips. Usually they enter the field with a bachelor's degree. Management may be an option later in their careers. Electricity is not likely to be replaced as a power source anytime soon, but international competition and the use of engineering services performed in other countries will limit employment growth. Electrical engineers working in firms providing engineering expertise and design services to manufacturers should have better job prospects.

Related Jobs

Job Title	Average Earnings	Job Growth	Job Openings
1. Electrical Engineers	$83,110	1.7%	4,000
2. Electronics Engineers, Except Computer	$89,310	0.30%	3,000
3. Engineering Managers	$117,000	6.2%	5,000
4. Engineering Teachers, Postsecondary	$85,830	15.1%	ROUGHLY 1,000

Characteristics of the Related Jobs: Personality Type—Investigative, Realistic. **Skills**—Science, operations analysis, mathematics, repairing, equipment maintenance, technology design, quality control analysis, equipment selection. **Work Conditions**—More often indoors than outdoors; sitting; hazardous conditions.

Elementary Education

Prepares individuals to teach students in the elementary grades, which may include kindergarten through grade eight, depending on the school system or state regulations. **Related CIP Program:** 13.1202 Elementary Education and Teaching.

Specializations in the Major: Art education, music education, science education, mathematics education, reading, bilingual education.

Typical Sequence of College Courses: Introduction to psychology, English composition, oral communication, history and philosophy of education, human growth and development, teaching methods, educational alternatives for exceptional students, educational psychology, reading assessment and teaching, mathematics education, art education, physical education, social studies education, health education, science education, language arts and literature, student teaching. **Typical Sequence of High School Courses:** English, algebra, geometry, trigonometry, science, foreign language, public speaking.

Career Snapshot: In elementary education, it is usually possible to specialize in a particular subject, such as reading or science, or to get a general background. Everyone in this field needs to learn general principles of how young people develop physically and mentally, as well as the teaching and classroom-management techniques that work best with children of this age. A bachelor's degree is often sufficient to enter this career, but in many school districts it is expected that you will continue your education as far as a master's degree. Enrollments in elementary schools are expected to decline for some time, but there will be job growth in Sunbelt communities and many openings to replace teachers who retire.

Related Jobs

Job Title	Average Earnings	Job Growth	Job Openings
1. Elementary School Teachers, Except Special Education	$50,510	15.8%	60,000

Characteristics of the Related Jobs: Personality Type—Social, Artistic, Conventional. **Skills**—Learning strategies, social perceptiveness, monitoring, service orientation, writing, instructing, judgment and decision making, coordination. **Work Conditions**—More often indoors than outdoors;

standing; close to coworkers; exposed to disease or infections; walking and running; noisy; kneeling, crouching, stooping, or crawling.

English

Focuses on the English language, including its history, structure, and related communications skills and the literature and culture of English-speaking peoples. **Related CIP Programs:** 23.1401 General Literature; 23.0101 English Language and Literature, General; 23.1301 Writing, General; 23.1302 Creative Writing; 23.1304 Rhetoric and Composition; 23.1402 American Literature (United States); 23.1403 American Literature (Canadian); 23.1303 Professional, Technical, Business, and Scientific Writing; 23.1404 English Literature (British and Commonwealth).

Specializations in the Major: Literature, language, creative writing, English education.

Typical Sequence of College Courses: English composition, introduction to literary study, foreign language, survey of British literature, survey of American literature, a major writer (e.g., Shakespeare, Romantic poets), a genre (e.g., drama, short story, poetry), creative writing, history of the English language, comparative literature. **Typical Sequence of High School Courses:** English, foreign language, literature, history, public speaking, social science.

Career Snapshot: English majors not only learn about a great literary tradition, but they also develop first-rate writing and critical-thinking skills that can be valuable in a variety of careers. Besides teaching, many of them go into business, law, and library science, usually with an appropriate master's or law degree. They are said to make excellent trainees in computer programming. In a wide range of careers, their humanistic skills often allow them to advance higher than those who prepare through more specifically career-oriented curricula.

Related Jobs

Job Title	Average Earnings	Job Growth	Job Openings
1. Editors	$50,800	–0.3%	3,000
2. English Language and Literature Teachers, Postsecondary	$58,870	15.1%	Roughly 2,000

Characteristics of the Related Jobs: Personality Type—Artistic, Enterprising, Conventional. **Skills**—Writing, reading comprehension, negotiation, quality control analysis, management of personnel resources, time management, speaking, active learning. **Work Conditions**—Indoors; sitting; making repetitive motions.

Environmental Science

Focuses on the application of biological, chemical, and physical principles to the study of the physical environment and the solution of environmental problems, including subjects such as abating or controlling environmental pollution and degradation, the interaction between human society and the natural environment, and natural resources management. **Related CIP Programs:** 03.0104 Environmental Science; 03.0103 Environmental Studies.

Specializations in the Major: Land resources, natural history, environmental technology, environmental policy, environmental education.

Typical Sequence of College Courses: English composition, college algebra, general biology, general chemistry, organic chemistry, oral communication, statistics, introduction to computer science, introduction to geology, ecology, introduction to environmental science, natural resource management and water quality, microbiology, introduction to economics, introduction to ground water/hydrology, regional planning and environmental protection, environmental impact assessment, environmental economics, environmental law, environmental chemistry. **Typical Sequence of High School Courses:** Biology, chemistry, algebra, geometry, trigonometry, computer science, English, public speaking, geography.

Career Snapshot: Environmental science (or studies) is a multidisciplinary subject that involves a number of sciences such as biology, geology, and chemistry, as well as social sciences such as economics and geography. It also touches on urban/regional planning and on law and public policy. Those with a bachelor's degree may work for an environmental consulting business or a government planning agency or may go on to get a graduate or professional degree in one of these related fields.

Related Jobs

Job Title	Average Earnings	Job Growth	Job Openings
1. Environmental Science and Protection Technicians, Including Health	$40,790	28.9%	3,000
2. Environmental Science Teachers, Postsecondary	$65,540	15.1%	Roughly 200
3. Environmental Scientists and Specialists, Including Health	$61,010	27.9%	5,000

Characteristics of the Related Jobs: Personality Type—Investigative, Realistic, Conventional. **Skills**—Science, programming, mathematics, reading comprehension, operations analysis, writing, complex problem solving, learning strategies. **Work Conditions**—In a vehicle; more often outdoors than indoors; sitting; high places; noisy; very hot or cold.

Family and Consumer Sciences

Focuses on how individuals develop and function in family, work, and community settings and how they relate to their physical, social, emotional, and intellectual environments. **Related CIP Programs:** 19.0201 Business Family and Consumer Sciences/Human Sciences; 19.0401 Family Resource Management Studies, General; 19.0101 Family and Consumer Sciences/Human Sciences, General; 19.0202 Family and Consumer Sciences/Human Sciences Communication; 13.1308 Family and Consumer Sciences/Home Economics Teacher Education; 19.0403 Consumer Services and Advocacy; 19.0203 Consumer Merchandising/Retailing Management; 19.0402 Consumer Economics.

Specializations in the Major: Family financial management, clothing and textiles, child care and family life, foods and nutrition, human sciences communication, consumer merchandising, consumer services and advocacy.

Typical Sequence of College Courses: Introduction to psychology, English composition, oral communication, history and philosophy of education, human growth and development, foods, textiles, introduction to nutrition, introduction to interior design, marriage and the family, consumer economics, housing, clothing and fashion, student teaching. **Typical**

Sequence of High School Courses: English, algebra, geometry, trigonometry, science, foreign language, home economics, public speaking.

Career Snapshot: Family and consumer sciences, which used to be called home economics, is a combination of several concerns related to families and their economic needs and behaviors. Some programs are designed to prepare home economics educators and therefore include courses on teaching strategies and classroom management, plus student teaching. Some graduates work in industries that market to families. Some become financial advisors. Others pursue a higher degree with the goal of working for the federal government as a cooperative extension agent.

Related Jobs

Job Title	Average Earnings	Job Growth	Job Openings
1. Editors	$50,800	–0.3%	3,000
2. Education Teachers, Postsecondary	$58,300	15.1%	ROUGHLY 1,800
3. Farm and Home Management Advisors	$44,180	1.1%	FEWER THAN 500
4. First-Line Supervisors/Managers of Retail Sales Workers	$34,900	5.2%	45,000
5. Home Economics Teachers, Postsecondary	$64,470	15.1%	ROUGHLY 200
6. Marketing Managers	$110,030	12.5%	6,000
7. Middle School Teachers, Except Special and Vocational Education	$50,770	15.3%	25,000
8. Public Relations Specialists	$51,960	24.0%	13,000
9. Sales Managers	$96,790	14.9%	13,000
10. Secondary School Teachers, Except Special and Vocational Education	$52,200	8.9%	41,000
11. Writers and Authors	$53,900	14.8%	5,000

Characteristics of the Related Jobs: Personality Type—Social, Artistic, Enterprising. **Skills**—Learning strategies, instructing, social perceptiveness, writing, service orientation, speaking, negotiation, active learning. **Work Conditions**—Indoors; standing; exposed to disease or infections; close to coworkers.

Film/Cinema Studies

Focuses on the study of the history, development, theory, and criticism of the film/video arts, as well as the basic principles of filmmaking and film production. **Related CIP Programs:** 50.0601 Film/Cinema/Video Studies; 50.0602 Cinematography and Film/Video Production.

Specializations in the Major: Criticism, directing/producing, screenwriting, editing.

Typical Sequence of College Courses: English composition, foreign language, world history in the modern era, introduction to psychology, film as a narrative art, history of film, film styles and genres, major film directors, literature and media, film theory and criticism, gender and film, seminar (reporting on research). **Typical Sequence of High School Courses:** English, foreign language, literature, history, photography.

Career Snapshot: Film is one of the newest art forms and can be viewed as both popular culture and high art. The American film and video industry continues to grow and remains dominant in the world market, but there is keen competition for creative jobs in this field. The rapidly falling cost of video equipment has increased the amount of video content competing for viewers, but it has also made business uses of video more affordable. Some graduates of film programs become critics or work in industrial or educational film production. Students can usually tailor the academic program to emphasize the aspect of film that interests them; therefore, they may do a lot of writing about film or a lot of hands-on work producing film.

Related Jobs

Job Title	Average Earnings	Job Growth	Job Openings
1. Art, Drama, and Music Teachers, Postsecondary	$60,400	15.1%	ROUGHLY 2,500
2. Camera Operators, Television, Video, and Motion Picture	$42,940	9.2%	1,000
3. Film and Video Editors	$50,790	11.9%	1,000
4. Producers and Directors	$66,720	9.8%	4,000

Characteristics of the Related Jobs: Personality Type—Artistic, Enterprising. **Skills**—Technology design, time management, coordination, negotiation, operations analysis, active learning, learning strategies, management of personnel resources. **Work Conditions**—Indoors; sitting; using hands; making repetitive motions.

Finance

Prepares individuals to plan, manage, and analyze the financial and monetary aspects and performance of business enterprises, banking institutions, or other organizations. **Related CIP Program:** 52.0801 Finance, General.

Specializations in the Major: Securities analysis, corporate finance, public finance.

Typical Sequence of College Courses: English composition, business writing, introduction to psychology, principles of microeconomics, principles of macroeconomics, calculus for business and social sciences, statistics for business and social sciences, introduction to management information systems, introduction to accounting, legal environment of business, principles of management and organization, operations management, strategic management, business finance, introduction to marketing, corporate finance, money and capital markets, investment analysis. **Typical Sequence of High School Courses:** English, algebra, geometry, trigonometry, science, foreign language, computer science.

Career Snapshot: Finance is the study of how organizations acquire funds and use them in ways that maximize their value. The banking and insurance industries, as well as investment service companies, employ graduates of this field. A bachelor's degree is good preparation for entry-level jobs. Because quantitative skills are very important in finance, firms sometimes employ graduates of engineering or science majors. Jobs with Wall Street firms may continue to experience some instability as the risk-taking culture bounces back from recession.

Related Jobs

Job Title	Average Earnings	Job Growth	Job Openings
1. Budget Analysts	$66,660	15.1%	2,000
2. Business Teachers, Postsecondary	$73,320	15.1%	ROUGHLY 2,000
3. Credit Analysts	$57,470	15.0%	2,000
4. Financial Analysts	$73,670	19.8%	10,000
5. Financial Managers	$101,190	7.6%	14,000
6. Loan Officers	$54,880	10.1%	7,000
7. Personal Financial Advisors	$68,200	30.1%	9,000

Characteristics of the Related Jobs: Personality Type—Conventional, Enterprising, Investigative. **Skills**—Management of financial resources, mathematics, operations analysis, judgment and decision making, writing, active learning, negotiation, reading comprehension. **Work Conditions**—Indoors; sitting.

Food Science

Focuses on the application of biological, chemical, and physical principles to the study of converting raw agricultural products into processed forms suitable for direct human consumption and the storage of such products. **Related CIP Programs:** 01.1001 Food Science; 01.1002 Food Technology and Processing.

Specializations in the Major: Food research, product development, management of food processing, food quality assurance.

Typical Sequence of College Courses: English composition, college algebra, general biology, general chemistry, organic chemistry, oral communication, statistics, introduction to computer science, microbiology, introduction to economics, general physics, introduction to biochemistry, introduction to food science and technology, food analysis, food chemistry, food analysis, food processing, food bacteriology, nutrition, food plant engineering. **Typical Sequence of High School Courses:** Biology, chemistry, algebra, geometry, trigonometry, computer science, English, public speaking.

Career Snapshot: A glance at the label on a package of food will tell you that the science of making, packaging, and ensuring the quality of foods involves both biology and chemistry. Food science graduates work in research, product development, and quality control. A bachelor's degree is usually sufficient for an entry-level job in quality control. But for advancement and for research jobs, a graduate degree is a help. Food manufacturing is more stable than most other manufacturing industries.

Related Jobs

Job Title	Average Earnings	Job Growth	Job Openings
1. Agricultural and Food Science Technicians	$34,410	8.8%	1,000
2. Chemical Technicians	$42,070	–0.8%	1,000
3. Food Scientists and Technologists	$59,630	16.3%	500

Characteristics of the Related Jobs: Personality Type—Realistic, Investigative, Conventional. **Skills**—Science, mathematics, quality control analysis, writing, reading comprehension, equipment maintenance, complex problem solving, repairing. **Work Conditions**—Indoors; common protective or safety equipment; hazardous conditions; contaminants; very hot or cold; hazardous equipment; wear specialized protective or safety equipment; standing.

Forestry

Prepares individuals to manage and develop forest areas for economic, recreational, and ecological purposes. **Related CIP Program:** 03.0501 Forestry, General.

Specializations in the Major: Forest management, urban forestry, forest product production, forest restoration.

Typical Sequence of College Courses: English composition, calculus, general biology, general chemistry, organic chemistry, introduction to geology, oral communication, statistics, computer applications in agriculture, introduction to soil science, ecology, introduction to forestry, dendrology, forest ecology, silviculture, forest resources policy, forest inventory and growth, forest surveying and mapping, tree pests and diseases, wood properties and utilization, forest economics and valuation, forest watershed management, timber harvesting, introduction to wildlife conservation, remote sensing. **Typical Sequence of High School Courses:** Biology, chemistry, algebra, geometry, trigonometry, computer science, English, public speaking, geography.

Career Snapshot: Foresters manage wooded land. Most of them work for governments and are concerned with conservation and fire prevention. Some work for logging companies and plan how to harvest timber economically, safely, and in keeping with environmental laws. Foresters also help plant and grow trees to regenerate forests. A bachelor's degree is usually a good preparation for this field, and the job outlook is good because of increased conservation efforts and continued pressure to maximize efficient use of natural resources.

Related Jobs

Job Title	Average Earnings	Job Growth	Job Openings
1. Conservation Scientists	$60,160	11.9%	FEWER THAN 500
2. Forest and Conservation Technicians	$32,860	8.6%	2,000
3. Forest and Conservation Workers	$25,580	8.5%	FEWER THAN 500
4. Foresters	$53,840	12.1%	FEWER THAN 500

Characteristics of the Related Jobs: Personality Type—Realistic, Investigative, Enterprising. **Skills**—Science, coordination, management of material resources, monitoring, mathematics, management of financial resources, judgment and decision making, complex problem solving. **Work Conditions**—In a vehicle; outdoors; sitting; very hot or cold; minor burns, cuts, bites, or stings; hazardous equipment; common protective or safety equipment; keeping or regaining balance.

French

Focuses on the French language and related dialects and creoles. **Related CIP Program:** 16.0901 French Language and Literature.

Specializations in the Major: Literature, translation, history and culture, language education.

Typical Sequence of College Courses: French language, conversation, composition, linguistics, French literature, French history and civilization, European history and civilization, grammar, phonetics. **Typical Sequence**

of High School Courses: English, public speaking, French, history, literature, social science.

Career Snapshot: French is a native tongue on several continents and in parts of the United States, and it has a rich cultural heritage associated with the arts and literature. French majors may go into careers in international business, travel, or teaching. Teaching at the secondary level requires education courses and, in many districts, a master's; college teaching requires a graduate degree.

Related Jobs

Job Title	Average Earnings	Job Growth	Job Openings
1. Foreign Language and Literature Teachers, Postsecondary	$56,740	15.1%	Roughly 900
2. Interpreters and Translators	$40,860	22.2%	2,000

Characteristics of the Related Jobs: Personality Type—Artistic, Social. **Skills**—Writing, reading comprehension, speaking, social perceptiveness, learning strategies, service orientation, active learning, monitoring. **Work Conditions**—Indoors; sitting; close to coworkers; exposed to disease or infections; exposed to radiation; making repetitive motions.

Geography

Focuses on the systematic study of the spatial distribution and interrelationships of people, natural resources, and plant and animal life. **Related CIP Program:** 45.0701 Geography.

Specializations in the Major: Management and policy, environmental science, geographic information systems, development, urban planning.

Typical Sequence of College Courses: English composition, American history, foreign language, introduction to economics, introduction to sociology, statistics, introduction to computer science, introduction to geology, introduction to human geography, economic geography, world history in the modern era, thematic cartography, geography of a region, physical geography, field geography, research techniques in geography, quantitative methods in geography, remote sensing, geographic information systems (GIS). **Typical Sequence of High School Courses:** Art, English, social science, foreign language, trigonometry, history, geography, computer science.

Career Snapshot: Geography studies how people and their environments relate to one another. It analyzes the human habitat spatially and records information about it in various forms, with an increasing emphasis on databases. Geographers work for governments, public-interest organizations, and businesses. They help with site planning, environmental impact studies, market research, competitive intelligence, and military intelligence. Best job opportunities will be for those who know how to use geographic information system (GIS) technology.

Related Jobs

Job Title	Average Earnings	Job Growth	Job Openings
1. Geographers	$71,470	26.2%	FEWER THAN 500
2. Geography Teachers, Postsecondary	$65,420	15.1%	ROUGHLY 100

Characteristics of the Related Jobs: Personality Type—Investigative, Social, Artistic. **Skills**—Science, writing, operations analysis, instructing, reading comprehension, active learning, learning strategies, speaking. **Work Conditions**—Indoors; sitting.

Geology

Focuses on the scientific study of the earth; the forces acting upon it; and the behavior of the solids, liquids and gases comprising it. **Related CIP Program:** 40.0601 Geology/Earth Science, General.

Specializations in the Major: Petroleum geology, stratigraphy, engineering geology, mineralogy, paleontology, volcanology, geophysics, oceanography.

Typical Sequence of College Courses: English composition, calculus, introduction to computer science, general chemistry, general physics, introduction to geology, invertebrate paleontology, summer field geology, structural geology, mineralogy, optical mineralogy, igneous and metamorphic petrology, sedimentary petrology, stratigraphy. **Typical Sequence of High School Courses:** English, algebra, geometry, trigonometry, chemistry, physics, pre-calculus, computer science, calculus.

Career Snapshot: Geology is the study of the physical makeup, processes, and history of the earth. Geologists use knowledge of this field to locate water, mineral, and petroleum resources; to protect the environment; and to offer advice on construction and land-use projects. A bachelor's degree opens the door for many entry-level jobs, but a master's degree helps for advancement and is thought to be the degree that now leads to the best opportunities. Many research jobs in universities and the government require a PhD. Some field research requires going to remote places, but it is also possible to specialize in laboratory sciences.

Related Jobs

Job Title	Average Earnings	Job Growth	Job Openings
1. Atmospheric, Earth, Marine, and Space Sciences Teachers, Postsecondary	$78,660	15.1%	ROUGHLY 300
2. Geoscientists, Except Hydrologists and Geographers	$81,220	17.5%	2,000
3. Hydrologists	$73,670	18.3%	FEWER THAN 500
4. Natural Sciences Managers	$114,560	15.4%	2,000

Characteristics of the Related Jobs: Personality Type—Investigative, Realistic. **Skills**—Science, operations analysis, reading comprehension, mathematics, writing, complex problem solving, management of personnel resources, coordination. **Work Conditions**—More often indoors than outdoors; sitting; in a vehicle.

Geophysics

Focuses on the scientific study of the physics of solids and its application to the study of the earth and other planets. **Related CIP Program:** 40.0603 Geophysics and Seismology.

Specializations in the Major: Atmospheric physics, physical oceanography, seismology, volcanology, remote sensing, geomagnetism, paleomagnetism, environmental geophysics.

Typical Sequence of College Courses: English composition, calculus, introduction to computer science, general chemistry, general physics, introduction to geology, summer field geology, structural geology, mineralogy, remote sensing, exploration geophysics, physical oceanography, stratigraphy, igneous and metamorphic petrology. **Typical Sequence of High School Courses:** English, algebra, geometry, trigonometry, chemistry, physics, pre-calculus, computer science, calculus.

Career Snapshot: Geophysics uses physical measurements and mathematical models to describe the structure, composition, and processes of the earth and planets. Geophysicists study seismic waves and variations in gravitation and terrestrial magnetism, thus learning where petroleum and minerals are deposited, where (and sometimes even when) earthquakes and volcanic eruptions are likely to strike, and how to solve environmental problems such as pollution. A bachelor's degree can lead to entry-level jobs, but a higher degree opens greater potential for advancement in research, as well as opportunities in college teaching.

Related Jobs

Job Title	Average Earnings	Job Growth	Job Openings
1. Atmospheric, Earth, Marine, and Space Sciences Teachers, Postsecondary	$78,660	15.1%	Roughly 300
2. Geoscientists, Except Hydrologists and Geographers	$81,220	17.5%	2,000
3. Natural Sciences Managers	$114,560	15.4%	2,000

Characteristics of the Related Jobs: Personality Type—Investigative, Realistic. **Skills**—Science, operations analysis, reading comprehension, mathematics, writing, management of personnel resources, time management, technology design. **Work Conditions**—Indoors; sitting; in a vehicle.

German

Focuses on the German language and related dialects as used in Austria, Germany, Switzerland, neighboring European countries containing German-speaking minorities, and elsewhere. **Related CIP Program:** 16.0501 German Language and Literature.

Specializations in the Major: Literature, translation, history and culture, language education.

Typical Sequence of College Courses: German language, conversation, composition, linguistics, German literature, German history and civilization, European history and civilization, grammar, phonetics. **Typical Sequence of High School Courses:** English, public speaking, German, history, literature, social science.

Career Snapshot: Germany is the dominant economic force in Europe and an important center of culture. A degree in German can open many doors in international business, travel, and law. Many employers are looking for graduates with an understanding of a second language and culture. Those with a graduate degree in German may go into translation or college teaching. With coursework in education, high school teaching is an option; many districts require a master's.

Related Jobs

Job Title	Average Earnings	Job Growth	Job Openings
1. Foreign Language and Literature Teachers, Postsecondary	$56,740	15.1%	Roughly 900
2. Interpreters and Translators	$40,860	22.2%	2,000

Characteristics of the Related Jobs: Personality Type—Artistic, Social. **Skills**—Writing, reading comprehension, speaking, social perceptiveness, learning strategies, service orientation, active learning, monitoring. **Work Conditions**—Indoors; sitting; close to coworkers; exposed to disease or infections; exposed to radiation; making repetitive motions.

Graphic Design, Commercial Art, and Illustration

Prepares individuals to use artistic techniques to effectively communicate ideas and information to business and consumer audiences via illustrations and other forms of digital or printed media, documents, images, graphics, sound, and multimedia products on the Web. **Related CIP Programs:** 50.0410 Illustration; 50.0411 Game and Interactive Media Design; 11.0801 Web Page, Digital/Multimedia, and Information Resources Design; 50.0402 Commercial and Advertising Art.

Specializations in the Major: Illustration, letterform, typography, cartooning, Web page design.

Typical Sequence of College Courses: English composition, college algebra, basic drawing, oral communication, art history: prehistoric to Renaissance, art history: Renaissance to modern, introduction to graphic design, visual thinking and problem solving, presentation graphics, history of graphic design, letterform, two-dimensional design, three-dimensional design, visual communication, typography, computer applications in graphic design, senior design project. **Typical Sequence of High School Courses:** Algebra, geometry, trigonometry, pre-calculus, English, public speaking, art, computer science, mechanical drawing, photography.

Career Snapshot: Many consumer goods, such as books, magazines, and Web pages, consist primarily of graphic elements—illustrations and text. Other goods, such as cereal boxes, use graphic elements conspicuously. Graphic design teaches you how to represent ideas graphically and give maximum visual appeal to text and pictures. The program involves considerable studio time, and an important goal is creating a good portfolio of work. Graduates with an associate or bachelor's degree work for publishers and design firms. Some freelance. Competition is expected to be keen; opportunities will be best for those with a bachelor's degree and experience with Web page design or animation.

Related Jobs

Job Title	Average Earnings	Job Growth	Job Openings
1. Commercial and Industrial Designers	$58,060	9.0%	2,000
2. Computer Programmers	$70,940	−2.9%	8,000
3. Computer Specialists, All Other	$77,010	13.1%	7,000
4. Graphic Designers	$43,180	12.9%	12,000
5. Multi-Media Artists and Animators	$58,250	14.1%	3,000
6. Set and Exhibit Designers	$45,400	16.6%	500

Characteristics of the Related Jobs: Personality Type—Artistic, Realistic, Enterprising. **Skills**—Operations analysis, technology design, negotiation, management of financial resources, time management, complex problem solving, reading comprehension, programming. **Work Conditions**—Indoors; sitting; making repetitive motions; using hands.

Health Information Systems Administration

Prepares individuals to plan, design, and manage systems, processes, and facilities used to collect, store, secure, retrieve, analyze, and transmit medical records and other health information used by clinical professionals and health-care organizations. **Related CIP Program:** 51.0706 Health Information/Medical Records Administration/Administrator.

Specializations in the Major: Management, information technology.

Typical Sequence of College Courses: English composition, introduction to computer science, college algebra, oral communication, introduction to psychology, accounting, introduction to business management, statistics for business and social sciences, epidemiology, introduction to medical terminology, financial management of health care, human resource management in health-care facilities, legal aspects of health care, American health-care systems, introduction to health records, health data and analysis, clinical classification systems, fundamentals of medical science, health data research, seminar (reporting on research). **Typical Sequence of High School Courses:** Algebra, English, geometry, trigonometry, pre-calculus, biology, chemistry, computer science, office computer applications, public speaking, foreign language, social science.

Career Snapshot: Health information systems are needed for much more than billing patients or their HMOs. Many medical discoveries have been made when researchers have examined large collections of health information. Therefore, health information systems administrators must know about the health-care system, about various kinds of diseases and vital statistics, about the latest database technologies, and about how researchers compile data to test hypotheses. Some people enter this field with a bachelor's degree, whereas others get a bachelor's degree in another field (perhaps related to health, information systems, or management) and complete a postgraduate certification program.

Related Jobs

Job Title	Average Earnings	Job Growth	Job Openings
1. Medical and Health Services Managers	$81,850	16.0%	10,000

Characteristics of the Related Jobs: Personality Type—Enterprising, Social, Conventional. **Skills**—Science, operations analysis, management of material resources, management of personnel resources, management of financial resources, negotiation, instructing, service orientation. **Work Conditions**—Indoors; sitting; exposed to disease or infections; exposed to radiation; close to coworkers; wear specialized protective or safety equipment; cramped work space, awkward positions; hazardous conditions.

History

Focuses on the general study and interpretation of the past, including the gathering, recording, synthesizing, and criticizing of evidence and theories about past events. **Related CIP Programs:** 25.0103 Archives/Archival Administration; 54.0101 History, General; 54.0104 History and Philosophy of Science and Technology; 54.0103 European History; 54.0107 Canadian History; 54.0106 Asian History; 54.0102 American History (United States).

Specializations in the Major: Applied history, genealogy, history education.

Typical Sequence of College Courses: English composition, foreign language, introduction to philosophy, introduction to political science, world history to the early modern era, world history in the modern era, American history, theory and practice of history, introduction to international relations, seminar (reporting on research). **Typical Sequence of High School Courses:** Algebra, English, foreign language, social science, trigonometry, history.

Career Snapshot: History studies past civilizations in order to understand the present, preserve our heritage, and appreciate the richness of human accomplishment. Almost every field—whether it be arts, science, or health—includes some study of its past. Therefore, many job opportunities in this field are in teaching. At the secondary level, this requires coursework in education and often a master's. At the postsecondary level, a master's or PhD is necessary. Some historians work as archivists, genealogists, or curators. Some graduates use the critical-thinking skills they develop from history to go into administration or law.

Related Jobs

Job Title	Average Earnings	Job Growth	Job Openings
1. Archivists	$46,470	6.5%	Fewer than 500
2. Curators	$47,930	23.0%	500
3. Historians	$51,050	11.5%	Fewer than 500
4. History Teachers, Postsecondary	$63,490	15.1%	Roughly 700

Characteristics of the Related Jobs: Personality Type—Investigative, Social. **Skills**—Writing, learning strategies, speaking, reading comprehension, science, active learning, instructing, critical thinking. **Work Conditions**—Indoors; sitting; extremely bright or inadequate lighting; cramped work space, awkward positions.

Hospital/Health Facilities Administration

Prepares individuals to apply managerial principles to the administration of hospitals, clinics, nursing homes, and other health-care facilities. **Related CIP Program:** 51.0702 Hospital and Health-Care Facilities Administration/Management.

Specializations in the Major: Hospital management, long-term care management, health policy.

Typical Sequence of College Courses: English composition, introduction to economics, college algebra, oral communication, introduction to psychology, accounting, introduction to business management, statistics for business and social sciences, American health-care systems, introduction to medical terminology, introduction to management information systems, financial management of health care, human resource management in health-care facilities, strategy and planning for health care, legal aspects of health care, health care and politics. **Typical Sequence of High School Courses:** Algebra, English, geometry, trigonometry, pre-calculus, biology, chemistry, computer science, office computer applications, public speaking, social science, foreign language.

Career Snapshot: Hospital and health facilities administrators need to combine standard business management skills with an understanding of the American health-care system and its current issues and trends. They may be generalists who manage an entire facility, or they may specialize in running a department or some specific service of the facility. Generalists are usually expected to have a master's degree, especially in large facilities, whereas specialists or those seeking employment in small facilities may enter with a bachelor's degree. Best employment prospects are in home health agencies and practitioners' offices and clinics and for those who have experience in a specialized field, such as reimbursement.

Related Jobs

Job Title	Average Earnings	Job Growth	Job Openings
1. Medical and Health Services Managers	$81,850	16.0%	10,000

Characteristics of the Related Jobs: Personality Type—Enterprising, Social, Conventional. **Skills**—Science, operations analysis, management of material resources, management of personnel resources, management of financial resources, negotiation, instructing, service orientation. **Work Conditions**—Indoors; sitting; exposed to disease or infections; exposed to radiation; close to coworkers; wear specialized protective or safety equipment; cramped work space, awkward positions; hazardous conditions.

Hotel/Motel and Restaurant Management

Prepares individuals to manage operations and facilities that provide lodging or vacation services or serve food to the public. **Related CIP Programs:** 52.0904 Hotel/Motel Administration/Management; 52.0906 Resort Management; 52.0905 Restaurant/Food Services Management.

Specializations in the Major: Hotels/motels, restaurants, resorts and theme parks.

Typical Sequence of College Courses: English composition, business writing, introduction to psychology, principles of microeconomics, principles of macroeconomics, calculus for business and social sciences, statistics for business and social sciences, introduction to management information systems, introduction to accounting, legal environment of business, principles of management and organization, operations management, strategic management, business finance, introduction to marketing, introduction to the hospitality industry, food and beverage production and management, food service and lodging operations, law and the hospitality industry, hotel financial management, marketing hospitality and leisure services, hospitality human resource management, hospitality technology applications, field experience/internship. **Typical Sequence of High School Courses:** English, algebra, geometry, trigonometry, science, foreign language, computer science, public speaking.

Career Snapshot: Students of hotel/motel and restaurant management learn many skills required in any management program—economics, accounting, human resources, finance—plus the specialized skills needed for the hospitality industry. Some enter the field with an associate degree, but opportunities are better with a bachelor's degree. Usually new hires enter an on-the-job training program where they learn all aspects of the business. The outlook for employment is mostly good, particularly at upscale and luxury hotels.

Related Jobs

Job Title	Average Earnings	Job Growth	Job Openings
1. Food Service Managers	$47,210	5.3%	8,000
2. Lodging Managers	$46,300	4.7%	2,000

Characteristics of the Related Jobs: Personality Type—Enterprising, Conventional, Social. **Skills**—Management of financial resources, management of material resources, management of personnel resources, operations analysis, negotiation, equipment maintenance, service orientation, repairing. **Work Conditions**—Indoors; standing; walking and running; minor burns, cuts, bites, or stings; close to coworkers; exposed to radiation; common protective or safety equipment; high places; using hands; very hot or cold.

Human Resources Management

Prepares individuals to manage the development of human capital in organizations and to provide related services to individuals and groups. **Related CIP Program:** 52.1001 Human Resources Management/Personnel Administration, General.

Specializations in the Major: Job analysis, compensation/benefits, labor relations, training.

Typical Sequence of College Courses: English composition, business writing, introduction to psychology, principles of microeconomics, principles of macroeconomics, calculus for business and social sciences, statistics for business and social sciences, introduction to management information systems, introduction to accounting, legal environment of business, principles of management and organization, operations management, strategic management, business finance, introduction to marketing, organizational theory, human resource management, compensation and benefits administration, training and development, employment law, industrial relations and labor management. **Typical Sequence of High School Courses:** English, algebra, geometry, trigonometry, science, foreign language, computer science, public speaking.

Career Snapshot: Human resource managers are responsible for attracting the right employees for an organization, training them, keeping them productively employed, and sometimes severing the relationship through outplacement or retirement. Generalists often enter the field with a bachelor's degree, although specialists may find a master's degree (or perhaps a law degree) advantageous. Generalists most often find entry-level work with small organizations. There is a trend toward outsourcing many specialized functions, such as training and outplacement, to specialized service firms.

Related Jobs

Job Title	Average Earnings	Job Growth	Job Openings
1. Business Teachers, Postsecondary	$73,320	15.1%	Roughly 2,000
2. Compensation and Benefits Managers	$88,050	8.5%	1,000
3. Compensation, Benefits, and Job Analysis Specialists	$55,620	23.6%	6,000
4. Employment, Recruitment, and Placement Specialists	$46,200	27.9%	11,000
5. Training and Development Managers	$88,090	11.9%	1,000
6. Training and Development Specialists	$52,120	23.3%	11,000

Characteristics of the Related Jobs: Personality Type—Enterprising, Social, Conventional. **Skills**—Science, service orientation, operations analysis, speaking, social perceptiveness, management of personnel resources, writing, reading comprehension. **Work Conditions**—Indoors; sitting.

Humanities

Focuses on combined studies and research in the humanities subjects as distinguished from the social and physical sciences, emphasizing languages, literatures, art, music, philosophy, and religion. **Related CIP Program:** 24.0103 Humanities/Humanistic Studies.

Specializations in the Major: Language, literature, the arts, history, religion, peace and justice studies, philosophy.

Typical Sequence of College Courses: Foreign language, major thinkers and issues in philosophy, literature, art and culture, European history and civilization, writing, seminar (reporting on research). **Typical Sequence of High School Courses:** English, algebra, foreign language, history, literature, public speaking, social science.

Career Snapshot: Humanities (sometimes called liberal arts) is an interdisciplinary major that covers a wide range of the arts and other nonscientific modes of thought, such as history, philosophy, religious studies, and language. Graduates of this major usually have strong skills for communicating and critical thinking, and they often advance further in the business world than those who hold more business-focused degrees. Some pursue careers in teaching, media, or the arts. Others get professional degrees in the law or medicine.

Related Jobs

Job Title	Average Earnings	Job Growth	Job Openings
1. Anthropology and Archeology Teachers, Postsecondary	$69,520	15.1%	Roughly 200
2. Area, Ethnic, and Cultural Studies Teachers, Postsecondary	$65,030	15.1%	Roughly 200
3. Art, Drama, and Music Teachers, Postsecondary	$60,400	15.1%	Roughly 2,500
4. Communications Teachers, Postsecondary	$58,890	15.1%	Roughly 800

(continued)

(continued)

Job Title	Average Earnings	Job Growth	Job Openings
5. Economics Teachers, Postsecondary	$81,170	15.1%	ROUGHLY 400
6. Education Teachers, Postsecondary	$58,300	15.1%	ROUGHLY 1,800
7. English Language and Literature Teachers, Postsecondary	$58,870	15.1%	ROUGHLY 2,000
8. Foreign Language and Literature Teachers, Postsecondary	$56,740	15.1%	ROUGHLY 900
9. Geography Teachers, Postsecondary	$65,420	15.1%	ROUGHLY 100
10. Graduate Teaching Assistants	$31,540	15.1%	ROUGHLY 4,000
11. History Teachers, Postsecondary	$63,490	15.1%	ROUGHLY 700
12. Library Science Teachers, Postsecondary	$60,650	15.1%	ROUGHLY 100
13. Philosophy and Religion Teachers, Postsecondary	$61,240	15.1%	ROUGHLY 600
14. Political Science Teachers, Postsecondary	$68,790	15.1%	ROUGHLY 500
15. Psychology Teachers, Postsecondary	$65,760	15.1%	ROUGHLY 1,000
16. Sociology Teachers, Postsecondary	$64,430	15.1%	ROUGHLY 500

Characteristics of the Related Jobs: Personality Type—Social, Artistic. **Skills**—Instructing, learning strategies, writing, speaking, reading comprehension, monitoring, active learning, critical thinking. **Work Conditions**—Indoors; sitting; close to coworkers.

Industrial and Labor Relations

Focuses on employee-management interactions and the management of issues and disputes regarding working conditions and worker benefit packages and may prepare individuals to function as labor or personnel relations specialists. **Related CIP Program:** 52.1002 Labor and Industrial Relations.

Specializations in the Major: Labor law, mediation, arbitration, worker compensation, worker safety.

Typical Sequence of College Courses: English composition, business writing, introduction to psychology, principles of microeconomics, principles of macroeconomics, calculus for business and social sciences, statistics for business and social sciences, introduction to management information systems, introduction to accounting, legal environment of business, business finance, introduction to marketing, organizational behavior, human resource management, industrial relations and labor management, employment law, training and development, systems of conflict resolution. **Typical Sequence of High School Courses:** English, algebra, geometry, trigonometry, foreign language, computer science, public speaking, social science.

Career Snapshot: Although labor unions are not as widespread as they once were, they still play an important role in American business. The "just in time" strategy that is popular in the manufacturing and transportation industries means that a strike lasting only a few hours can seriously disrupt business. Employers are eager to settle labor disputes before they start, and this creates job opportunities for labor-relations specialists working for either the employer or the union. Other job openings are found in government agencies that deal with labor. Many of these specialists hold bachelor's degrees, but a master's degree or law degree can be helpful for jobs involving contract negotiations and mediation.

Related Jobs

Job Title	Average Earnings	Job Growth	Job Openings
1. Business Teachers, Postsecondary	$73,320	15.1%	Roughly 2,000
2. Compensation and Benefits Managers	$88,050	8.5%	1,000
3. Compensation, Benefits, and Job Analysis Specialists	$55,620	23.6%	6,000
4. Employment, Recruitment, and Placement Specialists	$46,200	27.9%	11,000

Characteristics of the Related Jobs: Personality Type—Enterprising, Conventional, Social. **Skills**—Operations analysis, management of financial resources, speaking, management of personnel resources, social perceptiveness, writing, reading comprehension, negotiation. **Work Conditions**—Indoors; sitting.

Industrial Design

Prepares individuals to use artistic techniques to effectively communicate ideas and information to business and consumer audiences via the creation of effective forms, shapes, and packaging for manufactured products. **Related CIP Program:** 50.0404 Industrial and Product Design.

Specializations in the Major: Product design, computer modeling.

Typical Sequence of College Courses: English composition, college algebra, basic drawing, oral communication, introduction to economics, art history: Renaissance to modern, general physics, introduction to marketing, introduction to graphic design, visual thinking and problem solving, presentation graphics, industrial design materials and processes, human factors in design (ergonomics), computer modeling, history of industrial design, professional practices for industrial design, senior design project. **Typical Sequence of High School Courses:** Algebra, geometry, trigonometry, precalculus, English, public speaking, art, computer science, mechanical drawing, photography.

Career Snapshot: Industrial designers develop every conceivable kind of manufactured product, from cars to computers to children's toys. They need to understand the technology that will make the product work, the human context in which the product will be used—such as the way it will be held in the hand—as well as the marketplace in which the product will compete. Therefore, this field requires students to learn a combination of technical, creative, and business skills. Knowledge of computer-assisted design (CAD) has become essential, and skill with this tool can help in a field that is often keenly competitive and can suffer from outsourcing of work to foreign design firms.

Related Jobs

Job Title	Average Earnings	Job Growth	Job Openings
1. Art, Drama, and Music Teachers, Postsecondary	$60,400	15.1%	Roughly 2,500
2. Commercial and Industrial Designers	$58,060	9.0%	2,000
3. Graphic Designers	$43,180	12.9%	12,000

Characteristics of the Related Jobs: Personality Type—Artistic, Enterprising, Realistic. **Skills**—Operations analysis, technology design, active learning, complex problem solving, reading comprehension, writing, speaking, management of financial resources. **Work Conditions**—Indoors; sitting; making repetitive motions; using hands.

Industrial Engineering

Prepares individuals to apply scientific and mathematical principles to the design, improvement, and installation of integrated systems of people, material, information, and energy. **Related CIP Programs:** 14.3501 Industrial Engineering; 14.3701 Operations Research.

Specializations in the Major: Operations research, quality control.

Typical Sequence of College Courses: English composition, technical writing, calculus, differential equations, general chemistry, introduction to computer science, general physics, statics, dynamics, numerical analysis, thermodynamics, materials engineering, engineering economics, human factors and ergonomics, engineering systems design, operations research, quality control, facilities design, simulation, analysis of industrial activities, senior design project. **Typical Sequence of High School Courses:** English, algebra, geometry, trigonometry, pre-calculus, calculus, chemistry, physics, computer science.

Career Snapshot: Industrial engineers plan how an organization can most efficiently use staff, equipment, buildings, raw materials, information, and energy to output a product or service. They often are responsible for safety and quality-control procedures. They occupy the middle ground between management and the technology experts—for example, the mechanical or chemical engineers. Sometimes they make a career move into management positions. A bachelor's degree is good preparation for this field. The job outlook for industrial engineers is expected to be good, especially in non-manufacturing industries, as U.S. employers attempt to boost productivity to compete in the global workplace.

Related Jobs

Job Title	Average Earnings	Job Growth	Job Openings
1. Engineering Managers	$117,000	6.2%	5,000
2. Engineering Teachers, Postsecondary	$85,830	15.1%	Roughly 1,000
3. Industrial Engineers	$75,110	14.2%	9,000
4. Natural Sciences Managers	$114,560	15.4%	2,000
5. Operations Research Analysts	$70,070	22.0%	3,000

Characteristics of the Related Jobs: Personality Type—Investigative, Enterprising, Conventional. **Skills**—Management of material resources, mathematics, management of financial resources, complex problem solving, reading comprehension, writing, technology design, programming. **Work Conditions**—More often indoors than outdoors; sitting; hazardous equipment; common protective or safety equipment; noisy; hazardous conditions; contaminants.

Industrial/Technology Education

Prepares individuals to teach technology education/industrial arts programs at various educational levels. **Related CIP Program:** 13.1309 Technology Teacher Education/Industrial Arts Teacher Education.

Specializations in the Major: A technology (such as welding), agriculture.

Typical Sequence of College Courses: Introduction to psychology, English composition, oral communication, history and philosophy of education, human growth and development, history and philosophy of industrial education, methods of teaching industrial education, evaluation in industrial education, instructional materials in industrial education, classroom/laboratory management, special needs in industrial education, safety and liability in the classroom, student teaching. **Typical Sequence of High School Courses:** English, algebra, geometry, trigonometry, science, foreign language, industrial arts, mechanical drawing, public speaking.

Career Snapshot: As American industry progresses into a new century, the traditional "shop teacher" is evolving into a technology educator who teaches young people the high-tech skills they need to succeed in the new economy. In industrial/technology education, as in other teaching fields, a bachelor's degree is usually required for job entry, but a master's is often needed to build a career. In addition, it is helpful to get some genuine work experience in industry or agriculture. The job outlook is better for this field than for many other secondary-school specializations. Some graduates pursue careers in sales or training.

Related Jobs

Job Title	Average Earnings	Job Growth	Job Openings
1. Education Teachers, Postsecondary	$58,300	15.1%	Roughly 1,800
2. Middle School Teachers, Except Special and Vocational Education	$50,770	15.3%	25,000
3. Secondary School Teachers, Except Special and Vocational Education	$52,200	8.9%	41,000
4. Vocational Education Teachers, Middle School	$49,320	3.2%	Fewer than 500
5. Vocational Education Teachers, Postsecondary	$47,950	15.1%	Roughly 4,000
6. Vocational Education Teachers, Secondary School	$52,550	9.6%	4,000

Characteristics of the Related Jobs: Personality Type—Social. **Skills**—Learning strategies, instructing, writing, negotiation, speaking, social perceptiveness, active learning, reading comprehension. **Work Conditions**—Indoors; standing; close to coworkers; exposed to disease or infections; walking and running; noisy.

Insurance

Prepares individuals to manage risk in organizational settings and provide insurance and risk-aversion services to businesses, individuals, and other organizations. **Related CIP Program:** 52.1701 Insurance.

Specializations in the Major: Property and liability insurance, life and health insurance, commercial risk management.

Typical Sequence of College Courses: English composition, business writing, introduction to psychology, principles of microeconomics, principles of macroeconomics, calculus for business and social sciences, statistics for business and social sciences, introduction to management information systems, introduction to accounting, legal environment of business, principles of management and organization, operations management, strategic management, business finance, introduction to marketing, property and liability insurance, life and health insurance, commercial risk management, insurance law, employee benefit planning. **Typical Sequence of High School Courses:** English, algebra, geometry, trigonometry, science, foreign language, computer science.

Career Snapshot: A bachelor's degree in insurance may lead to employment in an insurance company or agency as an underwriter or sales agent. Good job prospects are expected for underwriters and for sales agents with good interpersonal skills. Graduates with outstanding mathematical ability may be hired for training as actuaries.

Related Jobs

Job Title	Average Earnings	Job Growth	Job Openings
1. Business Teachers, Postsecondary	$73,320	15.1%	ROUGHLY 2,000
2. Claims Adjusters, Examiners, and Investigators	$57,130	7.1%	10,000
3. Insurance Appraisers, Auto Damage	$55,390	0.5%	FEWER THAN 500
4. Insurance Sales Agents	$45,500	11.9%	15,000
5. Insurance Underwriters	$57,820	–4.1%	3,000
6. Purchasing Agents, Except Wholesale, Retail, and Farm Products	$54,810	13.9%	12,000
7. Sales Representatives, Wholesale and Manufacturing, Except Technical and Scientific Products	$50,920	6.6%	46,000
8. Telemarketers	$21,810	–11.1%	9,000
9. Wholesale and Retail Buyers, Except Farm Products	$48,650	–2.2%	4,000

Characteristics of the Related Jobs: Personality Type—Conventional, Enterprising. **Skills**—Negotiation, management of financial resources, critical thinking, speaking, mathematics, reading comprehension, writing, service orientation. **Work Conditions**—Indoors; sitting; in a vehicle; making repetitive motions.

Interior Design

Prepares individuals to apply artistic principles and techniques to the professional planning, designing, equipping, and furnishing of residential and commercial interior spaces. **Related CIP Program:** 50.0408 Interior Design.

Specializations in the Major: Residential design, kitchens, bathrooms, public spaces, restoration, acoustics, computer-aided design.

Typical Sequence of College Courses: Basic drawing, history of architecture, introduction to interior design, interior materials, history of interiors, presentation graphics, computer-aided design, color and design, lighting design, interior design studio, construction codes and material rating, senior design project. **Typical Sequence of High School Courses:** English, algebra, literature, history, geometry, art, physics, trigonometry, pre-calculus, computer science.

Career Snapshot: Interior designers plan how to shape and decorate the interiors of all kinds of buildings, including homes and commercial structures. They may design new interiors or renovate existing places. They respond to their clients' needs and budgets by developing designs based on traditional forms, innovative uses of layout and materials, sound principles of engineering, and safety codes. A bachelor's degree in the field is not universally required, but it contributes to your qualifications for licensure (in some states) and for membership in a professional association. It also gives you an edge over self-taught competitors, which can be important in this very competitive field.

Related Jobs

Job Title	Average Earnings	Job Growth	Job Openings
1. Art, Drama, and Music Teachers, Postsecondary	$60,400	15.1%	Roughly 2,500
2. Interior Designers	$46,180	19.4%	4,000

Characteristics of the Related Jobs: Personality Type—Artistic, Enterprising, Social. **Skills**—Management of financial resources, management of material resources, operations analysis, negotiation, service orientation, speaking, writing, coordination. **Work Conditions**—Indoors; sitting; in a vehicle.

International Business

Prepares individuals to manage international businesses and/or business operations. **Related CIP Program:** 52.1101 International Business/Trade/Commerce.

Specializations in the Major: A particular aspect of business, a particular part of the world.

Typical Sequence of College Courses: English composition, business writing, introduction to psychology, foreign language, principles of microeconomics, principles of macroeconomics, calculus for business and social sciences, statistics for business and social sciences, introduction to management information systems, introduction to accounting, international management, legal environment of business, principles of management and organization, operations management, international economics, business finance, introduction to marketing, organizational behavior, human resource management, international finance. **Typical Sequence of High School Courses:** English, algebra, geometry, trigonometry, science, foreign language, geography, computer science, public speaking.

Career Snapshot: The global economy demands businesspeople who are knowledgeable about other cultures. This major prepares you to work in businesses here and abroad and in the government agencies that deal with them. In addition to studying standard business subjects, you'll probably study or intern abroad to become proficient in a foreign language and gain a global perspective. The work usually requires a lot of travel and a sensitivity to cultural differences.

Related Jobs

Job Title	Average Earnings	Job Growth	Job Openings
1. Business Teachers, Postsecondary	$73,320	15.1%	ROUGHLY 2,000
2. Chief Executives	$160,720	−1.4%	11,000
3. General and Operations Managers	$92,650	−0.1%	50,000

Characteristics of the Related Jobs: Personality Type—Enterprising, Conventional, Social. **Skills**—Management of financial resources, management of material resources, management of personnel resources, operations analysis, negotiation, coordination, judgment and decision making, monitoring. **Work Conditions**—Indoors; in a vehicle; sitting.

International Relations

Focuses on the systematic study of international politics and institutions and the conduct of diplomacy and foreign policy. **Related CIP Program:** 45.0901 International Relations and Affairs.

Specializations in the Major: Development, diplomacy, international political economy, U.S. foreign policy, a regional specialization, global security.

Typical Sequence of College Courses: English composition, world history to the early modern era, world history in the modern era, introduction to political science, introduction to international relations, foreign language, introduction to economics, microeconomic theory, macroeconomic theory, comparative governments, world regional geography, history of a non-Western civilization, international economics, American foreign policy, seminar (reporting on research). **Typical Sequence of High School Courses:** Algebra, English, foreign language, social science, trigonometry, history.

Career Snapshot: The study of international relations is a multidisciplinary effort that draws on political science, economics, sociology, and history, among other disciplines. It attempts to find meaning in the ways people, private groups, and governments relate to one another politically and economically. The traditional focus on sovereign states is opening up to include attention to other actors on the world stage, including nongovernmental organizations; international organizations; multinational corporations; and groups representing a religion, ethnic group, or ideology. Now that American business is opening to the world more than ever before, this major is gaining in importance. Graduates often go on to law or business school, graduate school in the social sciences, the U.S. Foreign Service, or employment in businesses or organizations with an international focus.

Related Jobs

Job Title	Average Earnings	Job Growth	Job Openings
1. Chief Executives	$160,720	–1.4%	11,000
2. Political Science Teachers, Postsecondary	$68,790	15.1%	Roughly 500
3. Political Scientists	$104,090	19.5%	Fewer than 500

Characteristics of the Related Jobs: Personality Type—Enterprising, Conventional, Social. **Skills**—Management of financial resources, management of material resources, management of personnel resources, judgment and decision making, operations analysis, monitoring, time management, coordination. **Work Conditions**—Indoors; in a vehicle; sitting; whole body vibration.

Japanese

Focuses on the Japanese language. **Related CIP Program:** 16.0302 Japanese Language and Literature.

Specializations in the Major: Literature, translation, history and culture, language education.

Typical Sequence of College Courses: Japanese language, conversation, composition, linguistics, Japanese literature, East Asian literature, East Asian studies, grammar, phonetics. **Typical Sequence of High School Courses:** English, public speaking, foreign language, history, literature, social science.

Career Snapshot: Japan is a major trading partner of the United States, but comparatively few English speakers have mastered the Japanese language. This means that a major in Japanese can be a valuable entry route to careers in international business, travel, and law. A graduate degree in Japanese is good preparation for college teaching or translation.

Related Jobs

Job Title	Average Earnings	Job Growth	Job Openings
1. Foreign Language and Literature Teachers, Postsecondary	$56,740	15.1%	ROUGHLY 900
2. Interpreters and Translators	$40,860	22.2%	2,000

Characteristics of the Related Jobs: Personality Type—Artistic, Social. **Skills**—Writing, reading comprehension, speaking, social perceptiveness, learning strategies, service orientation, active learning, monitoring. **Work Conditions**—Indoors; sitting; close to coworkers; exposed to disease or infections; exposed to radiation; making repetitive motions.

Journalism and Mass Communications

Focuses on the theory and practice of gathering, processing, and delivering news and prepares individuals to be professional print journalists, news editors, and news managers. **Related CIP Programs:** 09.0401 Journalism; 09.0102 Mass Communication/Media Studies.

Specializations in the Major: News reporting, photojournalism, radio and television news, media management, news editing and editorializing.

Typical Sequence of College Courses: English composition, oral communication, American government, introduction to economics, foreign language, introduction to psychology, introduction to mass communication, writing for mass media, news writing and reporting, copy editing, mass communication law, communication ethics, feature writing, photojournalism, media management, visual design for media. **Typical Sequence of High School Courses:** English, algebra, foreign language, art, literature, public speaking, social science.

Career Snapshot: Journalism is a good preparation not only for news reporting and writing, but also for advertising and (with specialized coursework) news media production. Competition for entry-level journalism jobs can be keen, especially for prestigious newspapers and media outlets. Expect to start in a smaller operation and move around to increasingly bigger employers as you build your career. Although many workers are losing jobs as media outlets merge, new media technologies (such as Web-based magazines) have created some new job openings. A strong background in another field, such as science or economics, improves your job prospects.

Related Jobs

Job Title	Average Earnings	Job Growth	Job Openings
1. Broadcast News Analysts	$50,400	4.1%	FEWER THAN 500
2. Communications Teachers, Postsecondary	$58,890	15.1%	ROUGHLY 800
3. Editors	$50,800	−0.3%	3,000
4. Reporters and Correspondents	$34,360	−7.6%	2,000
5. Writers and Authors	$53,900	14.8%	5,000

Characteristics of the Related Jobs: Personality Type—Artistic, Enterprising, Investigative. **Skills**—Writing, speaking, reading comprehension, critical thinking, social perceptiveness, active learning, negotiation, judgment and decision making. **Work Conditions**—More often indoors than outdoors; in a vehicle; sitting; noisy; close to coworkers.

Landscape Architecture

Prepares individuals for the independent professional practice of landscape architecture and research in various aspects of the field. **Related CIP Program:** 04.0601 Landscape Architecture (BS, BSLA, BLA, MSLA, MLA, PhD).

Specializations in the Major: Historical and cultural landscapes, international studies, small town and urban revitalization, urban design, ecotourism, arid lands.

Typical Sequence of College Courses: English composition, calculus, basic drawing, general biology, introduction to soil science, architectural graphics, ecology, history of landscape architecture, landscape architectural design, site analysis, introduction to horticulture, land surveying, landscape structures and materials, architectural computer graphics, land planning, professional practice of landscape architecture, senior design project. **Typical Sequence of High School Courses:** English, algebra, geometry, trigonometry, pre-calculus, calculus, physics, computer science, art, biology.

Career Snapshot: Landscape architects must have a good flair for design, ability to work with a variety of construction techniques and technologies, and knowledge of the characteristics of many plants, plus business sense. A bachelor's degree is the usual entry route; some people enter the field with a master's degree after a bachelor's in another field. Almost all states require licensure, which requires an appropriate degree from an accredited school, work experience, and passing an exam. Job opportunities are expected to be good, but entry-level job seekers should expect keen competition for openings in large firms. About 21 percent of landscape architects are self-employed.

Related Jobs

Job Title	Average Earnings	Job Growth	Job Openings
1. Architecture Teachers, Postsecondary	$73,550	15.1%	ROUGHLY 200
2. Engineering Managers	$117,000	6.2%	5,000
3. Landscape Architects	$60,560	19.7%	1,000

Characteristics of the Related Jobs: Personality Type—Enterprising, Investigative, Realistic. **Skills**—Operations analysis, science, management of financial resources, management of material resources, mathematics, management of personnel resources, coordination, complex problem solving. **Work Conditions**—More often indoors than outdoors; in a vehicle; sitting.

Law

Prepares individuals for the independent professional practice of law, for taking state and national bar examinations, and for advanced research in jurisprudence. **Related CIP Program:** 22.0101 Law (LLB, JD).

Specializations in the Major: Environmental law, international and comparative law, intellectual property, family law, litigation.

Typical Sequence of College Courses: English composition, oral communication, introduction to political science, introduction to philosophy, American history, foreign language, civil procedure, constitutional law, contracts, criminal law, legal communication, legal research, legal writing, property, torts, criminal procedures, evidence, professional responsibility, trusts and estates. **Typical Sequence of High School Courses:** Algebra, English, foreign language, social science, history, geometry, public speaking.

Career Snapshot: Lawyers enter their occupation by completing four years of college and three years of law school and then passing the bar exam. The undergraduate major may be almost anything that contributes to skills in writing and critical thinking. Often the undergraduate major helps open doors to the kinds of careers that will be options after law school—for example, a bachelor's degree in a business field may help prepare for a career in tax law, labor relations law, or antitrust law. Graduates of law school can expect keen competition for positions as lawyers. Most openings are expected to be for staff lawyers rather than self-employed lawyers. There is a wide gap in earnings, work hours, and stress between lawyers who work in high-powered industries such as finance and those who work in public-interest jobs. Some law school graduates take business and government jobs where they use knowledge of law but do not practice it.

Related Jobs

Job Title	Average Earnings	Job Growth	Job Openings
1. Administrative Law Judges, Adjudicators, and Hearing Officers	$83,920	8.0%	FEWER THAN 500
2. Arbitrators, Mediators, and Conciliators	$52,770	13.9%	FEWER THAN 500
3. Judges, Magistrate Judges, and Magistrates	$112,830	–2.6%	500
4. Law Clerks	$38,390	13.9%	1,000
5. Law Teachers, Postsecondary	$99,040	15.1%	ROUGHLY 400
6. Lawyers	$113,240	13.0%	24,000

Characteristics of the Related Jobs: Personality Type—Enterprising, Investigative. **Skills**—Negotiation, speaking, writing, critical thinking, judgment and decision making, active learning, reading comprehension, operations analysis. **Work Conditions**—Indoors; sitting; in a vehicle.

Library Science

Focuses on the knowledge and skills required to develop, organize, store, retrieve, administer, and facilitate the use of local, remote, and networked collections of information in print, audiovisual, and electronic formats; prepares individuals for professional service as librarians and information consultants. **Related CIP Program:** 25.0101 Library and Information Science.

Specializations in the Major: Instructional libraries, special interest libraries, map libraries, music libraries, online information retrieval, archives, children's libraries, cataloguing.

Typical Sequence of College Courses: English composition, oral communication, introduction to computer science, foreign language, introduction to library and information science, reference services and resources, management of libraries and information services, bibliographic control of library materials, library research and evaluation. **Typical Sequence of High School Courses:** English, foreign language, computer science, algebra, public speaking, office computer applications, keyboarding, social science.

Career Snapshot: This major is sometimes called library and information science because increasingly the information that is needed by businesses, governments, and individuals is not available in books. Library science programs teach not only how to serve library users and manage library collections, but also how to retrieve and compile information from online databases. The master's degree is the entry-level credential in this field; a special librarian often needs an additional graduate or professional degree. Master's degree programs prefer applicants who have a bachelor's in a different field. The best employment opportunities will probably be in online information retrieval and in nontraditional settings.

Related Jobs

Job Title	Average Earnings	Job Growth	Job Openings
1. Librarians	$53,710	7.8%	5,000
2. Library Science Teachers, Postsecondary	$60,650	15.1%	Roughly 100

Characteristics of the Related Jobs: Personality Type—Conventional, Social, Enterprising. **Skills**—Management of material resources, service orientation, instructing, operations analysis, negotiation, management of financial resources, writing, social perceptiveness. **Work Conditions**—Indoors; sitting; making repetitive motions; exposed to disease or infections.

Management Information Systems

Prepares individuals to provide and manage data systems and related facilities for processing and retrieving internal business information; to select systems and train personnel; and to respond to external data requests. **Related CIP Program:** 52.1201 Management Information Systems, General.

Specializations in the Major: Accounting, network programming, security and disaster recovery.

Typical Sequence of College Courses: English composition, business writing, introduction to psychology, principles of microeconomics, principles of macroeconomics, calculus for business and social sciences, statistics for business and social sciences, introduction to management information systems, introduction to accounting, legal environment of business, principles of management and organization, operations management, strategic management, business finance, introduction to marketing, database management systems, systems analysis and design, decision support systems for management, networks and telecommunications. **Typical Sequence of High School Courses:** English, algebra, geometry, trigonometry, science, foreign language, computer science.

Career Snapshot: The management information systems major is considered a business major, which means that students get a firm grounding in economics, accounting, business law, finance, and marketing, as well as the technical skills needed to work with the latest business computer systems. Students may specialize in MIS at either the bachelor's or master's level and may combine it with a degree in a related business field, such as accounting or finance, or in computer science. The job outlook is very good.

Related Jobs

Job Title	Average Earnings	Job Growth	Job Openings
1. Computer and Information Systems Managers	$113,720	16.9%	10,000
2. Computer Programmers	$70,940	−2.9%	8,000
3. Database Administrators	$71,550	20.3%	4,000

Characteristics of the Related Jobs: Personality Type—Enterprising, Conventional, Investigative. **Skills**—Programming, management of financial resources, management of material resources, technology design, operations analysis, equipment selection, repairing, instructing. **Work Conditions**—Indoors; sitting.

Marketing

Prepares individuals to undertake and manage the process of developing consumer audiences and moving products from producers to consumers. **Related CIP Program:** 52.1401 Marketing/Marketing Management, General.

Specializations in the Major: Marketing research, marketing management.

Typical Sequence of College Courses: English composition, business writing, introduction to psychology, principles of microeconomics, principles of macroeconomics, calculus for business and social sciences, statistics for business and social sciences, introduction to management information systems, introduction to accounting, legal environment of business, principles of management and organization, operations management, strategic management, business finance, introduction to marketing, marketing research, buyer behavior, decision support systems for management, marketing strategy. **Typical Sequence of High School Courses:** English, algebra, geometry, trigonometry, science, foreign language, computer science.

Career Snapshot: Marketing is the study of how buyers and sellers of goods and services find one another, how businesses can tailor their offerings to meet demand, and how businesses can anticipate and influence demand. It uses the findings of economics, psychology, and sociology in a business context. A bachelor's degree is good preparation for a job in marketing research. Usually some experience in this field is required before a person can move into a marketing management position. Job outlook varies, with some industries looking more favorable than others.

Related Jobs

Job Title	Average Earnings	Job Growth	Job Openings
1. Advertising and Promotions Managers	$82,370	−1.7%	1,000
2. Business Teachers, Postsecondary	$73,320	15.1%	Roughly 2,000
3. Marketing Managers	$110,030	12.5%	6,000
4. Sales Managers	$96,790	14.9%	13,000

Characteristics of the Related Jobs: Personality Type—Enterprising, Conventional. **Skills**—Management of financial resources, operations analysis, management of material resources, management of personnel resources, negotiation, social perceptiveness, monitoring, active learning. **Work Conditions**—Indoors; sitting; in a vehicle.

Materials Science

Focuses on the general application of mathematical and scientific principles to the analysis and evaluation of the characteristics and behavior of solids. **Related CIP Program:** 40.1001 Materials Science.

Specializations in the Major: Ceramics/glass, polymers, building materials, thin films.

Typical Sequence of College Courses: English composition, technical writing, calculus, differential equations, introduction to computer science, general chemistry, physical chemistry, general physics, thermodynamics, numerical analysis, introduction to electric circuits, statics, dynamics, phase equilibrium, introduction to materials science, mechanics of materials, microstructure and mechanical properties, materials characterization, kinetics of chemical and physical reactions, senior design project. **Typical Sequence of High School Courses:** English, algebra, geometry, trigonometry, pre-calculus, calculus, chemistry, physics, computer science.

Career Snapshot: Materials scientists research the physical and chemical properties of ceramics, plastics, and other materials. They devise technologically elegant and economically valuable ways of creating and forming these materials. A bachelor's degree is a common entry route to this field, although those who want to do basic research or teach in college will need to get an advanced degree. The job outlook is best for those working with exotic materials, such as nanomaterials (extremely small) or biomaterials.

Related Jobs

Job Title	Average Earnings	Job Growth	Job Openings
1. Engineering Managers	$117,000	6.2%	5,000
2. Engineering Teachers, Postsecondary	$85,830	15.1%	Roughly 1,000
3. Materials Scientists	$80,300	11.9%	Fewer than 500

Characteristics of the Related Jobs: Personality Type—Enterprising, Investigative, Realistic. **Skills**—Operations analysis, science, management of financial resources, mathematics, management of material resources, reading comprehension, complex problem solving, writing. **Work Conditions**—Indoors; sitting; hazardous conditions; noisy; common protective or safety equipment; exposed to radiation; hazardous equipment.

Mathematics

Focuses on the analysis of quantities, magnitudes, forms, and their relationships, using symbolic logic and language. **Related CIP Program:** 27.0101 Mathematics, General.

Specializations in the Major: Theoretical mathematics, applied mathematics, mathematical statistics, mathematics education.

Typical Sequence of College Courses: Calculus, differential equations, introduction to computer science, programming in a language (e.g., C, Pascal, COBOL), statistics, linear algebra, introduction to abstract mathematics. **Typical Sequence of High School Courses:** Algebra, geometry, trigonometry, pre-calculus, calculus, computer science, physics.

Career Snapshot: Mathematics is a science in its own right in which researchers with graduate degrees continue to discover new laws. It is also a tool for understanding and organizing many aspects of our world. Many mathematics majors apply their knowledge by getting additional education or training in a math-intense field, either in a master's program or on the job. For example, an insurance company might train them in actuarial science; a computer consulting company might train them in computer security; a bank might train them in financial modeling; they might get a graduate degree in economics, engineering, or accounting. Employment opportunities are very good for people who apply mathematical knowledge to other fields.

Related Jobs

Job Title	Average Earnings	Job Growth	Job Openings
1. Mathematical Science Teachers, Postsecondary	$63,640	15.1%	Roughly 1,000
2. Mathematicians	$93,580	22.5%	Fewer than 500
3. Natural Sciences Managers	$114,560	15.4%	2,000
4. Statisticians	$72,820	13.1%	1,000

Characteristics of the Related Jobs: Personality Type—Investigative, Conventional, Social. **Skills**—Mathematics, science, active learning, reading comprehension, writing, operations analysis, learning strategies, instructing. **Work Conditions**—Indoors; sitting.

Mechanical Engineering

Prepares individuals to apply mathematical and scientific principles to the design, development, and operational evaluation of physical systems used in manufacturing and end-product systems used for specific uses. **Related CIP Program:** 14.1901 Mechanical Engineering.

Specializations in the Major: Automotive design, heating and air conditioning, testing.

Typical Sequence of College Courses: English composition, technical writing, calculus, differential equations, general chemistry, introduction to computer science, general physics, introduction to engineering, statics, dynamics, thermodynamics, numerical analysis, fluid mechanics, materials science, materials engineering, mechanical engineering design, heat transfer, manufacturing processes, senior design project. **Typical Sequence of High School Courses:** English, algebra, geometry, trigonometry, pre-calculus, calculus, chemistry, physics, computer science.

Career Snapshot: Mechanical engineers design, test, and supervise the manufacture of various mechanical devices, including tools, motors, machines, and medical equipment. Their goal is to maximize both the technical efficiency and the economic benefits of the devices. Usually they enter their first job with a bachelor's degree. Sometimes they move from engineering to a managerial position. Despite the current decline in manufacturing, job opportunities are expected to be good because of increasing emphasis on efficiency. Additional opportunities outside of mechanical engineering will exist because the skills acquired through earning a degree in mechanical engineering often can be applied in other engineering specialties.

Related Jobs

Job Title	Average Earnings	Job Growth	Job Openings
1. Cost Estimators	$57,300	25.3%	10,000
2. Engineering Managers	$117,000	6.2%	5,000
3. Engineering Teachers, Postsecondary	$85,830	15.1%	ROUGHLY 1,000
4. Mechanical Engineers	$77,020	6.0%	8,000

Characteristics of the Related Jobs: Personality Type—Investigative, Realistic, Conventional. **Skills**—Science, technology design, mathematics, operations analysis, installation, programming, quality control analysis, management of material resources. **Work Conditions**—Indoors; sitting; common protective or safety equipment; hazardous equipment; noisy.

Medical Technology

Prepares individuals to conduct and supervise complex medical tests, clinical trials, and research experiments; manage clinical laboratories; and consult with physicians and clinical researchers on diagnoses, disease causation and spread, and research outcomes. **Related CIP Program:** 51.1005 Clinical Laboratory Science/Medical Technology/Technologist Training.

Specializations in the Major: Clinical chemistry, blood banking, hematology, clinical microbiology, immunology, body fluid analysis.

Typical Sequence of College Courses: English composition, general biology, general chemistry, organic chemistry, human anatomy and physiology, general microbiology, introduction to biochemistry, college algebra, introduction to computer science, statistics, body fluid analysis, parasitology, clinical chemistry, hematology and coagulation, clinical microbiology, immunohematology, clinical immunology and serology, medical technology education, medical technology management and supervision. **Typical Sequence of High School Courses:** Algebra, biology, chemistry, computer science, English, physics, geometry, trigonometry.

Career Snapshot: The detection, diagnosis, and prevention of disease depend heavily on various kinds of medical tests—of blood, urine, tissue samples, and so on. Medical technologists, also called clinical laboratory scientists, are trained to perform these tests after studying the principles of chemistry, microbiology, and other basic sciences, plus laboratory techniques that sometimes involve complex and sophisticated equipment. A bachelor's degree is the usual preparation. Although technology is automating some medical tests, it is also creating new forms of testing. The job outlook is excellent.

Related Jobs

Job Title	Average Earnings	Job Growth	Job Openings
1. Health Specialties Teachers, Postsecondary	$84,840	15.1%	ROUGHLY 4,000
2. Medical and Clinical Laboratory Technologists	$55,140	11.9%	5,000

Characteristics of the Related Jobs: Personality Type—Investigative, Realistic, Conventional. **Skills**—Science, reading comprehension, instructing, writing, learning strategies, mathematics, active learning, equipment maintenance. **Work Conditions**—Indoors; sitting; exposed to disease or infections; hazardous conditions; common protective or safety equipment; making repetitive motions; using hands; contaminants; wear specialized protective or safety equipment.

Medicine

Prepares individuals for the independent professional practice of medicine (or osteopathic medicine), involving the prevention, diagnosis, and treatment of illnesses, injuries, and other disorders of the human body. **Related CIP Programs:** 51.1901 Osteopathic Medicine/Osteopathy (DO); 51.1201 Medicine (MD).

Specializations in the Major: Internal medicine, pediatrics, family medicine, emergency medicine, obstetrics/gynecology, surgery, radiology, psychiatry.

Typical Sequence of College Courses: English composition, introduction to psychology, college algebra, calculus, introduction to sociology, oral communication, general chemistry, general biology, introduction to computer science, organic chemistry, human anatomy and physiology, general microbiology, genetics, introduction to biochemistry, pathology, pharmacology, abnormal psychology, medical interviewing techniques, patient examination and evaluation, clinical laboratory procedures, ethics in health care, clinical experience in internal medicine, clinical experience in emergency medicine, clinical experience in obstetrics/gynecology, clinical experience in family medicine, clinical experience in psychiatry, clinical experience in surgery, clinical experience in pediatrics, clinical experience in geriatrics. **Typical Sequence of High School Courses:** English, algebra, geometry, trigonometry, pre-calculus, biology, computer science, public speaking, chemistry, foreign language, physics.

Career Snapshot: Medicine requires long years of education—four years of college, four years of medical school, and three to eight years of internship and residency, depending on the specialty. Entrance to medical school is highly competitive. Although "pre-med" is often referred to as a major, many students meet the entry requirements for medical school while majoring in a nonscientific subject. This may be helpful to demonstrate that you are a well-rounded person and to prepare you for another career in case you are not admitted to medical school. Today, physicians are more likely than in the past to work as salaried employees of group practices or HMOs. Good opportunities are expected in rural and low-income areas. Job prospects will also be especially good for physicians in specialties that afflict the rapidly growing elderly population. Examples of such specialties are cardiology and radiology, because the risks for heart disease and cancer increase as people age.

Related Jobs

Job Title	Average Earnings	Job Growth	Job Openings
1. Anesthesiologists	$166,400+	21.8%	ROUGHLY 1,000
2. Family and General Practitioners	$160,530	21.8%	ROUGHLY 4,000
3. Internists, General	$166,400+	21.8%	ROUGHLY 2,000
4. Obstetricians and Gynecologists	$166,400+	21.8%	ROUGHLY 1,000
5. Pediatricians, General	$152,240	21.8%	ROUGHLY 1,000
6. Physicians and Surgeons, All Other	$166,400+	21.8%	ROUGHLY 10,000
7. Psychiatrists	$160,230	21.8%	ROUGHLY 1,000
8. Surgeons	$166,400+	21.8%	ROUGHLY 2,000

Characteristics of the Related Jobs: Personality Type—Investigative, Social, Realistic. **Skills**—Science, operations analysis, reading comprehension, judgment and decision making, social perceptiveness, service orientation, active learning, management of personnel resources. **Work**

Conditions—Indoors; exposed to disease or infections; close to coworkers; common protective or safety equipment; exposed to radiation; cramped work space, awkward positions; wear specialized protective or safety equipment.

Metallurgical Engineering

Prepares individuals to apply mathematical and metallurgical principles to the design, development, and operational evaluation of metal components of structural, load-bearing, power, transmission, and moving systems. **Related CIP Program:** 14.2001 Metallurgical Engineering.

Specializations in the Major: Materials research, physical metallurgy, process engineering, chemical metallurgy.

Typical Sequence of College Courses: English composition, calculus, differential equations, general chemistry, introduction to computer science, general physics, organic chemistry, introduction to electric circuits, thermodynamics, numerical analysis, materials engineering, materials thermodynamics, physics of metals, hydroprocessing of materials, metallurgical transport phenomena, metallurgical design, mechanical metallurgy, process modeling, optimization and control, senior design project. **Typical Sequence of High School Courses:** English, algebra, geometry, trigonometry, pre-calculus, calculus, chemistry, physics, computer science.

Career Snapshot: Metallurgy is the science of refining and alloying metals and shaping them to form structures and products. Metallurgical engineers apply principles of physics, chemistry, materials science, and economics to improve extractive and manufacturing processes. A bachelor's degree is often an entry route to this field, which may eventually lead to management. Best job growth in this field is expected for those who work with nanotechnology (extremely small materials).

Related Jobs

Job Title	Average Earnings	Job Growth	Job Openings
1. Engineering Managers	$117,000	6.2%	5,000
2. Engineering Teachers, Postsecondary	$85,830	15.1%	Roughly 1,000
3. Materials Engineers	$83,190	9.3%	1,000

Characteristics of the Related Jobs: Personality Type—Enterprising, Investigative, Realistic. **Skills**—Operations analysis, science, management of financial resources, mathematics, management of material resources, management of personnel resources, complex problem solving, reading comprehension. **Work Conditions**—Indoors; sitting; common protective or safety equipment; noisy; hazardous equipment; hazardous conditions.

Microbiology

Focuses on the scientific study of unicellular organisms and colonies, sub-cellular genetic matter, and their ecological interactions with human beings and other life. **Related CIP Programs:** 26.0503 Medical Microbiology and Bacteriology; 26.0502 Microbiology, General; 26.0504 Virology.

Specializations in the Major: Bacteria, fungi (mycology), algae, virology, immunology.

Typical Sequence of College Courses: English composition, calculus, introduction to computer science, general chemistry, general biology, organic chemistry, general physics, general microbiology, genetics, introduction to biochemistry, immunology, bacterial physiology, bacterial genetics. **Typical Sequence of High School Courses:** English, biology, algebra, geometry, trigonometry, pre-calculus, chemistry, physics, computer science, calculus.

Career Snapshot: A bachelor's degree in microbiology or bacteriology may be an entry route to clinical laboratory work or to nonresearch work in industry or government. It also is good preparation for medical school. For a position in research or college teaching, a graduate degree is expected.

Related Jobs

Job Title	Average Earnings	Job Growth	Job Openings
1. Biological Science Teachers, Postsecondary	$73,980	15.1%	Roughly 1,700
2. Medical Scientists, Except Epidemiologists	$74,590	40.3%	7,000
3. Microbiologists	$66,580	12.2%	1,000
4. Natural Sciences Managers	$114,560	15.4%	2,000

Characteristics of the Related Jobs: Personality Type—Investigative, Realistic. **Skills**—Science, operations analysis, reading comprehension, mathematics, active learning, management of personnel resources, writing, instructing. **Work Conditions**—Indoors; sitting; exposed to disease or infections; hazardous conditions; common protective or safety equipment; exposed to radiation; wear specialized protective or safety equipment.

Modern Foreign Language

Focuses on a language being used in the modern world and includes related dialects; the cultural and historical contexts; and applications to business, science/technology, and other settings. **Related CIP Programs:** 16.0704 Bengali Language and Literature; 16.0301 Chinese Language and Literature; 16.1301 Celtic Languages, Literatures, and Linguistics; 16.1101 Arabic Language and Literature; 16.1401 Australian/Oceanic/Pacific Languages, Literatures, and Linguistics; 16.0406 Czech Language and Literature; 16.0405 Bulgarian Language and Literature; 16.0901 French Language and Literature; 16.1403 Burmese Language and Literature; 16.0503 Danish Language and Literature; 16.0401 Baltic Languages, Literatures, and Linguistics; 16.0300 East Asian Languages, Literatures, and Linguistics, General; 16.0907 Catalan Language and Literature; 16.0501 German Language and Literature; 16.1001 American Indian/ Native American Languages, Literatures, and Linguistics; 16.0404 Albanian Language and Literature; 16.0201 African Languages, Literatures, and Linguistics; 16.0504 Dutch/Flemish Language and Literature; others.

Specializations in the Major: Literature, translation, history and culture, language education, regional studies.

Typical Sequence of College Courses: Foreign language, conversation, composition, linguistics, foreign literature and culture, grammar, phonetics, history of a world region. **Typical Sequence of High School Courses:** English, public speaking, foreign language, history, social science.

Career Snapshot: The most popular foreign language majors—Chinese, French, German, Japanese, Russian, and Spanish—are described elsewhere in this book. But many colleges offer majors in other modern languages, such as Arabic, Hebrew, Hindi, Portuguese, Swahili, Swedish, or Turkish, to name just a few. As global trade continues to increase, a degree in a foreign language can lead to many job opportunities in international business, travel, security, and law. Many employers are looking for graduates with an understanding of a second language and culture. Translation and college teaching are options for those with a graduate degree in a foreign language.

Related Jobs

Job Title	Average Earnings	Job Growth	Job Openings
1. Foreign Language and Literature Teachers, Postsecondary	$56,740	15.1%	Roughly 900
2. Interpreters and Translators	$40,860	22.2%	2,000

Characteristics of the Related Jobs: Personality Type—Artistic, Social. **Skills**—Writing, reading comprehension, speaking, social perceptiveness, learning strategies, service orientation, active learning, monitoring. **Work Conditions**—Indoors; sitting; close to coworkers; exposed to disease or infections; exposed to radiation; making repetitive motions.

Music

Focuses on the introductory study and appreciation of music and the performing arts and prepares individuals to master musical instruments and performing art as solo and/or ensemble performers. **Related CIP Programs:** 50.0904 Music Theory and Composition; 50.0908 Voice and Opera; 50.0910 Jazz/Jazz Studies; 50.0901 Music, General; 50.0906 Conducting; 50.0903 Music Performance, General; 50.0912 Music Pedagogy; 50.0905 Musicology and Ethnomusicology; 50.0902 Music History, Literature, and Theory.

Specializations in the Major: Composition, performance, music theory, music education.

Typical Sequence of College Courses: English composition, foreign language, piano proficiency, introduction to music theory, harmony and counterpoint, conducting, music history and literature, recital attendance, performance technique with instrument/voice, recital performance. **Typical Sequence of High School Courses:** Music, foreign language, English.

Career Snapshot: Music majors study theory, composition, and performance. They learn how the success of a work of music depends on certain principles of what appeals to the ear, on the skill of the arranger, and on the interpretation of the performers. Relatively few graduates are able to support themselves as composers, arrangers, or performers, but many teach in schools or universities or give private instruction.

Related Jobs

Job Title	Average Earnings	Job Growth	Job Openings
1. Art, Drama, and Music Teachers, Postsecondary	$60,400	15.1%	ROUGHLY 2,500
2. Music Directors and Composers	$45,090	9.9%	2,000
3. Musicians and Singers	NO DATA AVAILABLE	7.6%	5,000

Characteristics of the Related Jobs: Personality Type—Artistic, Enterprising. **Skills**—Social perceptiveness, coordination. **Work Conditions**—Indoors; sitting; close to coworkers; making repetitive motions; extremely bright or inadequate lighting.

Nursing (RN Training)

Prepares individuals in the knowledge, techniques, and procedures for promoting health and providing care for sick, disabled, infirm, or other individuals or groups. **Related CIP Program:** 51.3801 Registered Nursing/Registered Nurse Training.

Specializations in the Major: Community health nursing, pediatric nursing, mental health nursing, nursing administration.

Typical Sequence of College Courses: English composition, introduction to psychology, college algebra, introduction to sociology, oral communication, general chemistry, general biology, human anatomy and physiology, general microbiology, ethics in health care, patient examination and evaluation, pharmacology, reproductive health nursing, pediatric nursing, adult health nursing, mental health nursing, nursing leadership and management, community health nursing, clinical nursing experience. **Typical Sequence of High School Courses:** English, algebra, geometry, trigonometry, biology, computer science, public speaking, chemistry, foreign language.

Career Snapshot: The study of nursing includes a combination of classroom and clinical work. Students learn what science tells us about the origins and treatment of disease, how to care effectively for the physical and emotional needs of sick and injured people, and how to teach people to maintain health. Nurses work in a variety of health-care settings, including physicians' offices, patients' homes, schools and companies, and in desk jobs for HMOs. The employment outlook is excellent in all specialties.

Related Jobs

Job Title	Average Earnings	Job Growth	Job Openings
1. Nursing Instructors and Teachers, Postsecondary	$61,360	15.1%	Roughly 1,500
2. Registered Nurses	$63,750	22.2%	104,000

Characteristics of the Related Jobs: Personality Type—Social, Investigative. **Skills**—Science, social perceptiveness, service orientation, learning strategies, active learning, instructing, monitoring, reading comprehension. **Work Conditions**—Indoors; standing; exposed to disease or infections; exposed to radiation; close to coworkers; common protective or safety equipment; wear specialized protective or safety equipment; walking and running; cramped work space, awkward positions.

Occupational Health and Industrial Hygiene

Prepares public health specialists to monitor and evaluate health and related safety standards in industrial, commercial, and government workplaces and facilities. **Related CIP Program:** 51.2206 Occupational Health and Industrial Hygiene.

Specializations in the Major: Occupational health, safety, hazardous materials.

Typical Sequence of College Courses: English composition, oral communication, calculus, technical writing, general chemistry, introduction to computer science, general physics, general biology, introduction to environmental health, introduction to occupational health and safety, biostatistics, organic chemistry, pollution science and treatment, statistics, microbial hazards, chemistry of hazardous materials, safety organization and management, industrial fire prevention, occupational safety and health law, environmental regulations. **Typical Sequence of High School Courses:** English, algebra, geometry, trigonometry, pre-calculus, chemistry, physics, computer science, public speaking.

Career Snapshot: Graduates with a bachelor's or master's degree in occupational health and industrial hygiene are trained to protect workers from a variety of threats to their health and safety: chemical and biological contaminants, fire, noise, cramped bodily positions, dangerous machinery, and radiation. The major covers the nature of the risks from these and other hazards, the laws that exist to ban such hazards, how to recognize the presence and assess the risks of workplace hazards, and how to take steps to eliminate them. It is possible to get a job as a technician with an associate degree, but the federal government and many other employers require a bachelor's. Most job opportunities are in the private sector and are somewhat sensitive to economic ups and downs, but government jobs are much more secure.

Related Jobs

Job Title	Average Earnings	Job Growth	Job Openings
1. Health Specialties Teachers, Postsecondary	$84,840	15.1%	Roughly 4,000
2. Occupational Health and Safety Specialists	$63,230	11.2%	2,000
3. Occupational Health and Safety Technicians	$44,830	14.4%	500

Characteristics of the Related Jobs: Personality Type—Investigative, Conventional, Social. **Skills**—Science, operations analysis, reading comprehension, writing, learning strategies, quality control analysis, judgment and decision making, speaking. **Work Conditions**—More often outdoors than indoors; in a vehicle; common protective or safety equipment; high places; wear specialized protective or safety equipment; hazardous conditions; hazardous equipment.

Occupational Therapy

Prepares individuals to assist patients limited by physical, cognitive, psychosocial, mental, developmental, and learning disabilities, as well as adverse environmental conditions, to maximize their independence and maintain optimum health through a planned mix of acquired skills, performance motivation, environmental adaptations, assistive technologies, and physical agents. **Related CIP Program:** 51.2306 Occupational Therapy/Therapist.

Specializations in the Major: Pediatric occupational therapy, geriatric occupational therapy, prosthetics.

Typical Sequence of College Courses: English composition, statistics for business and social sciences, general chemistry, general biology, human anatomy and physiology, introduction to psychology, human growth and development, introduction to computer science, abnormal psychology, fundamentals of medical science, neuroscience for therapy, occupational therapy for developmental problems, occupational therapy for physiological diagnoses, occupational therapy for psychosocial diagnoses, administration of occupational therapy services, research methods in occupational therapy, methods of facilitating therapeutic adaptation, occupational therapy field-work experience, seminar (reporting on research). **Typical Sequence of High School Courses:** English, algebra, geometry, trigonometry, chemistry, physics, biology, foreign language, computer science.

Career Snapshot: Occupational therapists help people cope with disabilities and lead more productive and enjoyable lives. Some therapists enter the field with a bachelor's degree in occupational therapy; others get a master's after a bachelor's in another field. They learn about the nature of various kinds of disabilities—developmental, emotional, and so on—and how to help people overcome them or compensate for them in their daily lives. The long-range outlook for jobs is considered quite good, although in the short run it may be affected by cutbacks in Medicare coverage of therapies.

Related Jobs

Job Title	Average Earnings	Job Growth	Job Openings
1. Health Specialties Teachers, Postsecondary	$84,840	15.1%	Roughly 4,000
2. Occupational Therapists	$69,630	25.6%	5,000

Characteristics of the Related Jobs: Personality Type—Social, Investigative. **Skills**—Learning strategies, writing, instructing, reading comprehension, service orientation, science, social perceptiveness, active learning. **Work Conditions**—More often indoors than outdoors; in a vehicle; exposed to disease or infections; close to coworkers; keeping or regaining balance; walking and running.

Oceanography

Focuses on the scientific study of the ecology and behavior of microbes, plants, and animals inhabiting oceans, coastal waters, and saltwater wetlands and the chemical components, mechanisms, structure, and movement of ocean waters and their interaction with terrestrial and atmospheric phenomena. **Related CIP Programs:** 26.1302 Marine Biology and Biological Oceanography; 40.0607 Oceanography, Chemical and Physical.

Specializations in the Major: Ocean geology, ocean biology, ocean chemistry, ocean meteorology.

Typical Sequence of College Courses: English composition, introduction to computer science, calculus, differential equations, general chemistry, general physics, agricultural power and machines, physical oceanography, chemical oceanography, geological oceanography, biological oceanography, seminar (reporting on research). **Typical Sequence of High School Courses:** English, algebra, geometry, trigonometry, chemistry, pre-calculus, physics, computer science, biology, calculus.

Career Snapshot: Oceans cover more of the earth than does dry land, yet many of the physical and biological characteristics of the oceans are poorly understood. Oceanographers use techniques of physical sciences to study the properties of ocean waters and how these affect coastal areas, climate, and weather. Those who specialize in ocean life work to improve the fishing industry, to protect the environment, and to understand the relationship between oceanic and terrestrial life forms. It is possible to get started in this field with a bachelor's degree; for advancement and many research jobs, however, a master's degree or PhD is helpful or required.

Related Jobs

Job Title	Average Earnings	Job Growth	Job Openings
1. Atmospheric, Earth, Marine, and Space Sciences Teachers, Postsecondary	$78,660	15.1%	Roughly 300
2. Biological Science Teachers, Postsecondary	$73,980	15.1%	Roughly 1,700
3. Geoscientists, Except Hydrologists and Geographers	$81,220	17.5%	2,000
4. Hydrologists	$73,670	18.3%	Fewer than 500
5. Natural Sciences Managers	$114,560	15.4%	2,000

Characteristics of the Related Jobs: Personality Type—Investigative, Realistic. **Skills**—Science, reading comprehension, operations analysis, writing, mathematics, complex problem solving, learning strategies, speaking. **Work Conditions**—Indoors; sitting; in a vehicle.

Operations Management

Prepares individuals to manage and direct the physical or technical functions of a firm or organization, particularly those relating to development, production, and manufacturing. **Related CIP Programs:** 52.0203 Logistics, Materials, and Supply Chain Management; 52.0205 Operations Management and Supervision.

Specializations in the Major: Production supervision, logistics, process analysis, quality assurance, materials management.

Typical Sequence of College Courses: English composition, business writing, introduction to psychology, principles of microeconomics, principles of macroeconomics, calculus for business and social sciences, statistics for business and social sciences, introduction to management information systems, introduction to accounting, legal environment of business, principles of management and organization, operations management, business finance, introduction to marketing, introduction to logistics, organizational behavior, human resource management, ancient literate civilizations, inventory management, supply chain management. **Typical Sequence of High School Courses:** English, algebra, geometry, trigonometry, science, precalculus, computer science.

Career Snapshot: Whereas other managers focus on segments of the production and distribution process (such as marketing or finance), operations managers look at the entire process and devise ways to streamline it. They use quantitative methods and computer technology to study the inputs of materials, energy, and labor into production; the processes that create products; and the paths that products take to reach customers. Their skills are greatly valued in today's competitive global business environment.

Related Jobs

Job Title	Average Earnings	Job Growth	Job Openings
1. Business Teachers, Postsecondary	$73,320	15.1%	ROUGHLY 2,000
2. Computer and Information Systems Managers	$113,720	16.9%	10,000
3. Construction Managers	$82,330	17.2%	14,000
4. First-Line Supervisors/Managers of Mechanics, Installers, and Repairers	$58,610	4.3%	14,000

(continued)

(continued)

Job Title	Average Earnings	Job Growth	Job Openings
5. First-Line Supervisors/Managers of Production and Operating Workers	$52,060	–5.2%	9,000
6. Industrial Production Managers	$85,080	–7.6%	5,000
7. Logisticians	$67,960	19.5%	4,000
8. Transportation, Storage, and Distribution Managers	$79,490	–5.3%	3,000

Characteristics of the Related Jobs: Personality Type—Enterprising, Realistic, Conventional. **Skills**—Management of financial resources, management of material resources, management of personnel resources, operations analysis, negotiation, quality control analysis, coordination, time management. **Work Conditions**—Indoors; common protective or safety equipment; hazardous equipment; noisy; walking and running; contaminants; hazardous conditions; minor burns, cuts, bites, or stings; high places.

Optometry

Prepares individuals for the independent professional practice of optometry and focuses on the principles and techniques for examining, diagnosing, and treating conditions of the visual system. **Related CIP Program:** 51.1701 Optometry (OD).

Specializations in the Major: Contact lenses, low vision.

Typical Sequence of College Courses: English composition; introduction to psychology; calculus; introduction to sociology; oral communication; general chemistry; general biology; organic chemistry; general microbiology; introduction to biochemistry; microbiology for optometry; geometric, physical, and visual optics; ocular health assessment; neuroanatomy; ocular anatomy and physiology; pathology; theory and methods of refraction; general and ocular pharmacology; optical and motor aspects of vision; ophthalmic optics; environmental and occupational vision; assessment of oculomotor system; strabismus and vision therapy; visual information processing and perception; ocular disease; contact lenses; pediatric and developmental vision; ethics in health care; professional practice management; low vision and geriatric vision; clinical experience in optometry. **Typical Sequence of High School Courses:** English, algebra, geometry, trigonometry, pre-calculus, biology, computer science, public speaking, chemistry, calculus, physics, foreign language.

Career Snapshot: Optometrists measure patients' visual ability and prescribe visual aids such as glasses and contact lenses. They may evaluate patients' suitability for laser surgery or provide postoperative care, but they do not perform surgery. The usual educational preparation is at least three years of college, followed by a four-year program of optometry school. The job outlook is good because the aging population will need increased attention to vision. The best opportunities probably will be at retail vision centers and outpatient clinics.

Related Jobs

Job Title	Average Earnings	Job Growth	Job Openings
1. Optometrists	$96,140	24.4%	2,000

Characteristics of the Related Jobs: Personality Type—Investigative, Social, Realistic. **Skills**—Science, reading comprehension, management of financial resources, operations analysis, quality control analysis, management of material resources, service orientation, active learning. **Work Conditions**—Indoors; sitting; exposed to disease or infections; close to coworkers; using hands.

Orthotics/Prosthetics

Prepares individuals, in consultation with physicians and other therapists, to design and fit orthoses for patients with disabling conditions of the limbs and/or spine and prostheses for patients who have partial or total absence of a limb or significant superficial deformity. **Related CIP Program:** 51.2307 Orthotist/Prosthetist Training.

Specializations in the Major: Orthotics, prosthetics, fabrication, fitting.

Typical Sequence of College Courses: English composition, general chemistry, introduction to psychology, general biology, general physics, statistics for business and social sciences, human anatomy and physiology, human growth and development, introduction to computer science, abnormal psychology, kinesiology, fundamentals of medical science, function of the locomotor system, neuroanatomy, lower-extremity orthotics, upper-extremity orthotics, lower-extremity prosthetics, upper-extremity prosthetics, psychological aspects of rehabilitation, immediate postoperative and early fitting, spinal orthotics. **Typical Sequence of High School Courses:** English, algebra, geometry, trigonometry, chemistry, physics, biology, foreign language, computer science.

Career Snapshot: Orthotics is the design and fitting of supportive or corrective braces for patients with musculoskeletal deformity or injury. Prosthetics is the fabrication and fitting of artificial limbs. People enter this field by getting a bachelor's degree in one or both specializations or enrolling in a certification program after a bachelor's in another field (perhaps occupational therapy). The job outlook is expected to be good.

Related Jobs

Job Title	Average Earnings	Job Growth	Job Openings
1. Health Specialties Teachers, Postsecondary	$84,840	15.1%	Roughly 4,000
2. Medical Appliance Technicians	$35,010	10.9%	Fewer than 500
3. Orthotists and Prosthetists	$62,070	15.5%	Fewer than 500

Characteristics of the Related Jobs: Personality Type—Social, Investigative. **Skills**—Instructing, science, learning strategies, reading comprehension, writing, active learning, speaking, operations analysis. **Work Conditions**—Indoors; sitting; exposed to disease or infections; hazardous conditions; contaminants; hazardous equipment; close to coworkers.

Parks and Recreation Management

Prepares individuals to develop and manage park facilities and other indoor and outdoor recreation and leisure facilities. **Related CIP Program:** 31.0301 Parks, Recreation, and Leisure Facilities Management.

Specializations in the Major: Interpretation, resource management, tourism, exercise, outdoor leadership, therapeutic recreation.

Typical Sequence of College Courses: English composition, introduction to computer science, American government, oral communication, conservation of natural resources, introduction to economics, introduction to psychology, statistics for business and social sciences, introduction to sociology, introduction to business management, natural resource economics, ecology, foundations of parks and recreation, tourism management and planning, methods of environmental interpretation, evaluation and research in parks and recreation, parks, recreation and diverse populations, recreation and tourism programs, park planning and design, seminar (reporting on research). **Typical Sequence of High School Courses:** English, biology, social science, chemistry, geometry, public speaking.

Career Snapshot: Interest in the outdoors and in fitness is growing. Americans want to make the most of their recreational time and the parks and other facilities that are set aside for recreational use. Graduates with a bachelor's degree in parks and recreation management may find employment with government, commercial recreational, and tourism organizations, camps, or theme parks. However, many people are expected to compete for these jobs, so a master's degree may be an advantage.

Related Jobs

Job Title	Average Earnings	Job Growth	Job Openings
1. Recreation Workers	$22,280	14.7%	11,000

Characteristics of the Related Jobs: Personality Type—Social, Enterprising, Artistic. **Skills**—Management of material resources, management of personnel resources, service orientation, social perceptiveness, learning strategies, instructing, management of financial resources, coordination. **Work Conditions**—More often outdoors than indoors; in a vehicle; noisy; exposed to disease or infections; very hot or cold; extremely bright or inadequate lighting; keeping or regaining balance.

Petroleum Engineering

Prepares individuals to apply mathematical and scientific principles to the design, development, and operational evaluation of systems for locating, extracting, processing, and refining crude petroleum and natural gas. **Related CIP Program:** 14.2501 Petroleum Engineering.

Specializations in the Major: Drilling/extraction, refining, distribution, exploration.

Typical Sequence of College Courses: English composition, introduction to computer science, technical writing, calculus, differential equations, general chemistry, general physics, physical geology, introduction to engineering, statics, dynamics, fluid mechanics, thermodynamics, numerical analysis, materials engineering, engineering economics, heat transfer, sedimentary rocks and processes, petroleum geology, petroleum development, petroleum production methods, petroleum property management, formation evaluation, natural gas engineering, reservoir fluids, reservoir engineering, well testing and analysis, drilling engineering, reservoir stimulation, senior design project. **Typical Sequence of High School Courses:** English, algebra, geometry, trigonometry, pre-calculus, calculus, chemistry, physics, computer science.

Career Snapshot: Petroleum engineers devise technically effective and economically justifiable ways of locating, extracting, transporting, refining, and storing petroleum and natural gas. They apply basic principles of science to oil wells deep in the ground or high-towering refineries. Usually they begin with a bachelor's degree. Management is sometimes an option later in their careers. The job outlook is favorable in the United States and even better in foreign countries, where many American-trained petroleum engineers work.

Related Jobs

Job Title	Average Earnings	Job Growth	Job Openings
1. Engineering Managers	$117,000	6.2%	5,000
2. Engineering Teachers, Postsecondary	$85,830	15.1%	Roughly 1,000
3. Petroleum Engineers	$108,910	18.4%	1,000

Characteristics of the Related Jobs: Personality Type—Enterprising, Investigative, Realistic. **Skills**—Management of financial resources, science, management of material resources, mathematics, operations analysis, management of personnel resources, complex problem solving, reading comprehension. **Work Conditions**—Indoors; sitting; exposed to radiation.

Pharmacy

Prepares individuals for the independent or employed practice of preparing and dispensing drugs and medications in consultation with prescribing physicians and other health-care professionals and for managing pharmacy practices and counseling patients. **Related CIP Program:** 51.2001 Pharmacy (PharmD [USA], PharmD or BS/BPharm [Canada]).

Specializations in the Major: Pharmaceutical chemistry, pharmacology, pharmacy administration.

Typical Sequence of College Courses: English composition, introduction to psychology, calculus, introduction to sociology, oral communication, general chemistry, general biology, organic chemistry, introduction to biochemistry, human anatomy and physiology, pharmaceutical calculations, pharmacology, pharmaceutics, microbiology and immunology, patient assessment and education, medicinal chemistry, therapeutics, pharmacy law and ethics, pharmacokinetics, electrical inspection. **Typical Sequence of High School Courses:** English, algebra, geometry, trigonometry, biology, computer science, public speaking, chemistry, calculus, physics, foreign language.

Career Snapshot: Pharmacists dispense medications as prescribed by physicians and other health practitioners and give advice to patients about how to use medications. Pharmacists must be knowledgeable about the chemical and physical properties of drugs, how they behave in the body, and how they may interact with other drugs and substances. Schools of pharmacy take about four years to complete and usually require at least one or two years of prior college work. Some pharmacists go on to additional graduate training to prepare for research, administration, or college teaching. Some find work in sales for pharmaceutical companies or in marketing research for managed care organizations. The job outlook for pharmacists is expected to be good, thanks to the aging of the population, combined with the shift of medical care from the scalpel to the pill.

Related Jobs

Job Title	Average Earnings	Job Growth	Job Openings
1. Health Specialties Teachers, Postsecondary	$84,840	15.1%	ROUGHLY 4,000
2. Pharmacists	$109,180	17.0%	11,000

Characteristics of the Related Jobs: Personality Type—Investigative, Conventional, Social. **Skills**—Science, operations analysis, reading comprehension, writing, instructing, management of material resources, social perceptiveness, speaking. **Work Conditions**—Indoors; standing; exposed to disease or infections; using hands; making repetitive motions; close to coworkers; walking and running.

Philosophy

Focuses on ideas and their logical structure, including arguments and investigations about abstract and real phenomena. **Related CIP Program:** 38.0101 Philosophy.

Specializations in the Major: Logic, esthetics, ethics, history of philosophy.

Typical Sequence of College Courses: English composition, foreign language, introduction to logic, major thinkers and issues in philosophy, ethical/moral theory, classical philosophy, modern philosophy, contemporary philosophy, esthetics. **Typical Sequence of High School Courses:** Algebra, English, foreign language, social science, history, geometry.

Career Snapshot: Philosophy is concerned with the most basic questions about the human experience, such as what reality is, what the ultimate values are, and how we know what we know. Philosophy majors are trained to think independently and critically and to write clearly and persuasively. They may go to work in a number of business careers where these skills are appreciated—perhaps most of all in the long run as these former philosophy majors advance to positions of leadership. Some find that a philosophy major combines well with further training in law, computer science, or religious studies. Those with a graduate degree in philosophy may teach in college.

Related Jobs

Job Title	Average Earnings	Job Growth	Job Openings
1. Clergy	$42,950	12.7%	22,000
2. Directors, Religious Activities and Education	$36,190	12.6%	3,000
3. Philosophy and Religion Teachers, Postsecondary	$61,240	15.1%	Roughly 600

Characteristics of the Related Jobs: Personality Type—Social, Enterprising, Artistic. **Skills**—Management of financial resources, social perceptiveness, negotiation, learning strategies, management of material resources, service orientation, instructing, management of personnel resources. **Work Conditions**—More often indoors than outdoors; in a vehicle; sitting; exposed to disease or infections.

Physical Education

Prepares individuals to teach physical education programs or to coach sports at various educational levels. **Related CIP Program:** 13.1314 Physical Education Teaching and Coaching.

Specializations in the Major: Sports activities, coaching, recreation, health education.

Typical Sequence of College Courses: Introduction to psychology, English composition, oral communication, history and philosophy of education, human growth and development, introduction to special education, history and philosophy of physical education, first aid and CPR, methods of teaching physical education, human anatomy and physiology, kinesiology, special needs in physical education, psychomotor development, organization and administration of physical education, evaluation in physical education, methods of teaching dance, methods of teaching sports activities, methods of teaching aerobics and weight training, swimming and water safety, student teaching. **Typical Sequence of High School Courses:** English, algebra, geometry, trigonometry, science, foreign language, public speaking.

Career Snapshot: This major covers not only educational techniques, but also the workings of the human body. Thanks to a national concern for fitness and health, physical education graduates are finding employment not only as teachers, but also as instructors and athletic directors in health and sports clubs. Most jobs are still to be found in elementary and secondary schools, where a bachelor's degree is often sufficient for entry, but a master's may be required for advancement to a more secure and better-paid position. Some graduates may go on to get a master's in athletic training and work for a college or professional sports team.

Related Jobs

Job Title	Average Earnings	Job Growth	Job Openings
1. Coaches and Scouts	$28,380	24.8%	10,000
2. Education Teachers, Postsecondary	$58,300	15.1%	Roughly 1,800
3. Fitness Trainers and Aerobics Instructors	$30,670	29.4%	12,000

(continued)

(continued)

Job Title	Average Earnings	Job Growth	Job Openings
4. Middle School Teachers, Except Special and Vocational Education	$50,770	15.3%	25,000
5. Secondary School Teachers, Except Special and Vocational Education	$52,200	8.9%	41,000

Characteristics of the Related Jobs: Personality Type—Social, Enterprising. **Skills**—Learning strategies, instructing, management of personnel resources, monitoring, social perceptiveness, negotiation, management of material resources, judgment and decision making. **Work Conditions**—Indoors; standing; close to coworkers; exposed to disease or infections.

Physical Therapy

Prepares individuals to alleviate physical and functional impairments and limitations caused by injury or disease through the design and implementation of therapeutic interventions to promote fitness and health. **Related CIP Program:** 51.2308 Physical Therapy/Therapist Training.

Specializations in the Major: Orthopedics, sports medicine, geriatric physical therapy, neurological physical therapy, physical therapy education.

Typical Sequence of College Courses: English composition, statistics for business and social sciences, general chemistry, general biology, human anatomy and physiology, introduction to psychology, human growth and development, introduction to computer science, abnormal psychology, fundamentals of medical science, neuroanatomy, neuroscience for therapy, cardiopulmonary system, musculoskeletal system, clinical orthopedics, clinical applications of neurophysiology, therapeutic exercise techniques, physical and electrical agents in physical therapy, medical considerations in physical therapy, psychomotor development throughout the lifespan, psychosocial aspects of physical disability, research in physical therapy practice, research in physical therapy practice. **Typical Sequence of High School Courses:** English, algebra, geometry, trigonometry, chemistry, physics, biology, foreign language, computer science.

Career Snapshot: Physical therapists help people overcome pain and limited movement caused by disease or injury and help them avoid further disabilities. They review patients' medical records and the prescriptions of physicians, evaluate patients' mobility, and then guide patients through appropriate exercise routines and apply therapeutic agents such as heat and electrical stimulation. They need to be knowledgeable about many disabling conditions and therapeutic techniques. The master's program is becoming the standard requirement for entry into this field. Entry to master's programs is extremely competitive. The short-term job outlook has been hurt by cutbacks in Medicare coverage of therapy; however, the long-term outlook is expected to be good.

Related Jobs

Job Title	Average Earnings	Job Growth	Job Openings
1. Health Specialties Teachers, Postsecondary	$84,840	15.1%	Roughly 4,000
2. Physical Therapists	$74,480	30.3%	8,000

Characteristics of the Related Jobs: Personality Type—Social, Investigative. **Skills**—Science, operations analysis, instructing, reading comprehension, writing, service orientation, time management, social perceptiveness. **Work Conditions**—Indoors; standing; exposed to disease or infections; close to coworkers; keeping or regaining balance; walking and running; kneeling, crouching, stooping, or crawling; cramped work space, awkward positions.

Physician Assisting

Prepares individuals to practice medicine, including diagnoses and treatment therapies, under the supervision of a physician. **Related CIP Program:** 51.0912 Physician Assistant Training.

Specializations in the Major: Internal medicine, pediatrics, family medicine, emergency medicine.

Typical Sequence of College Courses: English composition, college algebra, general chemistry, general biology, introduction to psychology, human growth and development, general microbiology, human physiology, human anatomy, pharmacology, medical interviewing techniques, patient examination and evaluation, clinical laboratory procedures, ethics in health care, clinical experience in internal medicine, clinical experience in emergency medicine, clinical experience in obstetrics/gynecology, clinical experience in family medicine, clinical experience in psychiatry, clinical experience in surgery, clinical experience in pediatrics, clinical experience in geriatrics. **Typical Sequence of High School Courses:** English, algebra, geometry, trigonometry, pre-calculus, biology, computer science, public speaking, chemistry, foreign language.

Career Snapshot: Physician assistants work under the supervision of physicians, but in some cases they provide care in settings where a physician may be present only a couple of days per week. They perform many of the diagnostic, therapeutic, and preventative functions that we are used to associating with physicians. The typical educational program results in a bachelor's degree. It often takes only two years to complete, but entrants usually must have at least two years of prior college and often must have work experience in the field of health care. Employment opportunities are expected to be good.

Related Jobs

Job Title	Average Earnings	Job Growth	Job Openings
1. Health Specialties Teachers, Postsecondary	$84,840	15.1%	ROUGHLY 4,000
2. Physician Assistants	$84,420	39.0%	4,000

Characteristics of the Related Jobs: Personality Type—Social, Investigative. **Skills**—Science, instructing, reading comprehension, judgment and decision making, social perceptiveness, service orientation, writing, operations analysis. **Work Conditions**—Indoors; standing; exposed to disease or infections; exposed to radiation; close to coworkers; wear specialized protective or safety equipment; common protective or safety equipment.

Physics

Focuses on the scientific study of matter and energy and the formulation and testing of the laws governing the behavior of the matter-energy continuum. **Related CIP Program:** 40.0801 Physics, General.

Specializations in the Major: Theoretical physics, astronomy, nuclear physics, elementary particles, solid-state physics, optics, acoustics, plasma physics.

Typical Sequence of College Courses: English composition, introduction to computer science, calculus, differential equations, general chemistry, mechanics, optics, thermal physics, electricity and magnetism, modern physics, modern experimental physics, quantum and atomic physics.
Typical Sequence of High School Courses: English, algebra, geometry, trigonometry, chemistry, physics, pre-calculus, computer science, calculus.

Career Snapshot: Physics is the study of the basic laws of the physical world, including those that govern what matter and energy are and how they change form, move, and interact. This knowledge is the basis for our understanding of many fields, such as chemistry, biology, and engineering. Physics has direct applications in the technologies that we use every day for transportation, communication, and entertainment. For jobs in basic research and development, as well as for college teaching, a PhD is most commonly required. Unfortunately, research is not expected to grow fast, if at all, so there will be keen competition for jobs as physicists. Job opportunities will be better for physics graduates in applied settings, where they do work associated with engineering and computer science. High school teaching is also an option. Most states require that new teachers eventually get a master's degree.

Related Jobs

Job Title	Average Earnings	Job Growth	Job Openings
1. Natural Sciences Managers	$114,560	15.4%	2,000
2. Physicists	$106,390	15.9%	500
3. Physics Teachers, Postsecondary	$75,060	15.1%	Roughly 400

Characteristics of the Related Jobs: Personality Type—Investigative, Enterprising. **Skills**—Science, mathematics, technology design, programming, reading comprehension, operations analysis, active learning, writing. **Work Conditions**—Indoors; sitting; exposed to radiation; hazardous conditions.

Podiatry

Prepares individuals for the independent professional practice of podiatric medicine, involving the prevention, diagnosis, and treatment of diseases, disorders, and injuries to the foot and lower extremities. **Related CIP Program:** 51.2101 Podiatric Medicine/Podiatry (DPM).

Specializations in the Major: Sports medicine, orthopedics, surgery.

Typical Sequence of College Courses: English composition, introduction to psychology, college algebra, calculus, introduction to sociology, oral communication, general chemistry, general biology, introduction to computer science, organic chemistry, human anatomy and physiology, general microbiology, genetics, introduction to biochemistry, gross anatomy, histology, patient examination and evaluation, lower-extremity anatomy, neuroanatomy, human physiology, microbiology and immunology, pathology, biomechanics, radiology, podiatric surgery, dermatology, general medicine, traumatology, professional practice management, clinical experience in podiatric medicine. **Typical Sequence of High School Courses:** English, algebra, geometry, trigonometry, biology, computer science, public speaking, chemistry, foreign language, physics, pre-calculus.

Career Snapshot: Podiatrists are health-care practitioners who specialize in the feet and lower extremities. The educational process is much like that for medical doctors—for almost all students, first a bachelor's degree and then four years of study and clinical practice in a school of podiatric medicine, followed by one to three years of a hospital residency program. The bachelor's degree can be in any subject as long as it includes certain coursework in science and math. Job opportunities will probably be better in group medical practices, clinics, and health networks than in traditional solo practices.

Related Jobs

Job Title	Average Earnings	Job Growth	Job Openings
1. Podiatrists	$116,250	9.0%	Fewer than 500

Characteristics of the Related Jobs: Personality Type—Investigative, Social, Realistic. **Skills**—Science, management of financial resources, active learning, technology design, management of material resources, reading comprehension, service orientation, instructing. **Work Conditions**—Indoors; sitting; exposed to disease or infections; exposed to radiation; close to coworkers; common protective or safety equipment; wear specialized protective or safety equipment; using hands; contaminants.

Political Science

Focuses on the systematic study of political institutions and behavior. **Related CIP Program:** 45.1001 Political Science and Government, General.

Specializations in the Major: Political theory, comparative politics, international relations, public administration, public policy, public opinion.

Typical Sequence of College Courses: English composition, introduction to psychology, introduction to sociology, American government, foreign language, statistics, introduction to economics, statistics for business and social sciences, state and local government, comparative governments, introduction to international relations, political theory, political science research methods, public policy analysis, seminar (reporting on research). **Typical Sequence of High School Courses:** Algebra, English, foreign language, social science, trigonometry, history.

Career Snapshot: Political science is the study of how political systems and public policy are created and evolve. It is concerned with many levels of political activity, from the campaigns of candidates for representation of a city precinct to the maneuvers of nations trying to resolve regional conflicts. Most political scientists with graduate degrees work as researchers and teachers in universities; some work for nonprofits, political lobbyists, and social organizations. Many holders of the bachelor's degree use it as an entry route to law school or public administration.

Related Jobs

Job Title	Average Earnings	Job Growth	Job Openings
1. Political Science Teachers, Postsecondary	$68,790	15.1%	Roughly 500
2. Political Scientists	$104,090	19.5%	Fewer than 500

Characteristics of the Related Jobs: Personality Type—Social, Investigative, Artistic. **Skills**—Science, speaking, writing, active learning, reading comprehension, operations analysis, critical thinking, instructing. **Work Conditions**—Indoors; sitting.

Psychology

Focuses on the scientific study of individual and collective behavior, the physical and environmental bases of behavior, and the analysis and treatment of behavior problems and disorders. **Related CIP Program:** 42.0101 Psychology, General.

Specializations in the Major: Clinical/counseling psychology, industrial psychology, research clinical psychology, educational psychology.

Typical Sequence of College Courses: Introduction to psychology, English composition, statistics, research methods in speech pathology and audiology, experimental psychology, psychology of learning, abnormal psychology, social psychology, developmental psychology, sensation and perception, cognitive psychology, biopsychology, psychology of personality, quantitative analysis in psychology, psychological testing and measurements. **Typical Sequence of High School Courses:** Algebra, biology, English, foreign language, social science, trigonometry.

Career Snapshot: Psychology is the study of human behavior. It may take place in a clinical, educational, industrial, or experimental setting. Those with a bachelor's degree usually must find employment in another field, such as marketing research. A bachelor's degree can also be a good first step toward graduate education in education, law, social work, or another field. To be licensed as a clinical or counseling psychologist, you usually need a PhD. Industrial-organizational psychologists need a master's. School psychologists need an educational specialist degree and may enjoy the best job opportunities in this field. Competition for graduate school is expected to be keen. About half of psychologists are self-employed. Because psychology is about behavior, many people don't realize that it uses scientific methods and that students are expected to become competent in statistics.

Related Jobs

Job Title	Average Earnings	Job Growth	Job Openings
1. Clinical, Counseling, and School Psychologists	$66,040	11.1%	6,000
2. Industrial-Organizational Psychologists	$83,260	26.3%	Fewer than 500
3. Psychology Teachers, Postsecondary	$65,760	15.1%	Roughly 1,000

Characteristics of the Related Jobs: Personality Type—Investigative, Social, Artistic. **Skills**—Social perceptiveness, science, learning strategies, writing, reading comprehension, speaking, negotiation, service orientation. **Work Conditions**—Indoors; sitting; exposed to disease or infections; close to coworkers.

Public Administration

Prepares individuals to serve as managers in the executive arm of local, state, and federal government and focuses on the systematic study of executive organization and management. **Related CIP Program:** 44.0401 Public Administration.

Specializations in the Major: Policy analysis, program management, economic development, finance and budgeting, personnel and labor relations.

Typical Sequence of College Courses: English composition, oral communication, accounting, introduction to business management, American government, state and local government, college algebra, introduction to economics, organizational behavior, statistics for business and social sciences, organizational theory, introduction to psychology, urban politics, public policy-making process, public finance and budgeting, political science research methods, planning and change in public organizations, seminar (reporting on research). **Typical Sequence of High School Courses:** Algebra, English, foreign language, social science, trigonometry, history, public speaking, computer science.

Career Snapshot: The public sector includes many kinds of agencies, working in the fields of health, law enforcement, environmental protection, transportation, and taxation, to name just a few. Because of this variety of fields, graduates who have been trained in administrative skills (perhaps at the master's level) often find it helpful to combine that background with specific training in another field, such as health, science, engineering, or accounting. Public administration programs usually include internships that give students actual experience working in a public agency.

Related Jobs

Job Title	Average Earnings	Job Growth	Job Openings
1. Administrative Services Managers	$75,520	12.5%	9,000
2. Chief Executives	$160,720	−1.4%	11,000
3. Emergency Management Specialists	$52,590	21.7%	500
4. General and Operations Managers	$92,650	−0.1%	50,000
5. Legislators	$18,810	0.7%	2,000
6. Postmasters and Mail Superintendents	$58,770	−15.1%	500
7. Social and Community Service Managers	$56,600	13.8%	5,000
8. Transportation, Storage, and Distribution Managers	$79,490	−5.3%	3,000

Characteristics of the Related Jobs: Personality Type—Enterprising, Conventional, Social. **Skills**—Management of material resources, management of financial resources, operations analysis, management of personnel resources, negotiation, coordination, monitoring, social perceptiveness. **Work Conditions**—Indoors; sitting; in a vehicle; walking and running; high places.

Public Relations

Focuses on the theories and methods for managing the media image of a business, organization, or individual and the communication process with stakeholders, constituencies, audiences, and the general public and prepares individuals to function as public relations assistants, technicians, and managers. **Related CIP Program:** 09.0902 Public Relations/Image Management.

Specializations in the Major: Management, creative process, new media.

Typical Sequence of College Courses: English composition, oral communication, introduction to marketing, introduction to economics, principles of public relations, communications theory, public relations message strategy, communication ethics, public relations media, public relations writing, public relations techniques and campaigns, organizational communications, mass communication law, introduction to communication research, visual design for media. **Typical Sequence of High School Courses:** English, algebra, foreign language, art, literature, public speaking, social science.

Career Snapshot: Public relations specialists work for business, government, and nonprofit organizations and encourage public support for the employer's policies and practices. Often several "publics" with differing interests and needs have to be targeted with different messages. The work requires an understanding of psychology, the business and social environments, effective writing, and techniques used in various media for persuasive communications. A bachelor's degree is good preparation for an entry-level job in this competitive field, and an internship or work experience is an important advantage. On-the-job experience may lead to a job managing public relations campaigns; a master's degree can speed up the process of advancement.

Related Jobs

Job Title	Average Earnings	Job Growth	Job Openings
1. Advertising and Promotions Managers	$82,370	–1.7%	1,000
2. Communications Teachers, Postsecondary	$58,890	15.1%	Roughly 800
3. Public Relations Managers	$89,690	12.9%	2,000
4. Public Relations Specialists	$51,960	24.0%	13,000

Characteristics of the Related Jobs: Personality Type—Enterprising, Artistic, Social. **Skills**—Operations analysis, negotiation, social perceptiveness, writing, speaking, time management, service orientation, coordination. **Work Conditions**—Indoors; sitting; in a vehicle.

Religion/Religious Studies

Focuses on the nature of religious belief and specific religious and quasi-religious systems. **Related CIP Programs:** 39.0602 Divinity/Ministry (BD, MDiv); 38.0201 Religion/Religious Studies.

Specializations in the Major: Pastoral studies, pastoral counseling, missionary work, scriptural texts/language, ecumenical studies.

Typical Sequence of College Courses: English composition, foreign language, introduction to religious studies, introduction to philosophy, ethical/moral theory, Hebrew Bible, New Testament, non-Western religions, philosophy of religion, history of religion in the West, contemporary theologies, religious ethics. **Typical Sequence of High School Courses:** Algebra, English, foreign language, social science, history, geometry, public speaking.

Career Snapshot: Interest in religion continues to grow in America, and many colleges were founded by churches, so the religious studies major continues to attract students, some of whom do not feel the call to become professional clergy. A graduate of a religious studies major has skills in language, literature, critical thinking, and writing that are valuable in many careers in the secular world. The amount of education required to be ordained in the clergy depends on the person's religious denomination. For some, there may be no formal requirement; most require several years of seminary training, often following four years of college. Clergy find work in churches, synagogues, and religious schools; as chaplains for hospitals, prisons, and the military; and as missionaries.

Related Jobs

Job Title	Average Earnings	Job Growth	Job Openings
1. Clergy	$42,950	12.7%	22,000
2. Philosophy and Religion Teachers, Postsecondary	$61,240	15.1%	Roughly 600

Characteristics of the Related Jobs: Personality Type—Social, Artistic, Enterprising. **Skills**—Management of financial resources, social perceptiveness, negotiation, learning strategies, management of material resources, service orientation, instructing, management of personnel resources. **Work Conditions**—More often indoors than outdoors; in a vehicle; sitting; exposed to disease or infections.

Russian

Focuses on the Russian language. **Related CIP Program:** 16.0402 Russian Language and Literature.

Specializations in the Major: Literature, translation, history and culture, language education.

Typical Sequence of College Courses: Russian language, conversation, composition, linguistics, Russian literature, Russian history and civilization, European history and civilization, grammar, phonetics. **Typical Sequence of High School Courses:** English, public speaking, foreign language, history, literature, social science.

Career Snapshot: Despite the breakup of the Soviet Union, Russian is still an important world language that not many Americans know. As business and governmental ties with Russia continue to increase as it opens to free trade, a degree in Russian can lead to careers in international business, travel, and law. College teaching and translation are options for those with a graduate degree in Russian.

Related Jobs

Job Title	Average Earnings	Job Growth	Job Openings
1. Foreign Language and Literature Teachers, Postsecondary	$56,740	15.1%	Roughly 900
2. Interpreters and Translators	$40,860	22.2%	2,000

Characteristics of the Related Jobs: Personality Type—Artistic, Social. **Skills**—Writing, reading comprehension, speaking, social perceptiveness, learning strategies, service orientation, active learning, monitoring. **Work Conditions**—Indoors; sitting; close to coworkers; exposed to disease or infections; exposed to radiation; making repetitive motions.

Secondary Education

Prepares individuals to teach students in the secondary grades, which may include grades seven through twelve, depending on the school system or state regulations. May include preparation to teach a comprehensive curriculum or specific subject matter. **Related CIP Program:** 13.1205 Secondary Education and Teaching.

Specializations in the Major: Art education, music education, science education, mathematics education, remedial and developmental reading, bilingual education, social studies education, language education.

Typical Sequence of College Courses: Introduction to psychology, English composition, oral communication, history and philosophy of education, human growth and development, teaching methods, educational alternatives for exceptional students, educational psychology, courses in subject to be taught, student teaching. **Typical Sequence of High School Courses:** English, algebra, geometry, trigonometry, science, foreign language, public speaking.

Career Snapshot: A bachelor's is the minimum for starting a secondary teaching career, and a master's may be required or encouraged for job security and a pay raise. A teacher-education program covers not only the subjects you will teach, but also basic principles of how young people learn and how to run a classroom. Demand for secondary school teachers is expected to be better than that for lower grades, but it will vary according to subject field and geographic area. Job opportunities will be best in inner-city and rural locations.

Related Jobs

Job Title	Average Earnings	Job Growth	Job Openings
1. Secondary School Teachers, Except Special and Vocational Education	$52,200	8.9%	41,000

Characteristics of the Related Jobs: Personality Type—Social, Artistic, Enterprising. **Skills**—Learning strategies, instructing, social perceptiveness, service orientation, writing, speaking, judgment and decision making, monitoring. **Work Conditions**—Indoors; standing; close to coworkers; exposed to disease or infections.

Social Work

Prepares individuals for the professional practice of social welfare administration and counseling and focuses on the study of organized means of providing basic support services for vulnerable individuals and groups. **Related CIP Program:** 44.0701 Social Work.

Specializations in the Major: Mental health, substance abuse, child welfare, mental retardation, health care, school, domestic violence, advocacy.

Typical Sequence of College Courses: English composition, human growth and development, American government, introduction to psychology, introduction to sociology, introduction to philosophy, statistics for business and social sciences, cultural diversity, human anatomy and physiology, development of social welfare, human behavior and the social environment, social work methods, social welfare policy and issues, field experience/internship, social work research methods, foreign language, seminar (reporting on research). **Typical Sequence of High School Courses:** Algebra, biology, English, foreign language, social science, trigonometry.

Career Snapshot: Social workers improve people's lives by helping them cope with problems of bad health, substance abuse, disability, old age, family conflicts, mental illness, or poverty. A large number of them work for public agencies and health-care institutions. A master's degree is becoming standard preparation for this field. Job opportunities are expected to be best in rural areas and in the specializations of substance abuse and gerontology.

Related Jobs

Job Title	Average Earnings	Job Growth	Job Openings
1. Child, Family, and School Social Workers	$39,960	12.3%	11,000
2. Marriage and Family Therapists	$46,920	14.4%	1,000
3. Probation Officers and Correctional Treatment Specialists	$46,530	19.3%	4,000
4. Social Work Teachers, Postsecondary	$61,010	15.1%	Roughly 300

Characteristics of the Related Jobs: Personality Type—Social, Enterprising. **Skills**—Operations analysis, science, social perceptiveness, service orientation, negotiation, speaking, writing, coordination. **Work Conditions**—More often indoors than outdoors; in a vehicle; sitting; exposed to disease or infections; close to coworkers.

Sociology

Focuses on the systematic study of human social institutions and social relationships. **Related CIP Program:** 45.1101 Sociology.

Specializations in the Major: Anthropology, culture and social change, family and marriage, social problems, gerontology, human relations, social institutions/organizations, criminology.

Typical Sequence of College Courses: English composition, introduction to psychology, introduction to sociology, American government, introduction to economics, statistics, foreign language, social inequality, introduction to social research, history of social thought, contemporary social problems, seminar (reporting on research). **Typical Sequence of High School Courses:** Algebra, English, foreign language, social science, trigonometry.

Career Snapshot: Sociologists study how people behave within groups, such as families, religious denominations, social organizations, businesses, and political groups. Many graduates of bachelor's sociology programs go on to graduate school with the goal of research or teaching. Others branch out to a related field, perhaps with additional education, such as social work, the law, or marketing research.

Related Jobs

Job Title	Average Earnings	Job Growth	Job Openings
1. Sociologists	$69,620	21.9%	Fewer than 500
2. Sociology Teachers, Postsecondary	$64,430	15.1%	Roughly 500

Characteristics of the Related Jobs: Personality Type—Investigative, Social, Artistic. **Skills**—Science, writing, learning strategies, reading comprehension, instructing, speaking, active learning, operations analysis. **Work Conditions**—Indoors; sitting.

Soil Science

Focuses on the scientific classification of soils, soil properties, and their relationship to agricultural crops. **Related CIP Programs:** 01.1202 Soil Chemistry and Physics; 01.1203 Soil Microbiology; 01.1201 Soil Science and Agronomy, General.

Specializations in the Major: Soil conservation, waste/bioresource management, land-use management, soil surveying, sustainable agriculture.

Typical Sequence of College Courses: English composition, calculus, general biology, general chemistry, organic chemistry, general physics, introduction to geology, introduction to soil science, statistics, computer applications in agriculture, soil mechanics, soil chemistry, soil conservation engineering, soil morphology, soil analysis, soil fertility, ecology, introduction to ground water/hydrology, natural resource management and water quality, ecology and renewable resource management. **Typical Sequence of**

High School Courses: Biology, chemistry, algebra, geometry, trigonometry, computer science, English, public speaking.

Career Snapshot: Soil is a lot more than just dirt. It is a complex ecosystem with chemical, physical, mineralogical, and biological properties that affect agricultural productivity and the larger environment. Soil scientists survey and map soils, advise farmers and landowners on how to use land in productive and ecologically sound methods, and consult with civil engineers about construction projects that involve soil. Many work for governments; the federal government hires graduates of bachelor's-degree programs. Those with advanced degrees may go into college teaching or basic research.

Related Jobs

Job Title	Average Earnings	Job Growth	Job Openings
1. Agricultural Sciences Teachers, Postsecondary	$77,210	15.1%	Roughly 300
2. Biochemists and Biophysicists	$82,390	37.4%	2,000
3. Microbiologists	$66,580	12.2%	1,000
4. Soil and Plant Scientists	$59,180	15.5%	500

Characteristics of the Related Jobs: Personality Type—Investigative, Realistic. **Skills**—Science, mathematics, reading comprehension, operations analysis, programming, writing, active learning, learning strategies. **Work Conditions**—More often outdoors than indoors; sitting; hazardous conditions; in a vehicle; wear common and specialized protective or safety equipment.

Spanish

Focuses on the Spanish language and related dialects. **Related CIP Program:** 16.0905 Spanish Language and Literature.

Specializations in the Major: Literature, translation, history and culture, language education.

Typical Sequence of College Courses: Spanish language, conversation, composition, linguistics, Spanish literature, Spanish-American literature, Spanish history and civilization, European history and civilization, grammar, phonetics. **Typical Sequence of High School Courses:** English, public speaking, Spanish, history, literature, social science.

Career Snapshot: Spanish has become the second language in the United States, as well as maintaining its importance as a world language, especially in the Western hemisphere. A degree in Spanish can be useful preparation (perhaps with an additional degree) for many careers in business, travel, and public service, and not just with an international orientation. High school teaching usually requires a master's degree for security and advancement.

Related Jobs

Job Title	Average Earnings	Job Growth	Job Openings
1. Foreign Language and Literature Teachers, Postsecondary	$56,740	15.1%	Roughly 900
2. Interpreters and Translators	$40,860	22.2%	2,000

Characteristics of the Related Jobs: Personality Type—Artistic, Social. **Skills**—Writing, reading comprehension, speaking, social perceptiveness, learning strategies, service orientation, active learning, monitoring. **Work Conditions**—Indoors; sitting; close to coworkers; exposed to disease or infections; exposed to radiation; making repetitive motions.

Special Education

Focuses on the design and provision of teaching and other educational services to children or adults with special learning needs or disabilities and may prepare individuals to function as special education teachers. **Related CIP Programs:** 13.1001 Special Education and Teaching, General; 13.1003 Education/Teaching of Individuals with Hearing Impairments, Including Deafness; 13.1004 Education/Teaching of the Gifted and Talented; 13.1005 Education/Teaching of Individuals with Emotional Disturbances.

Specializations in the Major: Specific learning disabilities, multiple disabilities, speech-language impairments, visual impairments, autism, traumatic brain injury.

Typical Sequence of College Courses: Introduction to psychology, English composition, oral communication, history and philosophy of education, human growth and development, introduction to special education, curriculum and methods for special education, educational psychology,

psychology of the exceptional child, assessment in special education, classroom/laboratory management, behavior modification techniques in education, education for moderate and severe disabilities, reading assessment and teaching, mathematics education, student teaching. **Typical Sequence of High School Courses:** English, algebra, geometry, trigonometry, science, foreign language, public speaking.

Career Snapshot: Special education covers a wide variety of learning and developmental disabilities and other conditions that require nonstandard educational techniques. Many states require a master's degree for licensure, but some states are offering alternative entry routes. Job opportunity in this field is excellent, especially in rural areas and inner cities and for specializations such as multiple disabilities, autism, and bilingual special education.

Related Jobs

Job Title	Average Earnings	Job Growth	Job Openings
1. Interpreters and Translators	$40,860	22.2%	2,000
2. Special Education Teachers, Middle School	$51,970	18.1%	4,000
3. Special Education Teachers, Preschool, Kindergarten, and Elementary School	$50,950	19.6%	10,000
4. Special Education Teachers, Secondary School	$52,900	13.3%	6,000

Characteristics of the Related Jobs: Personality Type—Social, Artistic. **Skills**—Learning strategies, social perceptiveness, service orientation, instructing, monitoring, active learning, writing, reading comprehension. **Work Conditions**—Indoors; standing; close to coworkers; exposed to disease or infections; noisy.

Speech-Language Pathology and Audiology

Prepares individuals as audiologists and speech-language pathologists. **Related CIP Program:** 51.0204 Audiology/Audiologist and Speech-Language Pathology/Pathologist.

Specializations in the Major: Speech-language pathology, audiology.

Typical Sequence of College Courses: General biology, English composition, general physics, introduction to psychology, human growth and development, statistics, introduction to sociology, introduction to speech, language and hearing, phonetics, anatomy of the speech and hearing mechanism, linguistics, psychoacoustics, neuroscience, auditory anatomy and physiology, stuttering and other fluency disorders, voice disorders, hearing problems, psycholinguistics and speech perception, diagnostic procedures in audiology, aural rehabilitation, research methods in speech pathology and audiology, student teaching. **Typical Sequence of High School Courses:** English, algebra, geometry, trigonometry, biology, chemistry, physics, computer science, public speaking, social science, pre-calculus.

Career Snapshot: Speech-language pathologists and audiologists help people with a variety of communication disorders. About half of speech-language pathologists work in schools, and most of the rest work for health-care facilities. Among audiologists, about half work in health-care settings, with a smaller number in schools. A master's degree is the standard entry route for speech-language pathologists. For audiologists, a master's still suffices in many states, but a doctoral degree is expected to become the standard. It is possible to complete the requirements for entering both kinds of graduate program within a variety of undergraduate majors. Because of the aging of the population and an emphasis on early diagnosis, job opportunities are expected to be excellent for speech-language pathologists, though less certain for audiologists. Knowledge of a second language is an advantage.

Related Jobs

Job Title	Average Earnings	Job Growth	Job Openings
1. Audiologists	$63,230	25.0%	500
2. Health Specialties Teachers, Postsecondary	$84,840	15.1%	ROUGHLY 4,000
3. Speech-Language Pathologists	$65,090	18.5%	4,000

Characteristics of the Related Jobs: Personality Type—Social, Investigative, Artistic. **Skills**—Science, learning strategies, writing, social perceptiveness, active learning, monitoring, reading comprehension, instructing. **Work Conditions**—Indoors; sitting; exposed to disease or infections; close to coworkers; noisy; exposed to radiation.

Statistics

Focuses on the relationships, including similarities and differences, between groups of measurements, using probability theory and techniques derived from it. **Related CIP Programs:** 27.0502 Mathematical Statistics and Probability; 27.0501 Statistics, General.

Specializations in the Major: Mathematical statistics, probability, experimental design, computer applications, psychometrics.

Typical Sequence of College Courses: Calculus, introduction to computer science, programming in a language (e.g., C, Pascal, COBOL), statistics, linear algebra, experimental design and analysis, mathematical statistics, seminar (reporting on research). **Typical Sequence of High School Courses:** Algebra, geometry, trigonometry, pre-calculus, calculus, computer science, physics.

Career Snapshot: Statistical analysis is a valuable tool that is used by every discipline that deals in quantitative information—social sciences, laboratory sciences, and business studies. Statisticians find meaningful patterns in data sets that are harvested from experiments, surveys, and other procedures such as bookkeeping. Graduates of statistics programs are in demand in many parts of the economy, from basic research to business management, from government to academia. Some get advanced degrees to specialize in research or college teaching or get a degree in a second field such as psychology, computer science, or business.

Related Jobs

Job Title	Average Earnings	Job Growth	Job Openings
1. Mathematical Science Teachers, Postsecondary	$63,640	15.1%	Roughly 1,000
2. Mathematicians	$93,580	22.5%	Fewer than 500
3. Natural Sciences Managers	$114,560	15.4%	2,000
4. Statisticians	$72,820	13.1%	1,000

Characteristics of the Related Jobs: Personality Type—Investigative, Conventional. **Skills**—Programming, mathematics, science, operations analysis, reading comprehension, active learning, writing, instructing. **Work Conditions**—Indoors; sitting.

Transportation and Logistics Management

Prepares individuals to manage and coordinate all logistical functions in an enterprise, ranging from acquisitions to receiving and handling through internal allocation of resources to operations units to the handling and delivery of output. **Related CIP Programs:** 52.0203 Logistics, Materials, and Supply Chain Management; 52.0209 Transportation/Mobility Management.

Specializations in the Major: Inventory control, traffic and transportation management, location analysis, planning and forecasting, order fulfillment, management information systems, warehouse operations, materials handling.

Typical Sequence of College Courses: English composition, business writing, introduction to psychology, principles of microeconomics, principles of macroeconomics, calculus for business and social sciences, statistics for business and social sciences, introduction to management information systems, introduction to accounting, legal environment of business, business finance, introduction to marketing, human resource management, introduction to logistics, transportation management, inventory management, analysis and design of logistics systems. **Typical Sequence of High School Courses:** English, algebra, geometry, trigonometry, foreign language, computer science, public speaking, pre-calculus.

Career Snapshot: Transportation and logistics managers find the fastest and most cost-effective ways to keep materials flowing through our economy. Any business that produces goods or uses supplies—and that means practically every business—faces problems that these specialists are trained to solve. Some enter the field with a bachelor's in transportation and logistics management. On-the-job experience is important for advancement. Those interested in a technical specialization such as inventory control, packaging, or forecasting may major in (or get a master's degree in) management information systems, operations research, or industrial engineering.

Related Jobs

Job Title	Average Earnings	Job Growth	Job Openings
1. Administrative Services Managers	$75,520	12.5%	9,000
2. Business Teachers, Postsecondary	$73,320	15.1%	ROUGHLY 2,000
3. Chief Executives	$160,720	–1.4%	11,000
4. Logisticians	$67,960	19.5%	4,000
5. Transportation, Storage, and Distribution Managers	$79,490	–5.3%	3,000

Characteristics of the Related Jobs: Personality Type—Enterprising, Conventional. **Skills**—Management of financial resources, management of material resources, management of personnel resources, operations analysis, negotiation, coordination, time management, monitoring. **Work Conditions**—Indoors; sitting; in a vehicle.

Urban Studies

Focuses on the application of social science principles to the study of urban institutions and the forces influencing urban social and political life. **Related CIP Program:** 45.1201 Urban Studies/Affairs.

Specializations in the Major: Urban planning, community economic development, environmental design, ethnic studies, urban politics, urban economics.

Typical Sequence of College Courses: English composition, introduction to economics, introduction to sociology, statistics for business and social sciences, urban politics, history of cities, urban economics, introduction to urban planning, public policy analysis, seminar (reporting on research). **Typical Sequence of High School Courses:** Algebra, English, foreign language, social science, trigonometry, history.

Career Snapshot: Many different kinds of activities are concentrated in cities and towns—economic, social, political, architectural, and cultural—so urban studies is an interdisciplinary major. Usually you can shape the major to concentrate on whichever of these aspects is of greatest interest to you. Degree holders go on to a variety of different careers, most often after getting a graduate or professional degree. Some work in urban planning or redevelopment, law, public administration, environmental planning, social work, or journalism.

Related Jobs

Job Title	Average Earnings	Job Growth	Job Openings
1. Sociologists	$69,620	21.9%	FEWER THAN 500

Characteristics of the Related Jobs: Personality Type—Investigative, Artistic, Social. **Skills**—Science, reading comprehension, writing, speaking, mathematics, active learning, learning strategies, instructing. **Work Conditions**—Indoors; sitting.

Veterinary Medicine

Prepares individuals for the independent professional practice of veterinary medicine, involving the diagnosis, treatment, and health-care management of animals and animal populations and the prevention and management of diseases that may be transmitted to humans. **Related CIP Program:** 51.2401 Veterinary Medicine (DVM).

Specializations in the Major: Companion animals, large animals (horses, cattle), public health, research.

Typical Sequence of College Courses: English composition, introduction to psychology, college algebra, calculus, introduction to sociology, oral communication, general chemistry, general biology, introduction to computer science, organic chemistry, human anatomy and physiology, general microbiology, genetics, introduction to biochemistry, veterinary gross anatomy, neuroanatomy, veterinary histology and cell biology, veterinary radiology, animal nutrition and nutritional diseases, neuroanatomy, pathology, veterinary microbiology, pharmacology, veterinary ophthalmology, public health, veterinary surgery, reproduction, veterinary toxicology, clinical veterinary experience. **Typical Sequence of High School Courses:** English, algebra, geometry, trigonometry, biology, computer science, public speaking, chemistry, foreign language, physics, pre-calculus.

Career Snapshot: Veterinarians care for the health of animals—from dogs and cats to horses and cattle to exotic zoo animals—protect humans from diseases carried by animals, and conduct basic research on animal health. Most of them work in private practices. Some inspect animals or animal products for government agencies. Most students who enter the four-year veterinary school program have already completed a bachelor's degree that includes math and science coursework. Competition for entry to veterinary school is keen, but the job outlook is expected to be good.

Related Jobs

Job Title	Average Earnings	Job Growth	Job Openings
1. Health Specialties Teachers, Postsecondary	$84,840	15.1%	ROUGHLY 4,000
2. Veterinarians	$80,510	33.0%	3,000

Characteristics of the Related Jobs: Personality Type—Investigative, Social, Realistic. **Skills**—Science, reading comprehension, instructing, active learning, operations analysis, writing, learning strategies, judgment and decision making. **Work Conditions**—Indoors; standing; exposed to disease or infections; exposed to radiation; wear specialized protective or safety equipment; minor burns, cuts, bites, or stings; close to coworkers; contaminants; hazardous conditions.

Wildlife Management

Prepares individuals to conserve and manage wilderness areas and the flora, fauna, and marine and aquatic life therein and manage wildlife reservations and zoological/aquarium facilities for recreational, commercial, and ecological purposes. **Related CIP Program:** 03.0601 Wildlife, Fish, and Wildlands Science and Management.

Specializations in the Major: Terrestrial wildlife management, fisheries management, public policy.

Typical Sequence of College Courses: English composition, calculus, general biology, general chemistry, organic chemistry, oral communication, statistics, introduction to computer science, introduction to soil science, ecology, general zoology, ecology, introduction to wildlife conservation, invertebrate zoology, introduction to forestry, mammalogy, ornithology, natural resource biometrics, wildlife habitat management, animal population dynamics and management, animal physiology, ichthyology/herpetology, regional wildlife management and policy. **Typical Sequence of High School Courses:** Biology, chemistry, algebra, geometry, trigonometry, computer science, English, public speaking, geography.

Career Snapshot: The study of wildlife management combines a number of disciplines, including biology and public policy. Wildlife managers have to understand how wild creatures interact with their natural environment and how they react to the pressures put on them by human hunting and habitat destruction. Most wildlife managers work for governmental agencies. Students who specialize in fisheries management may find work in the growing field of aquaculture.

Related Jobs

Job Title	Average Earnings	Job Growth	Job Openings
1. Conservation Scientists	$60,160	11.9%	Fewer than 500
2. Fish and Game Wardens	$48,800	8.3%	Fewer than 500
3. Zoologists and Wildlife Biologists	$56,500	12.8%	1,000

Characteristics of the Related Jobs: Personality Type—Investigative, Realistic, Enterprising. **Skills**—Science, operations analysis, reading comprehension, writing, management of financial resources, speaking, mathematics, negotiation. **Work Conditions**—In a vehicle; more often outdoors than indoors; sitting; very hot or cold; minor burns, cuts, bites, or stings; extremely bright or inadequate lighting.

Women's Studies

Focuses on the history, sociology, politics, culture, and economics of women and the development of modern feminism in relation to the roles played by women in different periods and locations in North America and the world. **Related CIP Program:** 05.0207 Women's Studies.

Specializations in the Major: Women's issues in art and culture, women's political issues, history of feminism, feminist theory.

Typical Sequence of College Courses: English composition, foreign language, American history, introduction to women's studies, women of color, theories of feminism, historical and philosophical origins of feminism, feminism from a global perspective, seminar (reporting on research). **Typical Sequence of High School Courses:** English, algebra, foreign language, history, literature, public speaking, social science.

Career Snapshot: Women's studies is an interdisciplinary major that looks at the experience of women from the perspectives of history, literature, psychology, and sociology, among others. Graduates of this major may go into business fields where understanding of women's issues can be helpful—for example, advertising or human resources management. With further education, they may also find careers in fields where they can affect the lives of women, such as social work, law, public health, or public administration.

Related Jobs

Job Title	Average Earnings	Job Growth	Job Openings
1. Area, Ethnic, and Cultural Studies Teachers, Postsecondary	$65,030	15.1%	Roughly 200

Characteristics of the Related Jobs: Personality Type—Social, Investigative, Artistic. **Skills**—Science, writing, operations analysis, learning strategies, speaking, reading comprehension, active learning, instructing. **Work Conditions**—Indoors; sitting; exposed to disease or infections.

Zoology

Focuses on the scientific study of the biology of animal species and phyla, with reference to their molecular and cellular systems, anatomy, physiology, and behavior. **Related CIP Program:** 26.0701 Zoology/Animal Biology.

Specializations in the Major: Ornithology, mammalogy, herpetology, ichthyology, entomology.

Typical Sequence of College Courses: English composition, calculus, introduction to computer science, general chemistry, general biology, organic chemistry, genetics, general physics, cell biology, statistics, animal anatomy and physiology, evolution, ecology. **Typical Sequence of High School Courses:** English, biology, algebra, geometry, trigonometry, chemistry, pre-calculus, physics, computer science, calculus.

Career Snapshot: Zoologists study any form of animal life and therefore need a good background in biology and chemistry. A bachelor's degree in zoology can be a good first step toward a professional degree in medicine, veterinary science, or dentistry, or it may lead to entry-level work in some government and business fields. A graduate degree in zoology is good preparation for a career in research, college teaching, or agricultural extension service.

Related Jobs

Job Title	Average Earnings	Job Growth	Job Openings
1. Biological Science Teachers, Postsecondary	$73,980	15.1%	Roughly 1,700
2. Natural Sciences Managers	$114,560	15.4%	2,000
3. Zoologists and Wildlife Biologists	$56,500	12.8%	1,000

Characteristics of the Related Jobs: Personality Type—Investigative, Realistic, Enterprising. **Skills**—Science, reading comprehension, writing, management of financial resources, time management, mathematics, management of personnel resources, active learning. **Work Conditions**—More often outdoors than indoors; in a vehicle; sitting; hazardous conditions; minor burns, cuts, bites, or stings; exposed to disease or infections.

Key Points: Chapter 6

- Several majors described in this chapter are worth your consideration because they're a good match for you and are linked to careers that are attractive to you.

- When you consider a major, consider the whole package: the high school program that precedes it, the courses and specialization you'll study, and the careers it leads to. Be sure you feel comfortable with all of them.

- If the information you find in this chapter has raised some additional questions in your mind—good! Don't make a commitment until you have investigated further. But at least you've made a great start.

Chapter 7

Make Decisions
and Plans

Chapter 6 showed you lots of useful information about the college majors on your Hot List. Maybe you also read about some additional majors that seemed interesting. Now it's time for you to move toward the next step: decisions and plans for your college major.

Making decisions and plans is a good idea no matter what your particular situation is right now:

- **If you're still in high school,** you don't need to commit to a specific college major now. Nevertheless, deciding on a major (or a group of related majors) can help you decide which advanced high school courses to take and what colleges to apply to.

- **If you just started college or are about to,** you probably are being asked what major you expect to choose. Even if you're not being asked this, choosing a major (or a group of related majors) can help you decide which courses to take in your first year of college. Even if you can't decide between two alternatives, you can probably select courses that will be useful for completing either major. Another benefit of making a tentative decision is that you may be able to take a course that gives you a taste of the major. This experience will help you either confirm your decision or change your direction.

- **If you are now required to declare your major,** you obviously can't delay making a decision. But make sure that your decision is well thought out. Be sure you're choosing for the right reasons. And be sure to make plans for what lies beyond the decision. You want to avoid future surprises.

- **If you are now changing your mind about your previously declared major,** you should be especially careful. First, you want to make sure that your reasons for this new choice are better than the reasons for your original choice of a major. Also, you want to keep in mind that your new major is likely to impose a new set of course requirements. Some courses that you have taken may not help meet these new course requirements. As a result, you may be unable to stick to your original timetable for graduating. That means additional expense and a delay in getting on with your life. You will have to decide whether the advantages of the new major (such as greater satisfaction or the likelihood of a better career outcome) outweigh the damage being done to your timetable.

A Framework for Deciding

Most educational and career decisions involve trade-offs. That means you accept some things you don't like because you expect to get a lot more things you do like. Nobody can expect to be totally delighted during every hour of four years of college—or during every workday in the career that follows. Still, it's realistic to try to identify a major and career in which the good will outweigh the bad.

So let's assume that at this point you've identified two or more college majors that interest you. How do you decide among them?

Organize your thinking by following a two-step process: First, list what you want to get from your major (and the job it may lead to) and what you want to avoid. Second, give each major a score on how well it matches each preference; this might be as simple as plus and minus signs. Later in this section, you'll find a checklist that helps you through this process.

Start with preferences that relate to what you will experience in college. The most obvious matter to start with is your personality type. You achieved some insights into this in Chapter 2. Now, look at what Chapter 6 says about the majors you have in mind. Use this information to mark the checklist in this section, giving each major a plus or minus sign to indicate how good a match it is.

Second, do the same thing for your skills, which you clarified in Chapter 3. Use the information in Chapter 6 to give each major a rating on its match with your skills.

Now, review the favorite high school courses that you identified in Chapter 4. See which high school courses Chapter 6 mentions as typical requirements for the majors that interest you. Rate each major on its match.

What about the college courses that will be required? Look at the courses listed in Chapter 6 for each major. Think about how interesting they seem to you and how well you might do in them, based on your present understanding of your abilities. Then indicate a rating on the checklist.

The last issue relating directly to the college experience is any requirements at your college that may determine who is allowed to enter the major. Some colleges won't let you declare certain majors if your grade-point average is too low or if you get a low grade in a specified survey course. If you're aware of any such requirement for one of the majors you're considering, rate the major on how likely you are to get past this hurdle.

Next, it's time to consider your preferences for the careers you might pursue after graduation. Understand that these ratings are more tentative than the ratings for the majors because it's hard to predict your future job reliably. The job may turn out to be any of the jobs listed for the major in the description in Chapter 6 or an entirely different job. But even if you work in an occupation not listed, the job is likely to have a lot in common with the jobs listed there.

Begin by considering income in the jobs. Everybody wants to qualify for a career with decent pay, so how much is enough for you? A quick way to get a ballpark figure is to think of somebody you know who's living the kind of lifestyle, in terms of income, that you think is realistic for you to work for. How much is that person earning? It's considered rude to ask somebody outright, but if you know what that person does for a living, maybe you can find an advertisement (with a dollar figure) for a similar job. Maybe you can ask this person to point you to an advertisement for a similar job. Or you can find average earnings in a career resource such as the *Occupational Outlook Handbook (OOH)*. Once you have a rough idea of the income level you're aiming for, look at the earnings listed in Chapter 6 for the jobs related to your possible majors. Don't assume that you'll get the best-paying job listed. And remember that these figures are averages; new workers usually earn less.

Every day is not payday. Other aspects of your future job besides pay will please or displease you. Look at the career snapshot in Chapter 6 and perhaps get more detailed information from the *OOH* or another resource. (If a job you have in mind is not listed in Chapter 6, you'll definitely need to consult another resource.) Once you have an idea of what the job involves, think about whether you'd find the work tasks interesting. Do you think you can handle the skill requirements (after being suitably trained)? Are you comfortable with the work conditions? Is the amount of working with people right for you? Is there enough variety? Too much stress? Is the level of responsibility right for you? Does the work schedule suit you? You may be aware of other things you like or dislike. When you do, try to score *all* the majors on each job-related feature that you consider important.

As you evaluate the majors this way, especially if you judge on the basis of personal experience (such as a visit to a workplace), try to find out what is actually typical for the job. Sometimes conditions at one work site are unusual and give a mistaken impression of how the career feels to most workers.

The following checklist guides you through the process of scoring three majors and the related jobs. Use a plus sign to indicate features that match your preferences and a minus sign when a feature falls short. **This is just a model** for you to modify as you like. Feel free to change any of the features in the left column; add issues that are important *to you* and remove any that are not important.

Major Decision-Making Checklist

Feature	Major #1	Major #2	Major #3
The College Experience			
Match with my personality	——	——	——
Match with my skills	——	——	——
Match with my favorite high school courses	——	——	——
Appeal of college courses	——	——	——
Any local requirements	——	——	——
_____	——	——	——
_____	——	——	——
The Related Careers			
Earnings	——	——	——
Interesting work tasks	——	——	——
Types of skills	——	——	——
Work conditions	——	——	——
Work with people	——	——	——

Feature	Major #1	Major #2	Major #3
Variety	——	——	——
Stress	——	——	——
Responsibility	——	——	——
Work schedule	——	——	——
	——	——	——
	——	——	——

Once you have filled out this checklist, look at the pluses and minuses in each column. **Don't simply count them,** because they don't all deserve equal weight. For example, the ratings you gave for the college experience should carry more weight than the ratings you gave for the related careers. Remember, you can't be sure of what career you might go into.

Also, don't let other people decide which issues should be important. We all have different priorities. Think about which issues matter most to *you* and base your decision more on the pluses you gave to majors for these issues.

A Framework for Planning

Following are a series of questions you need to answer so you can make intelligent plans for your major and your future career:

- **Can I afford college?** The topic of paying for college deserves its own book, but this book would not be complete without advising you to answer this question. The cost of a college education keeps rising. If you're thinking of borrowing money to pay for college, be very cautious. Fortunately, financial aid is available. More than 6 in 10 full-time college students get aid from outside their families, and nearly half of these draw on more than one source. A good way to investigate your options is to use the interactive advisor at the Career InfoNet site, www.careerinfonet.org/acinet/finaidadvisor.

- **What are the specific requirements for the major at your college (or at a college you're considering attending)?** This includes requirements for both admission to the major and completion of it. You can find the answers to this question on the department's Web site. Also be sure to look at the college's requirements for the bachelor's degree.

- **What are my chances of completing the specific requirements for the major?** You have already looked at what Chapter 6 said about the skills and course requirements for the major, but you need to consider this question in greater detail. An academic advisor can help you make an informed estimate, based on your past academic performance, your test scores, and your commitment to the major. Some colleges also have a mentoring program, in which upper-division students offer advice to first- and second-year students.

- **Will I have enough opportunities to pursue my other interests?** For example, you may be thinking about minoring in a discipline that interests you. Can you fit the requirements for that minor into your schedule? You can get an idea of the answer by looking at the Web sites for both departments, but you should discuss your plans with an academic advisor. If you intend to hold a part-time job or participate in a sport, you need to consider whether the major will allow you sufficient free time.

- **For my career goal, what specializations have particularly good job openings now?** Talk to a counselor at the career advisement office at the college. If the college has an alumni network, you may be able to use that to contact someone in the career you're considering.

- **For a career goal that requires a graduate or professional degree, what should I do as an undergraduate to prepare for this next step?** Some graduate or professional programs expect you to have completed certain courses in college. Ask an academic advisor about this or consult the Web sites of several programs of the type you're aiming for.

- **After students with this major graduate, how successful are they at the next step: finding a job or getting additional education?** A counselor at the career advisement office may have suggestions. So may alumni who are working in your targeted career.

- **What activities besides coursework would be useful for me to engage in?** For some majors, you can help your future career by participating in a student club, doing relevant volunteer work, or doing an internship. For suggestions, talk to a counselor at the career advisement office or to someone in the alumni network who is working in your targeted career.

You won't be able to answer all of these questions today, but at least get started today.

Key Points: Chapter 7

- It's a good idea to get started now with decisions and plans about your major, even if you don't yet need to declare a major.

- When you're choosing between two or more majors, it helps to be systematic about your decision and consider all the pluses and minuses of each major.

- Your college has many resources to help you find answers to questions about your intended major: academic advisors, a career advisement office, a Web site, and probably an alumni network.

Index

A

Accountants and Auditors, 32, 56, 71

Accounting (college major), 32, 56, 70–71

Active Learning skill, 35, 38

Actors, 26, 59, 61, 111

Actuarial Science (college major), 32, 39, 41, 42, 55, 56, 61, 71–72

Actuaries, 32, 39, 41, 42, 55, 56, 61, 72

Administrative Law Judges, Adjudicators, and Hearing Officers, 30, 45, 49, 51, 58, 61, 62, 152

Administrative Services Managers, 31, 32, 42, 43, 45, 50, 95, 188, 201

Advertising and Promotions Managers, 30, 31, 39, 42, 43, 44, 49, 54, 73, 155, 189

Advertising (college major), 30, 45, 54, 61, 62, 72–73

Advertising Sales Agents, 30, 45, 61, 62, 73

Aeronautical/Aerospace Engineering (college major), 22, 38, 40, 44, 45, 46, 50, 55, 56, 60, 61, 73–74

Aerospace Engineers, 22, 38, 39, 41, 44, 45, 46, 50, 55, 56, 60, 61, 74

African-American Studies (college major), 27, 38, 39, 48, 49, 51, 57, 58, 59, 61, 62, 74–75

Agricultural and Food Science Technicians, 20, 39, 40, 46, 54, 55, 58, 79, 81, 123

Agricultural Business and Economics (college major), 20, 39, 40, 47, 54, 75–77

Agricultural Engineering (college major), 30, 38, 42, 43, 44, 45, 50, 55, 56, 61, 77–78

Agricultural Engineers, 30, 38, 39, 44, 45, 50, 55, 56, 60, 61, 78

Agricultural Sciences Teachers, Postsecondary, 20, 21, 42, 47, 54, 79, 81, 195

Agronomy and Crop Science (college major), 20, 39, 40, 46, 47, 54, 55, 78–79

Algebra (high school course). *See* Calculus (high school course); Pre-Calculus (high school course)

American Studies (college major), 27, 38, 39, 48, 49, 51, 57, 58, 59, 61, 62, 79–80

Anesthesiologists, 23, 54, 55, 60, 161

Animal Science (college major), 20, 39, 40, 46, 47, 54, 55, 80–81

Animal Scientists, 20, 46, 55, 58, 81

Anthropologists, 57, 58, 61, 62

Anthropologists and Archeologists, 22, 28, 39, 41, 48, 49, 51, 58, 61, 82, 83, 102

Anthropology and Archeology Teachers, Postsecondary, 22, 28, 48, 57, 58, 62, 82, 83, 137

Anthropology (college major), 22, 39, 41, 48, 49, 51, 57, 58, 61, 62, 81–82

Arbitrators, Mediators, and Conciliators, 30, 45, 49, 51, 61, 62, 152

Archeology (college major), 22, 39, 41, 48, 49, 51, 57, 58, 61, 62, 82–83

Architects, 54, 55

215

B

C

D

G

Public Administration (college major), 32, 39, 42, 43, 45, 187–188

Public Relations (college major), 30, 45, 49, 57, 188–189

Public Relations Managers, 30, 45, 57, 189

Public Relations Specialists, 28, 30, 49, 103, 119, 189

Public Speaking (high school course), 61–62

Purchasing Agents and Buyers, Farm Products, 20, 58, 76

Purchasing Agents, Except Wholesale, Retail, and Farm Products, 32, 45, 144

Q

Quality Control Analysis skill, 36, 46–47

R

Reading Comprehension skill, 36, 47

Realistic personality type, 16, 20

Recreation Management (college major), 61

Recreation Workers, 29, 62, 175

Registered Nurses, 27, 44, 49, 54, 56, 167

Religion/Religious Studies (college major), 29, 39, 41, 42, 45, 48, 49, 57, 58, 61, 62, 189–190

Repairing skill, 37, 47–48

Reporters and Correspondents, 26, 51, 59, 62, 149

resources for information, 4–5

Russian (college major), 25, 57, 58, 59, 61, 190–191

S

Sales Managers, 28, 31, 43, 44, 49, 95, 119, 155

Sales Representatives, Wholesale and Manufacturing, Except Technical and Scientific Products, 32, 144

Science skill, 37, 48

Secondary Education (college major), 29, 42, 57, 61, 191–192

Secondary School Teachers, Except Special and Vocational Education, 26, 28, 29, 42, 62, 94, 119, 143, 180, 192

Service Orientation skill, 37, 48–49

Set and Exhibit Designers, 25, 41, 48, 130

Shortz, Will, 10

skills

checklist, 35–37

relating to college majors and careers

Active Learning skill, 38

Complex Problem Solving skill, 38

Coordination skill, 38–39

Critical Thinking skill, 39

Equipment Maintenance skill, 39–40

Equipment Selection skill, 40

Installation skill, 40–41

Instructing skill, 41

Judgment and Decision Making skill, 41–42

Learning Strategies skill, 42

Management of Financial Resources skill, 42–43

Management of Material Resources skill, 43

Management of Personnel Resources skill, 43–44

T